DATE DUE			
Jan 9 79			
SPR 79			

THE MYTH OF
PSYCHOTHERAPY

Other books by *Thomas Szasz*

PAIN AND PLEASURE
THE MYTH OF MENTAL ILLNESS
LAW, LIBERTY, AND PSYCHIATRY
PSYCHIATRIC JUSTICE
THE ETHICS OF PSYCHOANALYSIS
THE MANUFACTURE OF MADNESS
*IDEOLOGY AND INSANITY
*THE AGE OF MADNESS (ED.)
*THE SECOND SIN
*CEREMONIAL CHEMISTRY
*HERESIES
KARL KRAUS AND THE SOUL-DOCTORS
SCHIZOPHRENIA
PSYCHIATRIC SLAVERY
THE THEOLOGY OF MEDICINE

* available from Anchor Press

THE MYTH OF PSYCHOTHERAPY

Mental Healing as Religion, Rhetoric, and Repression

Thomas Szasz

Anchor Press/Doubleday
GARDEN CITY, NEW YORK
1978

We gratefully acknowledge permission to reprint:

Excerpts from *Psychoanalysis and Faith: The Letters of Sigmund Freud and Oskar Pfister,* edited by Heinrich Meng and Ernst L. Freud, translated by Eric Mosbacher. Copyright © 1963 by Sigmund Freud Copyrights, Ltd., London. Reprinted by permission of Basic Books, Inc., Publishers, New York, and Sigmund Freud Copyrights, Ltd., London. Excerpts from *Letters of Sigmund Freud,* selected and edited by Ernst L. Freud, translated by Tania and James Stern. Copyright © 1960 by Sigmund Freud Copyrights, Ltd., London. Reprinted by permission of Basic Books, Inc., Publishers, New York. Excerpts from *The Discovery of the Unconscious: The History and Evolution of Dynamic Psychiatry,* by Henri F. Ellenberger. Copyright © 1970 by Henri F. Ellenberger. Reprinted by permission of Basic Books, Inc., Publishers, New York. Excerpts from *Studies on Hysteria,* by Josef Breuer and Sigmund Freud, translated from the German and edited by James Strachey in collaboration with Anna Freud. Published in the United States by Basic Books, Inc., Publishers, New York, by arrangement with The Hogarth Press, Ltd., London. Reprinted by permission of Basic Books, Inc., Publishers, New York. Excerpts from *Three Essays on the Theory of Sexuality,* by Sigmund Freud, translated and newly edited by James Strachey. Copyright © 1962 by Sigmund Freud Copyrights, Ltd. Reprinted by permission of Basic Books, Inc., Publishers, New York. Excerpts from *A Psychoanalytic Dialogue: The Letters of Sigmund Freud and Karl Abraham, 1907–1926,* edited by Hilda C. Abraham and Ernst L. Freud, translated by Bernard Marsh and Hilda C. Abraham. Copyright © 1965 by Hilda C. Abraham and Ernst L. Freud. Reprinted by permission of Basic Books, Inc., Publishers, New York. Excerpts from "On the History of the Psycho-Analytic Movement" (Volume I, 15), "Heredity and the Aetiology of the Neuroses" (Volume I, 8), "The Future Prospects of Psycho-Analytic Therapy" (Volume II, 25), "On Narcissism: An Introduction" (Volume IV, 3), "Contributions to the Psychology of Love. A Special Type of Choice of Object made by Men" (Volume IV, 13), in *The Collected Papers of Sigmund Freud,* edited by Ernest Jones, M.D., authorized translation under the supervision of Joan Riviere. Published by Basic Books, Inc., Publishers, New York, by arrangement with The Hogarth Press, Ltd., and The Institute of Psycho-Analysis, London. Reprinted by permission of Basic Books, Inc., Publishers, New York, and The Hogarth Press, Ltd. "Psycho-Analysis and Religious Origins" (Volume V, 8c), "Some Additional Notes upon Dream-Interpretation as a Whole" (Volume V, 13), "Postscript to a Discussion on Lay Analysis" (Volume V, 19), in *The Collected Papers of Sigmund Freud,* edited by James Strachey, published by Basic Books, Inc., Publishers, New York, by arrangement with

For
Beverly Jarrett

"Strictly speaking, the question is not how to get cured, but how to live."

—Joseph Conrad

Acknowledgments

My family, friends, and editors have been generous with their advice and help in the preparation of this book. I should like to thank in particular Ronald Carino, Joseph DeVeaugh-Geiss, Beverly Jarrett, Joan Kass, Elizabeth Knappman, George Szasz, Susan Szasz—and my secretary, Barbara Pallone, who typed the manuscript and attended to other tasks connected with writing a book with unflagging energy.

Contents

Preface

When, more than twenty years ago, I began to work on *The Myth of Mental Illness,* I unwittingly undertook an enterprise that soon assumed a life of its own. My initial aim was merely to demonstrate that mental illness was fake or metaphorical illness and that psychiatry was fake or metaphorical medicine.

But there was no stopping. It followed from this that mental hospitalization was not the therapeutic intervention it was officially claimed to be. If involuntary, as had been typical throughout the history of psychiatry, hospitalization was expulsion from society; and if voluntary, as was sometimes the modern arrangement, then it was escape from society. Accordingly, I next devoted myself to an examination and exposition of the complex historical, linguistic, moral, and sociological aspects of various psychiatric ideas and interventions, many of which are characterized by an insidious and pervasive combination of disease with deviance, illness with immorality, cure with control, treatment with torture.

The present work is an effort to complete the demythologizing of psychiatry begun in *The Myth of Mental Illness.* As mental illness is the core concept of what psychiatrists allegedly study, so psychotherapy is the paradigmatic practice in which they supposedly engage. The task of psychiatric demythologizing would thus remain incomplete without scrutinizing the ideas and interventions that psychiatrists designate by the term *psychotherapy*.

The conclusions of this inquiry are, of course, foreshadowed by the conclusions of my earlier inquiries into matters psychiatric. Disease, I have argued, means, and should only mean, a disorder of the body. It is a term that should be used to refer to physicochemical events or processes—for example, genetic defects, invasions of the body by microorganisms, alterations in metabolism—manifesting themselves in functional or structural changes in the body which are deemed undesirable. In short, disease is an abnormal biological condition of the body. The term *mental disease,* insofar as it refers to behaviors that imitate illness or to some other conduct regarded as undesirable—for example, claims of being unable to move an extremity or of being able to move the whole world—designates conditions that are not diseases. To be sure, mental illness may be thought and said to resemble bodily illness; but it is not such an illness. Medical disease stands in the same relation to mental disease as literal meaning stands to metaphorical meaning.

In this book I shall argue that treatment means, and should only mean, a physicochemical intervention in the structure and function of the body aimed at combating or curing disease. The term *psychotherapy,* insofar as it is used to refer to two or more people speaking and listening to each other, is therefore a misnomer, and a misleading category. Because it may help people, psychotherapy may be thought and said to resemble regular medical treatment; but it is not such a treatment. There is, properly speaking, no such thing as psychotherapy. Like mental illness, psychotherapy is a metaphor and a myth. Hypnosis, suggestion, psychoanalysis, whatever the so-called psychotherapy might be labeled, are names we give to people speaking and listening to each other in certain ways. By calling some types of human encounters "psychotherapy," we only impede our capacity to understand them.

Introduction

I

It is widely believed today that just as some diseases and patients are, and ought to be, treated by means of chemotherapy or radiation therapy, others are, and ought to be, treated by means of psychotherapy. Our language, the mirror of our mind, reflects this equation of the medical and the mental. Fears and foibles are "psychiatric symptoms"; persons exhibiting these and countless other manifestations of "psychiatric diseases" are "psychiatric patients"; and the interventions sought by or imposed on them are "psychiatric treatments" among which "psychotherapies" occupy a prominent rank.

In several previous books, I have argued that this entire system of interlocking concepts, beliefs, and practices is incorrect and immoral. In *The Myth of Mental Illness* I showed why the concept of mental illness is erroneous and misleading; in *Law, Liberty, and Psychiatry,* why many of the legal uses to which psychiatric ideas and interventions are put are immoral and inimical to the ideals of individual freedom and responsibility; in *The Manufacture of Madness,* why the moral beliefs and social practices based on the concept of mental illness constitute an ideology of intolerance, with belief in mental illness and the persecution of mental patients having replaced belief in witchcraft and the persecution of witches. In the present work, I extend this critical perspective to the principles and practices of mental healing, in an effort to show that psychotherapeutic interventions are not medical but moral in character and are, therefore, not literal but metaphorical treatments.

There are three fundamental reasons for holding that psychotherapies are metaphorical treatments. First, if the conditions psychotherapists seek to cure are not diseases, then the procedures they use are not genuine treatments. Second, if such procedures are imposed on persons against their will, then they are tortures rather than treatments. And third, if the psychotherapeutic procedures consist of nothing but listening and talking, then they constitute a type of conversation which can be therapeutic only in a metaphorical sense.

In the eighteenth and nineteenth centuries, when people spoke of the "cure of souls," everyone knew that the diseases such cures were supposed to heal were spiritual, that the therapists were clerical, and that the cures were metaphorical. Whereas today—with the soul securely displaced by the mind and the mind securely subsumed as a function of the brain—people speak of the "cure of minds," and everyone knows that the diseases psychiatrists treat are basically similar to ordinary medical diseases, that the therapists who administer such treatment are physicians, and that the cures are the results of literal treatments.

This is neither the first nor most likely the last time in history that people have mistaken the metaphorical meaning of a word for its literal meaning and have then used the literalized metaphor for their own personal and political purposes. In this book I shall try to show how coercion and conversation became analogized to medical treatment. The results are now all around us: dance therapy and sex therapy, art therapy and aversion therapy, behavior therapy and reality therapy, individual psychotherapy and group psychotherapy. Virtually anything anyone might do in the company of another person may now be defined as psychotherapeutic. If the definer has the proper credentials, and if his audience is sufficiently gullible, any such act will be publicly accepted and accredited as a form of psychotherapy.

II

Mental illness and mental treatment are symmetrical and indeed symbiotic ideas. The extension of somatic therapy into psychotherapy and the metaphorization of personal influence as psychotherapeutic coincide with the extension of pathology into psychopathology and the metaphorization of personal problems as mental diseases. Since the Freudian revolution, and especially since the Second World War, the secret formula has been this: If you want to debase what a person is doing, call his act psychopathological and call him mentally ill; if you want to exalt what a person is doing, call his act psychotherapeutic and call him a mental healer. Examples of this sort of speaking and writing abound.

It used to be that the forcible abduction of one person by another constituted kidnapping. The captor's efforts to change the moral beliefs of his captive constituted coerced religious conversion. Now these acts are called "deprogramming" and "reality therapy."

"Moonies' parents given custody; 'Deprogramming' sessions begin today," reads the headline of a typical recent newspaper story.[1] From an Associated Press dispatch, we learn that "five young followers of the Rev. Sun Myung Moon today begin 'deprogramming' sessions their parents hope will change their lives. 'This is very scary,' said John Hovard, 23, of Danville, California, after a court decision Thursday returned him and four others to the custody of their parents for 30 days. 'This is like the mental institutions they put dissidents in in Russia.' . . . Wayne Howard, an attorney for the parents, told reporters that 'reality therapy'—procedures commonly called deprogramming—'will begin immediately.' "[2]

Although an appeals court stayed the judicial order for "deprogramming," it upheld the order placing the "children" in their parents' custody.[3] " 'This is a case about the very essence of life—mother, father, and children,' said Judge Vavuris in his decision. 'There is nothing closer in our society than the family. A child is a child, even though the parent might be 90 and the child 60.' "[4] Judge Vavuris was mistaken in asserting that there is, in our society, nothing "closer" (presumably meaning "more important") than the family: in modern American society psychiatry is even more important, just as in medieval European society Christianity was even more important. These, after all, are the institutions that legitimize the family and thus support society.

Of course, before there was deprogramming or reality therapy, there was incarceration in the good old-fashioned insane asylum.

In the recent best seller *Haywire,* Brooke Hayward describes how that method of psychiatric treatment was used by her father and by the famed Menninger Clinic on her brother Bill. It is an episode that proved strangely unsettling to several reviewers of her book.[5] John Leonard, for example, is dismayed that "[Leland] Hayward's [an important theatrical agent and producer] idea of being a father was to send his son to a mental institution in Topeka, Kansas, when 16-year-old Bill wanted to quit school."[6] Peter Prescott writes even more indignantly—indeed, libelously, were it not true—that "Bill, the youngest [child], angered his father, who had him thrown into the Menninger psychiatric clinic for two years. Sane when he entered, he quickly deteriorated."[7] For decades, the Menninger Clinic has been looked upon as the psychiatric equivalent of the Mayo Clinic, a veritable Lourdes for lunatics. Nevertheless, in the context of their book reviews, these noted commentators allow themselves, and their readers, a momentary glimpse behind the psychotherapeutic rhetoric. They do not say, as Leland Hayward probably would have said, that Bill Hayward was confined in a psychiatric hospital because he was mentally ill; nor do they say, as the mad-doctors at the Menninger Clinic probably would have said, that the psychiatrists accepted Bill as a patient because he needed mental treatment. (After all, Hayward could not have "thrown" his son into a mental hospital if the psychiatrists had not agreed that he was a fit subject for psychotherapy.) The point, of course, is that when a person views the proceedings approvingly, he calls imprisonment in institutions such as the Menninger Clinic "psychotherapeutic."

Not only is confinement in a mental hospital therapeutic, but so is temporary leave from it. In 1976, New York State Department of Health Regulation ₦76–128 redefined "trial visits" as "therapeutic leaves."[8] If being paroled from a mental hospital is a form of treatment, then of course Medicaid and insurance companies will pay for it. The justification for this piece of psychiatric legerdemain was articulated by an apologist for the American Psychiatric Association as follows: "Therapeutic leaves of increasing length as well as overnight leaves must be introduced as early as possible into the treatment plan. These leaves must be professionally monitored, regulated, and modified as clinical conditions require. . . . One has to conclude that not only are therapeutic leaves therapeutic, but that they are crucial to any rational treatment plan, and from a practical point of view they must be reimbursable."[9] The Hospital Association of New York State has endorsed this view and has advised area hospitals that "day passes would be reimbursed if they were a part of a therapeutic plan and fully documented."[10] Moreover, only so-called acute patients are limited to day passes; chronic patients can, apparently, have unlimited passes and their nonhospitalization may still be regarded as treatment and reimbursed by Medicaid. "Passes of greater than 24 hours duration were not possible under the present federal guidelines," according to the association, "except for chronic (hospitalization for more than 60 days) patients."[11] The therapeutic possibilities of psychiatric semantics are clearly boundless.

A more amusing recent example of psychotherapy is the use of profanity. Traditionally, foul language has been regarded as a sign of poor manners. Since the psychiatric enlightenment, it is no doubt also a symptom of the passive-aggressive personality, and perhaps of other as yet undiscovered and unnamed mental maladies. During the declining days of the Nixon presidency, it was elevated to the ranks of psychotherapy—by, of all people, a Jesuit priest! On May 9, 1974, the New York *Times* reported that Dr. John McLaughlin, a Jesuit priest who was a special assistant to President Nixon, held a news conference in which he defended the president against growing charges that the "Watergate transcripts portrayed 'deplorable, disgusting, shabby, immoral performances' by the President and his aides."[12] Referring specifically to the "liberal use of profanity" in the Watergate transcripts, Father McLaughlin declared that "that language had 'no meaning, no moral meaning,' but served as a 'form of emotional drainage. This form of therapy is not only understandable,' Father McLaughlin said, 'but, I think, if looked at closely, good, valid, sound.' "[13]

The most dramatic—and, at the same time, historically the most transparent—examples of how the language of psychopathology and psychotherapy is used to vilify and glorify various human acts lie in the area of sexual behavior. Three examples will suffice.

Throughout the nineteenth century masturbation was regarded

as a cause and symptom of insanity.[14] Today, it is a psychotherapeutic technique used by sex therapists. For example, Helen Kaplan emphasizes that even though "a patient can avoid talking about masturbation guilt in psychotherapy, she must come to terms with this issue if, in sex therapy, she is instructed to experiment with self-stimulation."[15] "Sexual tasks" play an important role in Kaplan's therapeutic armamentarium. For retarded ejaculation she prescribes the following treatment: "The patient is instructed to ejaculate in situations which in the past had evoked progressively more intense anxiety. Initially, he may masturbate to orgasm in the presence of his partner. Then she may bring him to orgasm manually."[16] In a similar vein, Jack Annon asserts that "masturbation may be therapeutically helpful in treating a wide variety of sexual problems and, therefore, it is important for the clinician to become knowledgeable and comfortable in the area if he or she wishes to take advantage of such a treatment modality."[17] It is indeed unfortunate that masturbation is a tax-deductible activity only if it is prescribed by a physician.

For decades, nudism was considered a form of exhibitionism and voyeurism—that is, a perversion and hence a mental illness. Today, it is an accepted form of medical treatment. In reply to an inquiry from a reader, an editorial note in the authoritative journal, *Modern Medicine,* explains that "according to the Internal Revenue Service, such [*i.e.,* nude] therapy is a deductible medical expense if the patient is referred to the group by his physician and a written statement to that effect by the physician accompanies the patient's tax return."[18]

One of the oldest tactics in the battle between the sexes must surely be the refusal of women to gratify the sexual desires of men. With the dawn of psychiatric enlightenment this behavior too has been attributed to mental illnesses, such as hysteria and frigidity; today, however, it is also enlisted in the struggle against mental illness, specifically as a cure for alcoholism. An item in *Parade* magazine begins with the following question: "How does a wife get a husband to stop drinking?" In Sydney, Australia, we learn, some wives do it by "withholding sex from their husbands." Lest the reader unscientifically conclude that these women do this because they do not like, or are angry with, their husbands, we learn that the wives' conduct is in fact a form of psychotherapy: "It's all part of a program directed by Professor S. H. Lovibond, a psychologist at the University of New South Wales. 'We don't tell the wives,' explains Professor Lovibond, 'that withholding sex is the only aversion technique, but each is left to devise her own method. Quite a few have devised sex withholding to help an alcoholically addicted husband conquer his weakness.'" Professor Lovibond's use of language is revealing: he calls alcoholism a weakness, and sex withholding an aversion technique. The article in *Parade* goes on to assure the reader that for husbands who might be happy with their wives' sexual withholding, Professor Lovibond has more persuasive therapeutic tools at his command: "Professor Lovibond also uses electroshock therapy on his problem drinkers to dissuade heavy drinkers from the bottle."[19]

I cite these examples here not to argue that all so-called psychotherapies are coercive, fraudulent, or otherwise evil. That view is as false and foolish an oversimplification as is the view that all such interventions are healing, helpful, or otherwise good, merely because they are called "therapeutic." My point is rather that many, perhaps most, so-called psychotherapeutic procedures are harmful for the so-called patients; that this simple fact is now obscured by the expanded, loose, metaphorical—in short, jargonized —contemporary use of the term *psychotherapy;* and that all such interventions and proposals should therefore be regarded as evil until they are proven otherwise.

III

Of course, people have always influenced each other, for better or for worse. With the development of modern psychotherapy, there arose a powerful tendency to view all previous attempts of this sort through the pseudomedical spectacles of psychiatry and to relabel them as psychotherapies. Accordingly, both psychiatrists and laymen now believe that magic, religion, faith-healing, witch-doctoring, prayer, animal magnetism, electrotherapy, hypnosis, suggestion, and countless other human activities are *actually* different forms of psychotherapy. I consider this view objectionable. Instead of claiming that we have finally discovered the real nature of interpersonal influence and given it its proper name, *psychotherapy*, I believe our task should be to uncover and understand how this concept arose and how it now functions. That is the task I have set myself in this volume.

More specifically, I shall try to show how, with the decline of religion and the growth of science in the eighteenth century, the cure of (sinful) souls, which had been an integral part of the Christian religions, was recast as the cure of (sick) minds, and became an integral part of medical science. My aim in this enterprise has been to unmask the medical and therapeutic pretensions of psychiatry and psychotherapy. I have done so not because I think that medicine and treatment are bad things, but rather because, in the so-called mental health field, I know that the psychiatric and psychotherapeutic mythology is now used to disguise deception and conceal coercion—by psychiatrists, patients, politicians, jurists, journalists, and people in general.

Since people need myths to sustain their existence, however, there must be restraints on the pursuit of demythologizing. Accordingly, I have—in my life and in my writings—tried to distinguish between the use of myth to sustain a person's own existence and its use to deceive and coerce others. Objecting to the personal use of a mythology in private, or between consenting adults, is objecting to religious freedom; objecting to the legal and political use of force and fraud concealed and justified by a mythology is objecting to religious persecution. One can, of course, believe in and defend freedom of religion without believing in the literal truth of any particular religion—theological, medical, or psychiatric. And one can object to religious coercion even though one might believe that some or all of the goals of that particular religion—theological, medical, or psychiatric—are desirable. In either case, one would be for freedom and against coercion—not for or against religion or medicine or psychiatry.

It is in this spirit that I have offered my previous efforts at demythologizing psychiatry, and in which I now offer my present effort at demythologizing psychotherapy.

I

The Problem of
Psychotherapy

1

The Myth of Psychotherapy: Metaphorizing Medical Treatment

I

What is psychotherapy? In the conventional view, it is, generally, the treatment of mental disease—particularly by psychological, social, or environmental, rather than physical or chemical, means. In this imagery, psychotherapy is real and objective in the same sense that prescribing penicillin, surgically removing a brain tumor, or setting a fracture are real and objective. Hence, we commonly speak of psychiatrists "giving," and patients "receiving," psychotherapy. In my opinion, this view is entirely false. Actually, psychotherapy refers to what two or more people do with, for, and to each other, by means of verbal and nonverbal messages.[1] It is, in short, a relationship comparable to friendship, marriage, religious observance, advertising, or teaching.

Accordingly, when I suggest that psychotherapy is a myth I do not mean to deny the reality of the phenomena to which that term is applied. People do suffer from all sorts of aches and pains, fears and guilts, depressions and futilities; many such persons do consult, or are compelled to consult, experts called psychotherapists; and one or more of the participants in the resulting transaction may consider it helpful, useful, or "therapeutic." The coming together of these two parties and the results of their coming together are conventionally called psychotherapy. All that exists and is very much a part of our social reality. But therein, precisely, lies the mythology of psychotherapy: for these comings together have nothing whatever to do with psyches and are not therapeutic.

Definitions, especially the power to construct definitions and to impose them on others, are of great importance in all aspects of human life. In psychiatry and psychotherapy, because these disciplines deal with human relations and with the influence of persons and groups on one another, how words are used is extremely important. It seems appropriate, therefore, to begin with a discussion of some definitions of psychotherapy.

Noyes' Modern Clinical Psychiatry, perhaps the single most generally accepted and widely used American psychiatric text, defines psychotherapy as:

> The treatment of emotional or personality disorders by psychological means. Although many different psychological techniques may be employed in an effort to relieve problems and disorders and make the patient a mature, satisfied, and independent person, an important therapeutic factor common to them all is the therapist-patient relationship, with its interpersonal experiences. Through this relationship the patient comes to know that he can share his feelings, attitudes, and experiences with the physician and that the latter, with his warmth, understanding, empathy, acceptance, and support, will not depreciate, censure, or judge him no matter what he may reveal, but will respect his dignity or worth.[2]

Perhaps the best that can be said about this definition—which offers a "technique" that will make its object mature, satisfied, and independent—is that it is naïvely self-congratulatory: it characterizes the psychotherapist as warm, understanding, empathic, accepting, and supporting, and indeed as all of this regardless of what his patient tells him! Perhaps the worst that can be said about this definition—which asserts that the therapists will not depreciate, censure, or judge the patient—is that it is deliberately mendacious: it not only conceals the complex moral and political character of psychotherapy behind a series of quasi-medical pronouncements, but actually flies in the face of the very real fact that the psychotherapist often belittles, censures, and judges his patient, and that he may, indeed, go much further than this by stigmatizing him with socially destructive psychiatric-diagnostic labels and imposing involuntary hospitalization and treatment on him.

According to the Canadian Psychiatric Association, psychotherapy is "a medical act by which a physician, through sessions of verbal or other communications, explores and attempts to influence the behavior of a psychiatrically disordered patient with the objective of reducing his disability."[3] That, of course, is a purely institutional definition: it does not identify x in terms of y, as does, for example, the definition of the centigrade scale of temperature; instead, it simply claims and defends a sphere of economic and political interest, as does, for example, the definition of a modern state's "national interest."

What conclusions can we draw from these and the other usual definitions of psychotherapy? We can conclude that they are purely verbal exercises, having incantatory, ritualistic, and strategic functions rather than identifying, as they ostensibly do, discrete forms of medical treatments.[4] In trying to understand psychotherapy (or psychopathology), we are confronted with masses of confusions and problems that result from the stubborn and strategic misuse of words, or, as Wittgenstein put it: "Your concept is wrong. However, I cannot illumine the matter by fighting against your words, but only by trying to turn your attention away from certain expressions, illustrations, images, and *towards* the *employment* of the words."[5] Let us heed Wittgenstein's advice and focus on the actual use of the vocabulary of psychotherapy. To do so, we must first consider the ways in which genuine medical treatments are described and classified.

II

Since I shall argue that psychotherapeutic interventions are metaphorical treatments, it is necessary that I indicate what I consider literal treatments. By literal treatments I mean medical or surgical treatments—that is, material or physicochemical interventions on a person's body with the aim of ameliorating or curing the disorder of that body.[6]

This definition is an essentially instrumental one: medical treatment is identified by *what is done,* not by *who does it.* Thus, when a person suffering from pneumonia or syphilis takes penicillin, he is receiving chemotherapy whether the drug is prescribed by a duly licensed physician, is dispensed by a quack, or is ingested by the patient on his own initiative. In some cases of medical treatment—as in chemotherapy, radiation therapy, inhalation therapy—the treatment is identified by the method employed; again, regardless of who gives it and regardless of who gets it, such treatment is clearly identified by *what is done.* In still other cases of treatment—especially those employing surgery—the procedure is usually identified by a combination of words that point both to the *method* of therapy and to the *organ* or part of the body treated. Thus, neurosurgery is surgery on the nervous system, abdominal surgery is surgery on intra-abdominal organs, and so forth.

Where, then, are the parallels between medical treatments and psychotherapies? To best demonstrate the illusory, fake, or metaphorical character of psychotherapy, we might begin by employing the broadest definition of this term—that is, the one which designates as psychotherapy all efforts to relieve or cure "mental illness." One such effort is psychosurgery.

Psychosurgery is a wonderfully revealing term. Perhaps because its developer received the Nobel prize in medicine rather than in literature, it has received more neurologic than semantic attention. Clearly, *psychosurgery* is a term fashioned after such other terms as *neurosurgery* or *urologic surgery.* But the qualifiers in the latter terms obviously refer to organ systems or body parts, whereas the term *psyche* refers to no such thing. I need not consider here what the psyche is or is not to assert that the very term *psychosurgery* is political rhetoric of the most dangerous kind: by creating and legitimizing a scientific-sounding term, physicians are in effect given permission to operate on perfectly healthy brains! After all, if a person's brain is diseased and if a surgeon operates on such a patient, he is said to be doing neurosurgery. Hence, the very invention of the word *psychosurgery* is deeply revealing of its character as fake therapy on a metaphorical organ.

To be sure, psychosurgery is real surgery, just as Clifford Irving's manuscript on Howard Hughes was a real manuscript. But the claim that such surgery is therapeutic for the patient rests solely on the fact that it *resembles* therapeutic surgery, just as the claim that Irving's book was a biography of Hughes rested solely on the fact that it resembled a genuine biography of Hughes. In the one case, a person claims to have recorded interviews with someone he never saw; in the other, a person claims to have operated on organs or tissues no one ever saw. The literary impostor is recognized as a confidence man, and his production as a fabric of lies fashioned to sound like the truth. The psychiatric impostor, on the other hand, is not so exposed; on the contrary—because he supports a common, culturally shared desire to equate and confuse brain and mind, nerves and nervousness—he is hailed as the discoverer of a new "treatment" for "mental illness."

III

In contrast to the foregoing definitions of medical treatment, the definitions of psychotherapy are quite imprecise. Does the term *psychotherapy* refer to the method used or to the organ or body part affected by disease and hence the target of remedial influence? Actually, it refers to both. Thus, in one of its uses, the term *psychotherapy* is analogous to the term *chemotherapy:* just as in the latter chemicals are used to treat disease, so in the former psyches are thus used. Indeed, we have come to accept as psychotherapy all conceivable practices and situations in which the soul, spirit, mind, or personality of an individual who claims to be a healer is employed to bring about some sort of change, called "therapeutic," in the soul, spirit, mind, or personality of another individual who is called the patient. The only thing these diverse enterprises have in common is that the method used is psychological—that is, nonphysical.[7]

The proposition that *psychotherapy* is a metaphor, an expansion of the customary use of the word *therapy* to cover things hitherto not meant by it, is evident if one takes the trouble to ex-

amine what psychotherapists actually do. A dramatic example of
the origin of one such metaphorical treatment—what some American therapists now brazenly call "love therapy"—may be found
in Freud's account of the history of the psychoanalytic movement.
When Freud was a young practitioner, Rudolf Chrobak, a famous
Viennese obstetrician and gynecologist, referred a woman to him.
Let us see what was wrong with this "patient," what Chrobak
regarded as the appropriate "therapy" for her, and what Freud
thought about the problem. In "On the History of the Psycho-
Analytic Movement," Freud reminisces:

> Although the patient had been married for eighteen years
> [she] was still *virgo intacta*. The husband was abso-
> lutely impotent. In such cases, he [Chrobak] said, there
> was nothing for a medical man to do but to shield this
> domestic misfortune with his own reputation, and put up
> with it if people shrugged their shoulders and said of
> him: "He's no good if he can't cure her after so many
> years." The sole prescription for such a malady, he
> added, is familiar enough to us, but we cannot order it.
> It runs:
>
> 'Rx
> Penis normalis
>   dosim
>   repetatur!'
>
> I have never heard of such a prescription, and felt in-
> clined to shake my head over my kind friend's cynicism.[8]

The imagery and vocabulary of treatment are used here in an
obviously metaphorical, even humorous way. But in the nearly
one hundred years that have elapsed since that episode, what was
said in jest came to be taken in earnest; what had been metaphor
was systematically redefined as literal.

To be sure, Freud never defined sexual intercourse as therapy.
But he did something that was, in a way, more far-reaching and
harmful: he defined listening and talking—that is, conversation—
as therapy. Furthermore, he defined the people to whom he talked
in his office—and, soon, everyone at whom he looked in terms of
his personal philosophy which he called "psychoanalysis" and
whom he described in the pseudomedical vocabulary of that phi-

losophy which he called "psychoanalytic theory"—as "patients" suffering from various types of "mental diseases." Instead of conquering what had been presented to him as mental diseases by curing these diseases, he conquered what is in effect the human condition by annexing it in its entirety to the medical profession.[9]

In summary, then, psychotherapy is the name we give to a particular kind of personal influence: by means of communication, one person identified as the psychotherapist exerts an ostensibly therapeutic influence on another person identified as the patient. This process is, of course, but a special member of a much larger class—indeed, a class so vast that virtually all human interactions fall within it. In countless other situations people influence one another. But who is to say whether or when such interactions are helpful or harmful, and to whom? The concept of psychotherapy betrays us by prejudging the interaction as "therapeutic" for the patient, in intent or effect or both.

People try to influence one another constantly. The question that concerns those interested in psychotherapy is: What kind of influence do psychotherapists exert on their clients? People influence one another to support some values and to oppose others. In the past, they promoted such overt values as chastity, obedience, thrift. Today, they advocate such covert values as the common good, mental health, welfare—blanks that may be filled in with any meaning the speaker or listener desires. Herein lies the great value of these vague terms for the demagogue, whether political or professional. Just as a presidential candidate may talk about restoring the nation's economy to a "healthy" condition, without specifying whether he is promoting a balanced budget or deficit financing, so a psychiatrist may talk about "mental health," without revealing whether he is promoting individualism or collectivism, autonomy or heteronomy.

Psychotherapists do many things; the professed goal is always to provide therapy. Often, however, attempts to treat a patient are really efforts to alter his conduct from one mode to another. Thus, there are psychiatrists who try to convert unhappily married couples into happily married ones; homosexuals into heterosexuals; criminals into noncriminals; or, in general, mentally sick patients into mentally healthy former patients. In short, psychotherapy is secular ethics. It is the religion of the formally irreligious—with its language, which is not Latin but medical jargon; with its codes of conduct, which are not ethical but legalistic; and with its theology, which is not Christianity but positivism.

2

Persuading Persons: Rhetoric as Remedy

Trying to demonstrate that psychotherapy is rhetoric is like trying to demonstrate that the cow is a mammal. Why do it, then? For two reasons: because it is now the official opinion of the dominant institutions of society that psychotherapy is a form of medical treatment;[1] and because an appreciation of rhetoric has all but disappeared from contemporary consciousness.[2] Seeing psychotherapy as conversation rather than cure thus requires that we not only consider the error of classifying it as a medical intervention, but that we also look anew at the subject of rhetoric and assess its relevance to mental healing.

In plain language, what do patient and psychotherapist actually do? They speak and listen to each other. What do they speak about? Narrowly put, the patient speaks about himself, and the therapist speaks about the patient. In a broader sense, however, both also speak about other persons and about various matters of concern to their lives. The point is that each tries to move the other to see or do things in a certain way. That is what qualifies their actions as fundamentally rhetorical. If the psychotherapist and his patient were not rhetoricians, they could not engage in the activity we now conventionally call *psychotherapy*—just as if cows did not suckle their young, we could not call them mammals.

One of the most important influences on Freud's development of psychoanalysis was the Socratic dialogues. Socrates engaged his perplexed interlocutors in a certain kind of conversation which the Greeks called *rhetoric*. And Socrates was hailed as a great *rhetorician*. Why, then, are Sigmund Freud, Carl Jung, and the other pioneer psychotherapists not also called rhetoricians, and why is their art not called rhetoric?

II

The sharp distinction in Western thought between body and mind, between bodily and mental diseases, goes back to Plato. It is to Plato, moreover, that we owe the view that the task of the physician of the body is to heal by biological or scientific means, whereas the task of the physician of the soul is to heal by verbal or rhetorical means. In the *Phaedrus,* Plato puts it, through Socrates, as follows: "It may be that the art of rhetoric follows the same methods as does the art of medicine. . . . In both cases you must analyze a nature, in the one that of the body, in the other that of the soul, if you are going to proceed scientifically, not merely by empirical routine, to apply medicine and diet to create health and strength in the one case—while in the other to apply proper words and rules of conduct to communicate such convictions and virtues as you may desire."[3] The nature of that division of labor could hardly be better expressed.

The Romans rearticulated not only the classic Platonic division between the cure of bodies and the cure of souls, but also reemphasized that whereas the methods of the former were "mute," those of the latter were "verbal." For Vergil, medicine is *muta ars,* the silent art;[4] and Vegetius, a fourth-century Roman writer, specifically enjoins that "animals and men must not be treated with vain words but by the sure art of medicine."[5] Indeed, the importance of the distinction between the silent art of the body-doctor and the semantic art of the soul-doctor cannot be over-emphasized in connection with our effort to clarify the historical origins of modern psychotherapy.

In his fine study, *The Therapy of the Word in Classical Antiquity,* Pedro Lain Entralgo traces those origins to the rhetoricians of Greece and Rome. The art of speaking well was then, of course, a matter of supreme importance, placing the orator or rhetorician foremost among men. Indeed, for the Greeks there was something divine about the art of persuasive speech; they had a goddess of persuasion, called Peitho.[6] Although Lain Entralgo's own views lead him to attempt to recombine the cure of bodies and the cure of souls, medicine and psychiatry, he notes nevertheless that in the classical Greek conception of rhetoric, the persuasive word could heal or harm depending on the intentions of the user. "But we have also heard," he writes, "that the persuasive word is a *pharmakon,* in the double sense, medicament and poison, of that Greek term."[7]

Lain Entralgo also shows that Plato recognized the crucial role of *katharsis,* in the dual sense of purgation and purification, in the cure of souls: "For Plato, the cathartic agent that the 'malady of the soul' specifically requires is the apt and effective word."[8] This idea is expressed most succinctly in *Charmides,* where Plato has Socrates saying: "The cure of the soul . . . has to be effected by the use of certain charms, and these charms are fair words."[9] Lain Entralgo thus concludes that we are obliged "to see Plato as the inventor of scientific, or *kata technen,* verbal psychotherapy. . . . Beyond the shadow of a doubt, Plato thus becomes the inventor of a rigorously technical verbal psychotherapy."[10] Although Lain Entralgo's evidence is right, I think he is quite wrong in concluding that Plato's invention is "scientific."

Aristotle has cautioned against confusing rhetoric with science. If we want to grasp the true nature of psychotherapy, we must revive Artistotle's ideas on rhetoric and relate them to the practices of modern mental healers.

Aristotle begins his book on *Rhetoric* with this observation: "Rhetoric is the counterpart of Dialectic. Both alike are concerned with such things as come, more or less, within the general ken of all men and belong to no definite science. Accordingly, all men make use, more or less, of both."[11] Aristotle here uses rhetoric and dialectic to refer to the arts of public speaking and logical discussion. Having identified rhetoric as persuasive speech, Aristotle distinguishes three varieties of it—political, forensic, and ceremonial:

Political speaking urges us either to do or not to do something: one of these two courses is always taken by private counsellors, as well as by men who address public assemblies. Forensic speaking either attacks or defends somebody: one or the other of these two things must always be done by the parties in a case. The ceremonial oratory of display either praises or censures somebody. These three kinds of rhetoric refer to three different kinds of time. The political orator is concerned with the future: it is about things to be done hereafter that he advises, for or against. The party in a case at law is concerned with the past; one man accuses the other, and the other defends himself, with reference to things already done. The ceremonial orator is, properly speaking, concerned with the present, since all men praise or blame in view of the state of things existing at the time, though they often find it useful also to recall the past and to make guesses at the future.[12]

Psychotherapists engage in all three types of rhetorical discourse; and, as a rule, so do their clients. Indeed, Aristotle casually remarks, as if it were quite obvious—which, in classical Greece it no doubt was—that private counselors do the same things as men who address public assemblies. Here is the category error of modern psychiatry writ large: no one now believes that what politicians do constitutes a form of medical treatment, but many believe that what psychiatrists do does.

Aristotle describes the various ways in which the rhetorician does his job, which is to persuade his interlocutor or audience. Among his methods, the use of enthymemes—which Aristotle considers the "substance of rhetorical persuasion"[13]—ranks very high. An enthymeme is a type of syllogism or argument in which one of the propositions, usually the premise, is understood but is not stated. The enthymeme is thus closely related to the metaphor. For example, the argument that the psychotherapist is a type of medical healer and should be a qualified physician is an enthymeme: the unstated premise is that a person who makes a seemingly sick individual feel better by a seemingly medical method is performing a treatment and is therefore practicing medicine. Having stated the premise, one can debate it. For example, one could maintain that just as not everything that makes people feel badly constitutes illness, so not everything that makes them feel well constitutes treatment.

Aristotle also considers the relation of rhetoric to science. "The truth is," he writes, "that rhetoric is a combination of the science of logic and of the ethical branch of politics; and it is partly like dialectic, partly like sophistical reasoning. But the more we try to make either dialectic or rhetoric not what they really are, practical faculties, but sciences, the more we shall inadvertently be destroying their true nature; for we shall be refashioning them and shall be passing into the region of sciences dealing with definite subjects rather than simply with words and forms of reasoning."[14]

Since rhetoric is the art of persuasive discourse, considerations of rhetoric necessarily raise the issue of the rhetorician's aims. The ends of political rhetoric, Aristotle explains, vary just as do those of government. "The end of democracy," he writes, "is freedom; of oligarchy, wealth; of aristocracy, the maintenance of education and national institutions; of tyranny, the protection of the tyrant."[15] Similarly, the end of medicine is health; and of psychotherapy, mental health. This latter statement, however, is itself an enthymeme, concealing the premise that mental health is as readily identifiable as freedom or wealth.

Indeed, immediately after the passage quoted above, Aristotle explicitly rejects such a nominalist approach to human affairs, opting instead for a refreshingly empirical position. "We shall learn the qualities of governments," he declares, "in the same way as we learn the qualities of individuals, since they are revealed in their deliberate acts of choice; and these are determined by the ends that inspire them."[16] Just so for mental patients and mental healers: the symptoms of the former and the treatments of the latter are, themselves, acts of choice made by moral agents. Of course, they may not be deliberate acts in quite the same sense in which we choose to put on one tie rather than another; but they are "deliberate acts of choice" nevertheless, and they reveal, as indeed nothing else does, the actors' aims. That simple idea is the key Freud and Jung used for unlocking the meaning of mental symptoms; and it is the key that we can use to unlock the meaning of mental treatments as well. We cannot assimilate mental illnesses and treatments to a medical model; through their symptoms, mental patients seek to attain certain ends, as do mental healers, through their treatments. Insofar as these two parties join forces, it is necessary to reinspect their acts toward each other and to infer from them what ends each is pursuing separately, and what end both are pursuing together. In actuality, these ends vary just as do the ends pursued by politicians and people generally.

Aristotle has thus provided us with firm foundations for seeing and studying human beings as moral agents. He even anticipated some of the modern positivistic-reductionistic "explanations" of the "causes" of human actions, which were, even in his day, evidently not lacking for supporters. "Nor, again, is action due to wealth or poverty," declares Aristotle, as if he were answering the modern mental-health rhetorician making excuses on behalf of "disadvantaged" muggers and murderers. "It is of course true that poor men, being short of money, do have an appetite for it, and that rich men, being able to command needless pleasures, do have an appetite for such pleasures: but here, again, their actions will be *due* not to wealth or poverty but to appetite."[17]

III

As the painter's medium is oil on canvas and the musician's medium is the vibration of the strings of a piano or violin, so the orator's and writer's medium is language. Clearly, Freud and his followers worked in this latter medium. Not only did the early psychoanalysts talk a great deal to their patients (much more than many people now imagine), they also wrote a great deal. Their interest in language was very much a part of their culture. To illuminate this latter point, I want to call attention to an all-but-forgotten aspect of the cultural milieu in which modern psychotherapy arose: namely, that in the German-speaking countries of Europe during the second half of the nineteenth century, it was not only physics and chemistry that were booming, but also philology and linguistics. The study of languages—historical, anthropological, religious, psychological, and structural studies of speech and writing—was popular in and outside of academic circles.

The idea of humanness, the demarcation between the human and nonhuman being, has apparently been connected with the idea of language as far back as history extends. This is not very surprising, but it is nevertheless of surpassing significance: in defining what a human being is or ought to be, language remains perhaps the single most important criterion. The idea that thought cannot exist without speech was implicit in the Greek language. *Phrazomai,* the Greek term for *I meditate,* means literally *I speak to myself. Logos,* the Greek term for *reason,* also means *speech.*[18]

Among nineteenth-century students of language whose work bears especially closely on the nature of psychotherapy is Fritz Mauthner (1849–1923). His basic thesis was that language is metaphorical through and through, and that therein lies its immense power. More specifically, Mauthner suggested that "metaphor and association are identical," that "thought-association . . . is fundamentally nothing but an insufferably pedantic expression . . . for the concept of metaphor."[19] In effect he had advanced an almost fully articulated linguistic-rhetorical account of the psychoanalytic method: Freud demands from his patients "free associations," the name he gives to their mental comparisons of one object or event with another; and he offers them in return "interpretations," the name he gives to his own mental comparisons of one object or event with another. The whole enterprise is linguistic, in the specific sense of having to do with the classification of comparisons—as literal or metaphoric, healthy or sick, legitimate or illegitimate.

Mauthner's second favorite theme was the power of words. He even invented a new term, *logocracy,* to identify it.[20] According to Gershon Weiler, Mauthner's point about logocracy—or rhetorical power—was "that it is precisely that characteristic of words which makes them inadequate for the description of things as they are, namely their historical load of associations, that makes them eminently suitable for inducing moods and feelings in people and for making them act. . . . To invoke 'the fatherland' or 'justice' is to rely on the great emotional appeal that such words have."[21]

Although Freud did not invent the idea, he was exceptionally adept at naming some of the complaints of physically healthy persons *symptoms* that pointed to underlying *diseases,* called *neuroses,* which he then offered to relieve by means of a species of conversation called *psychoanalysis.* In this view, Freud discovered new diseases and new treatments in much the same way that the leader of a legendary barbarian tribe (in the following story told by Mauthner) discovered a new species of dogs. According to that story, "The Emperor Marcus Aurelius sent lions into battle along with his soldiers, against a barbarian tribe. Members of this tribe had never seen lions so they asked their leader what these animals were. This leader, who 'knew the significance of names and words,' replied: 'These are dogs, Roman dogs.' Upon which they proceeded to treat them like dogs: they beat them to death with their clubs."[22]

Mauthner was perhaps the first modern thinker to clearly articulate the idea, for which contemporary linguistic philosophers now usually get the credit, that it is a fateful, possibly fatal, error to believe that just because someone uses a word there must be something in the world of which that word is the name. Mauthner regarded this natural tendency to reify abstraction "as the origin not just of speculative confusion, but also of practical injustice and evil in the world. . . . [He] considered metaphysics and dogmatism to be two faces of a single coin, which was also the fountainhead of intolerance and injustice."[23] Mauthner may have gone a little too far here in equating the origin of evil in the world with its linguistic justification; but he was clearly onto something important. Just how important is apparent from the following brief excerpts from his book, significantly titled *Sprache und Psychologie* (*Language and Psychology*), published in 1901:

> If language were a thing—sort of like a tool—then with use it would deteriorate and wear out. But language is not an object, not a tool—but a usage. Language is simply language-use. This is not a play on words, but a fact. It explains why the more language is used, the richer and stronger it grows.
>
> . . . .
>
> The deplorable condition of the world is reflected, as in a mirror, by language. Latin, at the height of the Empire, was a sick language before it became a dead language. The cultural languages of our age are similarly

sick, rotten to the core. . . . The languages of sophistication have all developed through metaphorization and have all become childish as the meanings of the metaphors were forgotten.[24]

IV

Probably no contemporary scholar has grasped the fundamentally rhetorical nature of language, especially the language of social science, as well as Richard Weaver. He never tired of warning us that with the decline of rhetoric a "great shift of valuation has taken place," the clearly value-laden languages of theology and tragedy being replaced with the seemingly value-free languages of science and technology. Language, Weaver insisted, "is intended to be sermonic. . . . It is always preaching. [Hence] the upholders of mere dialectic . . . are among the most subversive enemies of societies and culture."[25]

Among these subversive enemies Weaver ranked the social scientists very high, and rightly so. Why? Because science necessarily deals with the abstract and the universal, whereas rhetoric is always concerned with the particular and the individual.[26] Although Weaver never refers specifically to psychiatrists or psychotherapists, his admonition about the rhetorical character of social science applies with great force to psychiatry and psychotherapy. Where else do people engage more obviously in an ostensibly scientific activity—rationalized in terms of diseases, diagnoses, and treatments—in which, in fact, the only things that really matter are the "individual men in their individual situations?"[27] Psychotherapists may, and of course do, pontificate about instincts and ids, Oedipus complexes and infantile memories, unipolar and bipolar depressions, enzymes in the brain and endocrines in the blood, but all that is, in fact, "pure rhetoric." What matters, what is real and true, is what doctor and patient, psychotherapist and client, actually say and do.

We can thus see why the languages of psychiatry, psychoanalysis, and psychotherapy—as the ostensibly scientific languages of a science of man and of the cure of mental diseases—are necessarily anti-individualistic, and hence threats to human freedom and dignity. One cannot help but agree with Weaver's conclusion that "the recovery of value and of community in our time calls for a restatement of the broadly cultural role of rhetoric."[28] Weaver's remarks bring us back to the significance of rhetoric for psychotherapy, and to psychoanalysis as its paradigm. That Freud was a rhetorician may or may not be obvious, depending on one's point of view on psychoanalysis: it is obvious to those who view Freud as a great imaginative writer, or moralist, or myth-maker; but it is not obvious, may even seem incredible, to those who view him as a scientist of the human mind, especially of the "unconscious mind," and as the discoverer of a new form of treatment for mental diseases.[29]

If we accept the proposition that psychotherapists are rhetoricians, we must consider whether they are noble or base. That distinction hinges on whether we believe that a particular rhetorician moves his listeners toward what is good or what is evil, a judgment that will differ according to the values of those who render it. It is interesting to note, however, that Weaver identifies the base rhetorician as a person who is "always trying to keep [individuals] from the support which personal courage, noble associations, and divine philosophy provide a man."[30] Although his examples of the typical base rhetorician are the journalist and political propagandist, his characterization of them applies to the psychoanalyst or psychotherapist as well. "Nothing is more feared by him [that is, by the base rhetorician] than a true dialectic," writes Weaver. "By discussing only one side of an issue, by mentioning cause without consequence or consequence without cause, acts without agents or agents without agency, he often successfully blocks definition and cause-and-effect reasoning."[31]

As the base rhetorician uses language to increase his own power, to produce converts to his own cause, and to create loyal followers of his own person, so the noble rhetorician uses language to wean men from their inclination to depend on authority, to encourage them to think and speak clearly, and to teach them to be their own masters. It is thus, Weaver declares, that "rhetoric at its truest sense [that is, noble rhetoric] seeks to perfect men by showing them better versions of themselves, links in that chain extending up toward the ideal, which only the intellect can apprehend and only the soul have affection for. This is the justified affection of which no one can be ashamed, and he who feels no influence of it is truly outside the communion of minds."[32] That is my standard for judging Freud and the psychoanalysts and psychohistorians he spawned as base rhetoricians.

V

How has the medical, or rather pseudomedical, vocabulary of modern psychiatry displaced the vocabulary of oratory, ethics, and politics? In his celebrated book, *Battle for the Mind,* William Sargant, widely regarded as the leading organic psychiatrist in Britain, explains his choice of a subtitle for the book—*A Physiology of Conversion and Brainwashing.* Explicitly disavowing his concerns from those of the rhetorician, Sargant insists that he is interested in the brain, not the mind, while simultaneously reaffirming the incontrovertibly rhetorical and repressive nature of psychiatric interventions:

> My concern here is *not* with the immortal soul, which is the province of the theologian, nor even with the mind in the broadest sense of the word which is the province of the philosopher, but with the brain and the nervous system, which man shares with the dog and other animals. . . . This study discusses mechanistic methods influencing the brain which are open to many agencies, some obviously good and some obviously very evil indeed; but it is concerned with brain mechanics, not with the ethical and philosophical aspects of a problem which others are very much more competent to discuss than I am.[33]

This passage, and others I shall cite presently, bring to mind Hitler's famous recommendation that politicians use only big lies. Small lies, Hitler warned, are easily unmasked, discrediting the person who utters them; whereas big lies astound, commanding the acceptance of the lie as a truth and of the liar as a leader.

Much of Sargant's book is about "conversion," in the traditional religious sense. Yet this too, Sargant claims, he considers from a purely medical point of view: "It must not be held against me that I do not discuss some types of purely intellectual conversion, but only those physical or physiological stimuli, rather than intellectual arguments, which seem to help to produce conversion by causing alteration in the subject's brain function. Hence the term 'physiology' in the title."[34] One might conclude that Sargant is writing about neurophysiology. Actually, nothing could be further from the truth. As the very first paragraph of his book shows, he is discussing politics. However, Sargant insists that his subjects are physiology and brain mechanics:

> Politicians, priests and psychiatrists often face the same problem: how to find the most rapid and permanent means of changing a man's beliefs. When, towards the end of World War II, I first became interested in the similarity of the methods which have, from time to time, been used by the political, religious, and psychiatric disciplines, I failed to foresee the enormous importance now attaching to the problem—because of an ideological struggle that seems fated to decide the course of civilization for centuries to come. The problem of the doctor and his nervously ill patient, and that of the religious leader who sets out to gain and hold new converts, has now become the problem of whole groups of nations, who wish not only to confirm certain political beliefs within their boundaries, but to proselytize the outside world.[35]

This appears to be a straightforward statement about the similarities between politics and psychiatry—in particular, about their common basis in rhetoric. Not so, according to Sargant, who actually denies the role of rhetoric, or of repression, in any of it: "The conclusion reached is that simple physiological mechanisms of conversion do exist. . . . The politico-religious struggle for the mind of man may well be won by whoever becomes most conversant with the normal and abnormal functions of the brain, and is readiest to make use of the knowledge gained."[36]

Although Sargant uses the terms *persuasion* and *suggestion,* in his explanations and justifications of mental treatments he puts all his faith in physiological methods and models: "Psychotherapeutic techniques that involve merely talking to the patient generally prove ineffective in curing severe states of mental disorder, even when strong emotions can be aroused. . . . Far better results may be achieved by a combination of psychotherapy with one or another of the newly introduced modern shock treatments, or with operations on the brain."[37] Celebrating the brain as the organ of mental illness, he advocates altering it with mental treatment—and the more radical the treatment, the better: "In the present state of medical knowledge the only hopeful treatment of some chronic obsessional, chronic schizophrenic and chronic anxious or depressive patients, who respond to no form of shock therapy, psychotherapy or drug treatment is a surgical one to which, as a rule, recourse is only had when all else fails: the newer modifications of the operation called 'prefrontal leucotomy.' "[38]

Leucotomy, explains Sargant, makes psychotics more "open to suggestion and persuasion without stubborn resistance."[39] It also helps them to "think more logically, and examine new theories without emotional bias."[40] He offers this astonishing example: "One patient with a Messianic delusion had proved wholly unamenable to intensive psycho-analytic treatment, but after leucotomy was now able to discuss his Messianic claims with an intelligent male nurse and let them be argued away. Genuine religious conversions are also seen after the new modified leucotomy operations. For the mind is freed from its old strait-jacket and new religious beliefs and attitudes can now more easily take the place of the old."[41]

Sargant seems extremely fond of changing people's religious beliefs. Another case of "successful" leucotomy he reports was performed on a high-ranking Salvation Army officer: "She married a clergyman. For years she lay in a hospital, constantly complaining that she had committed sins against the Holy Ghost. She complained of it for weeks and months, and her poor husband did his best to distract her, but without success. Then we decided to operate upon her. . . . After the dressing had been taken off, I asked her, 'How are you now? What about the Holy Ghost?' Smiling, she answered, 'Oh, the Holy Ghost; there is no Holy Ghost.' "[42]

Nevertheless, Sargant insists that psychiatric religion, rhetoric, and repression are not religion, rhetoric, and repression; they are simply treatments restoring sick people to health: "Doctors—if I may speak for my profession—certainly do not claim that they are capable of formulating a new religious or political dispensation; it is merely their function to learn how to provide the health that will enable the most suitable of such dispensations to be fought for and won."[43]

That certainly puts the case for a medical psychiatry and psychotherapy clearly and well. I submit, however, that that case rests on nothing more substantial than the metaphors of mental health and mental illness and a psychotherapeutic rhetoric socially authenticated as embodying the principles and practices of psychiatric healing.

3

Curing Souls:
Religion as Remedy

I

The basic ingredients of psychotherapy are religion, rhetoric, and repression, which are themselves mutually overlapping categories. However, in keeping with the medical and scientific pretensions of psychiatry, the reader of modern psychiatric texts would not discover this from perusing their pages. Psychiatrists writing about the nature of their discipline medicalize its contents, operations, and vocabulary; those writing about its history, and especially about the history of psychotherapy, medicalize its origins and development. Thus, although most psychiatric historians make passing acknowledgments of the religious prehistory of psychotherapy, they liken its religious origins to the religious origins of all healing and completely ignore the true precursor of modern psychotherapy—namely, the pastoral cure of souls.*

---

* Texts such as Gregory Zilboorg's and Franz Alexander and Sheldon Selesnick's do not even mention this subject.[1] Henri Ellenberger's encyclopedic *Discovery of the Unconscious* is exceptional in that it contains a three-and-a-half-page section specifically on the cure of souls.[2] But Ellenberger distorts the essential nature of psychotherapy by bracketing the cure of souls with religion and then contrasting it with a modern psychotherapy, which he calls "scientific," thus reintroducing into psychiatry the fateful error of confusing rhetoric with science, against which Aristotle warned.[3] John T. McNeill notes that a typical psychiatric text, such as *A Short History of Psychiatric Achievement* by Nolan D. C. Lewis, defines psychiatry as "a highly specialized branch of the practice of medicine" and makes no men-

The English phrase "cure of souls" derives from the Latin *cura animarum,* a phrase that designated one of the most important functions of the Roman Catholic Church. The significance of this phrase is obvious. The soul is the essence of the human personality; it distinguishes persons from animals or things and "causes" them to be moral agents. "The cure of souls," writes John T. McNeill in his *History of the Cure of Souls,* is, then, "the sustaining and curative treatment of persons in those matters that reach beyond the requirements of the animal life."[5] As we shall see, it is impossible to improve on this simple but incisive conceptualization that distinguishes not so much between body and mind, as simplistic anti-Cartesians would have it, but rather between human beings as animals and as moral agents.

Actually, psychotherapy is a modern, scientific-sounding name for what used to be called the "cure of souls." The true history of psychiatry thus begins not with the early nineteenth-century psychiatrists, but with the Greek philosophers and the Jewish rabbis of antiquity; and it continues with the Catholic priests and Protestant pastors, over a period of nearly two millennia, before the medical soul-doctors appear on the stage of history.

II

There is no need to belabor here that in scientifically underdeveloped societies all healing, whether of the body or the mind, is religious. The character of this holistic approach to therapy is exemplified by the shrine of Asclepius at Epidaurus. The Asclepieion, as the shrine was called, consisted of temples, a theater, a stadium, a gymnasium, and a library where, as Theodore Papadakis in a modern guidebook to Epidaurus explains, "every pilgrim could purify and regenerate himself."[6]

The Greeks believed that health was natural and that disease was the unnatural consequence of some foreign influence that disturbs the harmony of the mind. In their view, moreover, the agency that disturbed natural harmony was not real—that is, had

tion at all of the cure of souls. "The dissociation of psychotherapy from the theological and philosophical traditions is here complete."[4] Every other authoritative psychiatric text illustrates the same bias.

no substance—but was an illusion or chimera. These enemies of our natural harmony, writes Papadakis, "are very dangerous because they assail our mind and our thinking. . . . First, they attack a man mentally, and if they find that he is unguarded or spiritually too weak to behead them immediately, they settle in his mind and from there they spread to incapacitate also his body."[7]

It followed from this view that the essence of all therapy was spiritual healing. "A radical healing is thus obtained only when the mind itself is cured; when there is a change of mind (*metanoia*). For together with the mind, the body also is necessarily healed."[8] The Greeks recognized, however, that the body may also be cured directly, with various medicinal agents for example; but they regarded that form of therapy as superficial, leaving the underlying disharmonies uncorrected and, hence, potentially capable of causing new diseases elsewhere in the body. The psychoanalytic approach to psychosomatic medicine revives this imagery, showing us that far from being the fruit of a modern scientific understanding of disease, it is actually a massive medical regression to early Hellenic, and pre-Hellenic, ideas and practices of healing. Actually the fundamental differences between medical and mental healing are already crystal clear in ancient Greece—Hippocrates (*ca.* 460–377 B.C.) exemplifying the medical healer and Socrates (*ca.* 470–399 B.C.) the mental healer.*

In the many centuries before the birth of Jesus, as well as in nineteen following it, mankind's knowledge of medicine lagged far behind its understanding of religion and philosophy. In ancient Israel and Greece the healer of the soul is thus not the physician, but the rabbi and the philosopher. Socrates, McNeill reminds us, "was, and wished to be, *iatros tes psuches,* a healer of the soul. These Greek syllables have been recast to form the word 'psychiatrist.' But Socrates would hardly recognize the medical psychiatrist as a member of his fraternity. A scientific psychiatry indifferent to religion and philosophy is a new and strange phenomenon."[10] New, yes; strange, hardly. Furthermore, medical psy-

---

* Werner Jaeger states that "Euripides (*ca.* 485–407 B.C.) was the first psychologist. It was he who discovered the soul . . . who revealed the troubled world of man's emotions and passions." And he explains that, "in Euripides' time, (in addition to doctors of the body) there existed 'doctors of the soul.' Such was Antiphon, the sophist, who also taught and wrote about the interpretation of dreams."[9]

chiatry is not merely indifferent to religion, it is implacably hostile to it. Herein lies one of the supreme ironies of modern psychotherapy: it is not merely a religion that pretends to be a science, it is actually a fake religion that seeks to destroy true religion.

III

Psychotherapy as the cure of souls issues directly from Socrates' life and work. The *Dialogues* are, of course, Plato's representations of his master's thoughts. Greek scholars generally agree, however, that it is an accurate representation, especially so far as Socrates' concern with the cure of souls is concerned. Werner Jaeger, for example, attributes the emergence of the idea of the care of the soul in Christianity to the influence of Socrates as Plato interprets him.[11]

In the *Apology,* Socrates articulates his vocation as philosopher, by which he means a person who cares for psyche or soul, thus identifying a social role indistinguishable from that carved out by Freud and Jung and adopted by modern psychotherapists. "Gentlemen," declares Socrates, echoing the Jewish cry of personal independence from worldly authority, "I owe a greater obedience to God than to you."[12] That, of course, has since been the resounding *cri de coeur* of every political protester and the repressed *cri de coeur* of every psychiatric patient.

Socrates defines the role of the physician of the soul as follows: "This I do assure you, is what my God commands, and it is my belief that no greater good has ever befallen you in this city than my service to my God. For I spend all my time going about trying to persuade you, young and old, to make your first and chief concern not for your bodies nor for your possessions, but for the highest welfare of your souls."[13] Socrates here clearly demarcates not two but three parallel concerns and social roles: that is, caring for the body, as sick patients and regular physicians do; caring for possessions, as rich persons and money-lenders do; and caring for the soul, as religious persons and their spiritual counselors do. He thus shows us that both the dichotomy between and the equation of body and mind, curing the body and curing the soul, are utterly misleading.

The idea that the philosopher's function is to be a physician of the soul is taken for granted by many post-Socratic philosophers, especially by the Stoics. Cicero (106–43 B.C.) provides what may be one of the earliest articulations of the idea that the person suffering from a sick soul cannot be his own healer but must entrust himself to the care of an expert: "The soul that is sick cannot rightly prescribe for itself, except by following the instruction of wise men."[14] These wise men, or physicians of the soul, should, of course, be philosophers, experts in the use of words. In summarizing the duties of comforters of the soul, Cicero recommends the use of "healing words," what Aeschylus (*ca.* 525–456 B.C.) called *iatroi logoi*.[15] Veritably, like pure water issuing from a spring that becomes contaminated as it courses downstream toward the oceans, we see psychotherapy as healing rhetoric here in its pristine purity, before it becomes contaminated and unfit for its function as it courses through history and empties into modern medicine.

With Seneca (*ca.* 4 B.C.–A.D. 65), the most famous of Stoics, begins the Western literature of consolation. The cure of grief by personal counsel, and even more often by consoling letter, becomes a mainstay of the cure of souls, both among the Stoics and the Christians who replace them. To his own mother grieving over his exile to Corsica, Seneca writes: "I resolved to conquer, not to minimize your woe." And he encourages her "to give herself to the study of philosophy, sovereign remedy for sadness."[16]

IV

The significance of the word and of the law in Judaism is obvious. The religious-rhetorical dimensions of Judaism were, indeed, so important that from early times there existed three distinct classes of Jewish religious experts: the priests, whose work was connected with public worship and ceremonies; the prophets, who spoke forth in the name of the Lord and sometimes rebuked the powerful; and the wise men (*hakhamim*) who counseled their fellows concerning matters of personal conduct.[17] These three social roles or vocations are clearly identified in Jeremiah: "The law shall not perish from the priest, nor the counsel from the wise, nor the word from the prophet."[18]

In this connection, it is impossible to overemphasize that in Judaism only the Lord has absolute authority over man. And His will is often inscrutable. Thus, in *Ecclesiasticus* those troubled in soul are specifically admonished to retain their autonomy and to refrain from excessive or ill-advised dependence on their counselors. Standing in remarkable contrast to the Roman Catholic injunction demanding total submission to the priestly confessor, and to the psychiatric injunction demanding similar submission to the physician, are these precepts, written in the second century B.C.:

> Every counselor says his own advice is best,
> but some have their own advantage in view.
> Beware of the man who offers advice,
> and find out beforehand where his interest lies.
> His interest will be weighted in his own favour
> and may tip the scales against you.[19]

To Jesus Ben Sirach, the author of *Ecclesiasticus,* the moral legitimacy of self-reliance as against dependence on the authority of the counselor is self-evident:

> But also trust your own judgment,
> for it is your most reliable counsellor.
> A man's own mind has sometimes a way of telling him more
> than seven watchmen posted high on a tower.[20]

Although I shall say more about it later, it is worth noting here that Christ's devotion to God and His fellow men was displayed by His denunciation of the psychotherapists of His time: He called the scribes "blind guides," charging them, and the Pharisees, with pretense, vanity, and oppressive legalism.[21]

V

In the history of the cure of souls, no less than in the history of civilization itself, Jesus Christ occupies a unique place. Indeed, in the Continental Reformation, He is represented first and foremost as a physician of the soul. In his study of Jesus as *Seelsorger,* Gerhard Kittel remarks: "He was not scribe and not rabbi, not teacher and master of wisdom; what men discovered in him was exactly this: healer of souls."[22]

Jesus' role as psychotherapist is important on several counts, not least among them being His disagreements with the established practices of the then officially recognized physicians of the soul, that is, the rabbis. Unlike the rabbis, Jesus had women followers and held conversations with publicans and social outcasts.[23] Moreover, Jesus not only departed from established practices of soul-healing, He also castigated and condemned the counseling establishment itself in the strongest terms. "For I tell you," He exclaims in a characteristic attack on His psychotherapist colleagues, "unless your righteousness exceeds that of the scribes and Pharisees, you will never enter the kingdom of heaven."[24] Jesus could, of course, become even more vehement in His denunciation of the psychotherapeutic quacks of His age.

In His repeated attacks on the scribes and Pharisees, Jesus' role as reformer could not be clearer. "Beware of the scribes," He warns, "who like to go about in long robes, and to have salutations in the market places and the best seats in the synagogues and the places of honor at feasts, who devour widows' houses and for a pretense make long prayers."[25] Similarly, He might now warn people to beware of psychiatrists who like to go about in the white coat of doctors, and to receive government grants and the best seats in the theater. Naturally, the Jewish priesthood did not relish being denounced in such terms by Jesus, any more than contemporary pillars of society relish such criticism.

As a healer of souls, Jesus went far beyond the rabbis, engaging in acts of exorcism uncharacteristic of Hebrew practices. Hence our image of Him as the Great Physician, the Divine Healer. Surveying Jesus' feats as a healer, McNeill aptly concludes that "we become inescapably aware of the emergence in early Christianity of a new dynamic for personal moral living, the releasing of power for a new therapy of souls with which nothing else in the ancient world could compete."[26] Indeed, nothing in the world could compete with it for the subsequent eighteen centuries. Only with the decline of the power of the Christian churches, of the Christian religion, and of the Christian principles and practices in the cure of souls could new methods of faith healing—such as Mesmerism, phrenology, psychiatry, and psychoanalysis—arise. But that conclusion gets us ahead of our story, for the cure of souls in Catholicism and Protestantism remains to be considered, at least briefly.

VI

The cure of souls is closely linked to a number of basic concepts, such as wrongdoing, guilt, repentance, confession, conversion, and change of mind. These concepts continue to play an important role in religion and psychiatry. In the vocabulary of religion, McNeill observes, "The 'disorders' of the soul are 'sins'; the guide, or physician, of souls diagnoses the patient's case in terms of sin, and applies the remedies in rebuke, counsel, and penance."[27] But when the disorders of the soul are changed from sin to sickness and the psychiatrist displaces the priest as the physician of the soul, the patient's case is diagnosed in terms of psychopathology; and the remedies now become constraint, electricity, and chemistry.[28]

The use of confession in early Christianity brought with it certain new problems and generated certain new solutions for them. One such question was whether confession should be public or private. And if confession was to be private, should vows of secrecy be required. There is no evidence in Church law before the ninth century of any insistence upon secret confession. However, an eleventh-century Church manual sternly warns that a priest violating the secrecy of the confessional "is to be deposed and made to do penance in perpetual pilgrimage, deprived of all honor."[29] An Irish Church manual goes even further, stipulating that divulgence of a confession is one of the four offenses so grave that no penance for it is possible.[30]

McNeill remarks on the frequent use of the medical metaphor in the Church vocabulary of confession and penance. The penitential discipline is called "the health-giving medicine of souls," priests are called "spiritual physicians," and the disorders they heal are called "the wounds, fevers, transgressions, sorrows, sicknesses, and infirmities of souls."[31]

Not until the twelfth century did confession and absolution become one of the sacraments of the Catholic Church. Concurrently, the inviolable secrecy of the confessional is firmly established. Since the secrecy of the confessional transformed into the confidentiality of the psychotherapeutic relationship remains a confused and contested subject in contemporary psychiatry, it behooves us to pay proper attention to the religious antecedents of this seemingly psychiatric problem. The edict of the Fourth Lateran Council of 1215 concerning the confessional stated: "Further, he [the priest] is to give earnest heed that he does not in any wise betray the sinner by word or sign or in any other way. . . . We decree that he who shall presume to reveal a sin made known to him in the adjudication of penance, is not only to be deposed from the priestly office but also to be thrust into a strict monastery to do perpetual penance."[32] Alas, again what irony: In the thirteenth century the priest who divulged his penitent's secrets was involuntarily confined—in a monastery; now the patient who divulges his own secrets to the psychiatrist is involuntarily confined—in a madhouse.

The Church fathers understood that the purpose of confession was repentance, penance, and absolution—not the enforcement of secular laws. And they understood, too, that secrecy is indispensable to a full and free confession, and that its absence would force the penitent to become either a liar or a fool, and would transform his confessor into a betrayer of the penitent's confidence and an agent of satanic retribution. Though elementary, these are lessons contemporary politicians and psychiatrists have yet to learn.

Like any social policy, the practice of secret confession was not without undesirable consequences of its own. The sexual exploitation of women by priests was one of them. The excessive interest of the confessors in sin was another. Yet, neither of these dangers constituted the gravest risk to this essential religious practice. It was the use of indulgences—especially the practice of selling them—that became the principal cause for the progressive deterioration of the sacramental discipline of confession and absolution, and gave the Protestant reformers their most effective weapon for their assault on the papacy.*

* Today, in the industrially advanced societies, the Roman Catholic Church has relinquished to the medical profession virtually all claims to

VII

When Luther attacked the sale of indulgences and the priestly corruption that countenanced it and profited from it, he assumed a position vis-à-vis the Christian establishment of his day that was, for all intents and purposes, the same as that which Jesus had assumed toward the Jewish establishment when he attacked the scribes and Pharisees. Luther—unlike earlier critics of the official upholders of morality—made his attack on these immoralities at a time that was more propitious for protestors.

Why were Luther and other Protestant reformers more successful than earlier critics in their efforts to cure the institution of the curers of souls? Nearly all students of the Reformation contend that the reformers' success was made possible by the introduction of the printing press and the propaganda war it enabled them to launch against the papal authorities. Every aspect of Luther's world-shaking "Ninety-five Theses" bears out the contention that its impact derives largely from its effort to restore the cure of souls to the people—a right they had been deprived of by the Church. What aroused Luther, writes McNeill, was "that simple people were being deceived; they were led to believe that if they bought indulgence certificates they could be sure of salvation, and that when the coin clinked in the box the souls of their loved ones in purgatory flew up to heaven."[34]

Revealingly, Luther entitled his "Ninety-five Theses" *Disputation of the Power and Efficacy of Indulgence.*[35] Ritualized indulgences, Luther insisted, have no real spiritual power, beyond that

---

healing. The priest as healer has thus become a fringe figure, an embarrassment to the contemporary Church's self-image as a medically enlightened institution. A leader in the modern revival of prayer for healing is Father Francis MacNutt, whose therapeutic claims revealingly center on cures of so-called mental diseases:

> The first person I prayed for was a sister who had been through shock treatment for mental depression and had been taken as far as psychiatry could take her. . . . To my surprise, at least partly, she was healed (through prayer). . . . About three-fourths of those we pray for are healed of emotional and spiritual problems. . . . In no way do I conceive prayer for healing as a negation of the need for doctors, nurses, counselors, psychiatrists, or pharmacists. God works in all these ways to heal the sick.[33]

which the penitent imputes to them. Ritualized psychiatric interventions, I maintain, have no real therapeutic power, beyond that which the patient imputes to them. Luther attacked the sale of indulgences as a degraded and degrading falsification of the true cure of souls. I attack the sale of prescriptions and the other fakeries of contemporary psychotherapy as degraded and degrading falsifications of the true cure of souls.[36]

Luther's obedient and orthodox colleagues practiced in accordance with the standards of their time. They thus made fantastic claims and collected substantial fees for their monopoly on indulgences. Although these claims are now often characterized as "quackery"—as they are, for example, by McNeill too—it was, in fact, Luther who was, by definition, the quack, since it was he who departed from the accepted practices and standards of his guild.[37] Luther's predicament and the predicament of his followers was thus the same as that which now confronts those who try, either as professionals or as patients, to depart from the practices of contemporary "scientific" psychiatry. "I grieve over the utterly false notions the people have conceived," writes Luther to the Archbishop of Mainz. "O, good God! I could keep silence no longer. Works of piety and love are infinitely better than indulgences."[38] Surely, works of piety and love, self-discipline and honest labor, are still infinitely better cures for what ails the human soul than medicines, mechanized psychotherapies, and mental health centers.

Luther was not protesting against true penance, but against the act of substituting for it the performance of an unspiritual, impersonal act. He insisted that the essence of penance was an ineffable transformation of the human soul, rather than some identifiable external performance. With that fundamental premise, the validity of which remains unshaken and unshakable, Luther was led to question the whole procedure of confession, in particular the requirement that the penitent recite every offense. By 1520, Luther expressly rejects the Lateran canon "with its demand for a total confession once a year. An exhaustive confession is, in fact, a sheer impossibility."[39] Alas, how all this is forgotten when the history of psychotherapy is written. For what else is Freud's fundamental rule that the patient "free associate," and hold nothing back from the analyst, if not a secularized repetition of the canonical requirement for the confessional recitation of all one's sins? And what else is Jung's rejection of this and the other "Catholic" trappings of psychoanalysis, and his insistence on the personal-spiritual character of psychotherapy, if not a secularized repetition of the Protestant Reformers' struggle against the arrogant assertions of fundamentally anti-Christian authorities. The fact that these anti-Christian authorities were, in the one case, the Roman Catholic Church and the papacy, and, in the other case, the medical-psychiatric establishment and its Jewish leaders, only heightens the ironies that abound in the history of man's struggle for the possession of his soul, his body, and his self.

The battle lines were as clearly drawn then as they are now. Luther was not opposed to the cure of souls in general, or to confession in particular; neither am I, even if it be called psychotherapy. "Of private confession," declares Luther, "I am heartily in favor. It is a cure without an equal for distressed consciences."[40] What Luther opposed, then, was the "despotism and extortion of the pontiff"[41]—that is, the institutionalization and monopolization of the cure of souls. I hold, similarly, that genuine psychotherapy—uncoerced and nonritualized, as religion or as rhetoric—is, as Luther put it, a cure without an equal for distressed consciences. But the despotism and extortion of institutional psychiatry and of the organized schools of psychotherapy are abominations comparable to the selling of indulgences.

What mattered to Luther, and what matters still to anyone who takes the spiritual life of man seriously, is the human being as moral agent, his repentance, and his resolution to improve himself. Luther thus denounced the then-accepted belief, repeated by Josef Breuer and Freud in their discovery of "cathartic therapy," that confession alone changes a person's life. It may or may not, depending entirely on why he confesses and on how he conducts his life after he confesses. That is why Luther also bitterly opposed the idea that confession should be compulsory. He understood that it is impossible to compel a person to confront himself as a moral agent. And he understood, too, that although a particular moral practice may be beneficial when undertaken voluntarily, it is worthless or harmful when it is imposed on a person against his will. Though denouncing compulsory confession, Luther emphasized that "I would let no man take confession away from me, and I would not give it up for all the treasures of the world, since I know what comfort and strength it has given me."[42] All this decency and wisdom have been cast aside in modern psychiatry and psychoanalysis, which are animated by the despicable totalitarian principle that if something is bad it ought to be forbidden and if something is good it ought to be compulsory. How else can we account for the flourishing of coercive psychiatry, the famous compulsory training analyses of psychoanalysts, and the massive medical, psychiatric, psychological, and legal apologetics written on behalf of such compulsory soul-curing?

Because Luther sought to restore confession to a voluntary act that would serve the penitent rather than the Church, he was forced to face the question of how to deal with persons who are morally unworthy of such dignified treatment. By making confession and penance noncoercive, Luther strengthened it as a procedure for inducing *metanoia*, but he inevitably also weakened it as a procedure for controlling wicked behavior. Psychiatrists continue to confront this dilemma, but confront it as though it were a modern scientific problem.

If a pastor of souls cannot or will not coerce penitents, then he must make use of another option vis-à-vis certain persons, lest they invade and destroy his autonomy and vocation. Who are these persons? Those who are not so much troubled in soul, but troubling to the souls of others; who are not so much disturbed, as disturbing. Luther was compelled to conclude that "shameless offenders in conduct, such as adulterers, drunkards, gamblers, usurers, and slanderers," writes McNeill, "are to be excluded from communion unless they give proof of repentance."[43] The modern psychotherapist faces the same dilemma. If he accepts, or is compelled to accept, all patients, then he must coerce those who misbehave. If he is to eschew coercion, then he must exclude from his practice those patients who, because of their own coercive tactics, render peaceful conduct toward them impossible.[44]

The early Lutherans were remarkably sensitive to the issue of coercion. A Lutheran directive dated 1528 specifically advises pastors against visiting the sick without request, and one from

1533 actually forbids it![45] Would that patients in our foremost teaching hospitals might be spared the anguish of being "interviewed" by uninvited psychiatrists. The Lutheran insistence that any kind of contact between pastor and parishioner be wholly voluntary—by which they meant that the relationship must be actively sought by the parishioner—has, of course, the most pressing relevance to the principles and practices of modern psychotherapists. In short, the cure of souls was extremely important in the early history of Lutheranism, and remained an important part of the whole history of Protestantism until, in the twentieth century, this function was relinquished to psychiatry.

VIII

Puritanism, first in England and then in New England, stands out as a movement singularly concerned with the cure of souls. In his definitive history of the rise of Puritanism, William Haller actually applies the term "physicians of the soul" to all Puritan preachers, because they sought "to arouse every man to ask and then to answer for himself that ancient question which the keeper of the prison asked of Paul and Silas, 'Sirs, what must I do to be saved?' "[46]

The crucial idea in the Puritan cure of souls did not differ much from the Catholic idea it displaced: men must acknowledge their sins and repent of them. Moreover, as in ancient Greece the soul-curing philosophers used the same rhetorical and dramatic devices as did the great tragedians, so in Elizabethan England the Puritan preachers were "confronted by their own peculiar artistic problem, a problem of rhetoric and poetic, in thus undertaking to treat the souls of men. Had they but known it or been capable of admitting it, precisely such a mirror [showing the moral blemishes of man] was being held up to nature in the theaters, though not with quite the same intention or effect."[47] It is precisely these similarities among priest, playwright, and psychotherapist that the doctrines of "scientific" psychiatry systematically obscure and obliterate.

As Freud and Benjamin Spock furnish prescriptions for psychologically healthy living in the twentieth century, so Puritan physicians of the soul furnished prescriptions for spiritually healthy living in the seventeenth. A typical tract, Richard Rogers' *Seven Treatises,* went through seven printings between 1603 and 1630; it counseled that "fear, weakness, self-deception, over-confidence, irresolution, the slackening of attention and will . . . were the things that must first be faced and overcome if evil were to be deprived of its power. They were . . . the consequences of Adam's fall. . . . They were the work of the devil."[48] The Puritans thus developed to its logical and spiritual extreme the idea that self-reliance is the key to salvation—the same idea that Luther and the other pioneer Protestants sought to pit against the Catholic idea of salvation through self-surrender. In the early Puritan view, explains Haller, "The grace of God was free, and so all men were born free as well as equal. . . . Thus there might be help for any man, but this help came only from God and worked only through a man's own self. He must become a new man . . . fight his own weakness, blame none but himself for his troubles and failures, endeavor to be strong, believe that providence was with him, persevere, and trust that all would be well in the end."[49] To the saved, the call of the preachers implied that every man could be saved if he truly chose to be saved.

But how quickly the call to self-reliance was altered by the introduction among New England's Puritans of the idea of "visible sainthood"—prefiguring the modern psychoanalytic idea of "mature (fully analyzed) personhood." Edmund Morgan describes the modification of Puritan doctrine as follows: "The English emigrants to New England were the first Puritans to restrict membership in the church to visible saints, to persons, that is, who had felt the stirrings of grace in their souls, and who could demonstrate this fact to the satisfaction of other saints."[50] This practice finds its contemporary analogue in the restriction of membership in psychoanalytic groups to persons who have themselves been psychoanalyzed and who can demonstrate their analytically secured mental health to the satisfaction of their similarly cured fellows.

As these Protestants reembraced precisely that passion for complete purity which Luther and the other early Protestants rejected in Catholicism, that passion was translated, in the real world, into religious and social intolerance. Luther maintained that good deeds were more important in God's eyes than ritualized repentance. But in the Puritan doctrine (as in the psychiatric) good behavior became subordinated to possessing a "saving faith" (or "true insight"), thus paving the way for the creation of a new elite of arrogant persecutors. "In New England," writes Morgan, "the Puritans, certain that their way was the only one, forbade the erection of other churches. If a man could not qualify as a visible saint, he was wholly outside any church. He could not be baptized. He could not have his children baptized. He could not take communion."[51] This monopolistic practice of the New England Puritans clearly anticipates the monopolistic practices of modern physicians, which restrict the cure of bodies as well as souls to those healers and sufferers who are faithful members of the state-accredited therapeutic church.[52]

IX

Viewed as the cure of souls, the history of psychotherapy—from ancient Judaism and Greece through early and Medieval Christianity and the Reformation—displays a continuity and consistency quite at odds with its history as psychiatric treatment understood in the medical sense of that term. Indeed, the latter view of psychiatry depends on a radical revision—or, better, a mutilation—of the religious and rhetorical nature of psychotherapy. McNeill has no illusions about this. "The physicians of the soul," he writes, "would be astonished if they could suddenly enter our world of today. They would find themselves in an environment in which their assumptions are ignored by many earnest and highly trained men."[53] McNeill underestimates, however, the extent to which the earnestness and competence of contemporary psychiatrists are measured by the degree of their rejection of any connection between psychiatry and religion—indeed, by their insistence that the psychiatric cure of souls is just as objective and scientific as is the medical cure of bodies.[54]

II

The Precursors
of Psychotherapy

4

Franz Anton Mesmer: Metaphorizing Magnetism

I

Franz Anton Mesmer (1733–1815) is of exceptional importance and interest in the history of psychotherapy. Insofar as psychotherapy as a modern "medical technique" can be said to have a discoverer, Mesmer was that person. Mesmer stands in the same sort of relation to Freud and Jung as Columbus stands in relation to Thomas Jefferson and John Adams. Columbus stumbled onto a continent that the founding fathers subsequently transformed into the political entity known as the United States of America. Mesmer stumbled onto the literalized use of the leading scientific metaphor of his age for explaining and exorcising all manner of human problems and passions, a rhetorical device that the founders of modern depth psychology subsequently transformed into the pseudomedical entity known as psychotherapy.

The connections between the New World and the new "science" are, indeed, arresting. Both the United States and Mesmerism came into being in 1776. Benjamin Franklin was both a founder of the American Republic and a brilliant representative of the new scientific man of the Enlightenment. Franklin invented the lightning rod, thus impressing upon the public mind the imagery of one of the leading scientific subjects of the age—electricity. As a member of the French scientific commission that investigated Mesmer's claims that he magnetized people, as well as objects,

Franklin declared that claim to be totally unsupported by evidence. Franz Anton Mesmer, for his part, was a scholar well trained in both medicine and theology. He was the first man to invent and merchandise the use of a literalized metaphor for popular healing. Mesmer rose to instant fame as a magnetizer in 1774; by 1784 he was a discredited charlatan. In those tumultuous ten years—during which the United States won its independence from Britain and France was incubating the Revolution that would shake the world—Mesmer conquered Europe and bequeathed to posterity an imagery, vocabulary, and style of healing the effects of which are still clearly discernible. The idea of a "rapport" between patient and doctor and the notion that the nervous patient must overcome an "obstacle" in order to recover are both Mesmer's; and both are easily traced to Freud's notions of transference and resistance, the core concepts of psychoanalysis.

II

In the second half of the eighteenth century, people believed that the magnet possessed special curative powers. (More than two hundred years earlier Paracelsus had named it "the monarch of secrets.") Medicine was then so undeveloped that it cannot even be said to have been in its infancy. Physicians still believed that diseases were caused by an imbalance among the four humors. Although sharper distinctions were beginning to be made between genuine bodily afflictions and faked diseases, as illustrated by the insights and popularity of Molière's great satires on medicine, physicians possessed few technically effective remedies for real bodily diseases. That fact created a peculiar ambivalence in the medical consciousness of the age. On the one hand, honest physicians with a genuine bent for science recognized their therapeutic impotence; they thus concentrated on advancing the science of medicine, ignoring the therapeutic needs of the patient. On the other hand, compassionate physicians with a genuine sympathy for human suffering understood intuitively the fake remedies of their age; they thus concentrated on helping people, ignoring the differences between rhetoric and science. The efforts of the latter gained immense support from the fact that the ministrations of

regular physicians were just as worthless as those of the charlatans, but were usually more painful and dangerous. As Robert
Darnton sagaciously observed, this is the background against
which we must view Mesmer's therapeutic successes (and the
successes of other eighteenth-century faith healers as well): "The
alliance between charlatanism and conventional medicine had
been exposed so often on the French stage that any admirer of
Molière might consider Mesmer's techniques less lethal than
those of orthodox doctors and barber-surgeons, secure in their
faith in the four humors and the animal spirits, and formidable in
their arsenal of remedies: purgatives, cauteries, resolutives, evac-
uants, humectants, vesicatories, and derivative, revulsive, and
spoliative bleeding."[1]

In short, the sick person was then usually made sicker, if he was
not killed, by the purgations and blood-lettings of the regular doctor. Mesmer did away with all the harmful practices of the doctors, which made his methods instantly attractive to a multitude of
actual and potential patients. To be sure, he could no more cure
real diseases than could the regular doctors. But what he did was
at least pleasant rather than painful for the patients. The situation
in psychiatry since the late nineteenth century is similar. The cures
of regular psychiatrists were and are so worthless and frightful
that anyone offering a new method based on the premise of doing
away with this entire therapeutic armamentarium is bound to appear compassionate. That is what largely accounted for the initial
appeal of the psychoanalysts, and for the subsequent appeal of
transactional analysts, scream therapists, anti-psychiatrists, and
radical therapists of all sorts. None has any truly effective methods
for treating mental illness, but each spares the patient the tortures
that regular psychiatrists call "treatment."

In opposing the fallacies of the regular therapists of his day,
Mesmer was right; but that, of course, did not make his own
theories or therapies right. In fact, Mesmer pitted his own charlatanism against that of the regular physicians, much as anti-
psychiatrists and radical psychiatrists now pit their own charla-
tanisms against those of the regular psychiatrists.

The similarities between Mesmerism and psychiatry and psychoanalysis have been noted by other authors, and I will remark

on them later. Here I want to call attention to one of its remarkable similarities to anti-psychiatry. In France in the decade before the outbreak of the Revolution, Mesmerism was transformed from a medical to a political movement. The Mesmerians were going to "regenerate France by destroying 'obstacles' to universal harmony," writes Darnton. "Mesmerism would remedy the pernicious effects of the arts (another idea adapted from Rousseau) by restoring a 'natural' society in which physico-moral laws of nature would drown aristocratic privileges and despotic governments in a sea of mesmeric fluid. First to go, of course, would be the doctors. . . . The elimination of the doctors would set natural laws at work to root out all social abuses, for the despotism of doctors and their academic allies represented the last attempt of the old order to preserve itself against the forces of the true science of nature and society."[2] The recurrence of these ideas, in almost identical form, in the writings of David Cooper and R. D. Laing illustrates the poverty of the revolutionary-messianic imagination.[3]

III

Who was Mesmer? What did he do, and what did he claim to be able to do? Franz Anton Mesmer was born on May 23, 1733, at Iznang, a small Austrian town on the Lake of Constance. He studied divinity before turning to medicine, earning a doctorate in both by 1766. His medical doctoral dissertation at the University of Vienna, "Influence of the Planets," was devoted to the supposed effects of celestial bodies on human physiology, a notion then gaining scientific respectability. In 1768, Mesmer married a wealthy widow ten years his senior, thus gaining entrance into Viennese high society.

As a young man, Mesmer lived a life of cultured and sophisticated ease. Stefan Zweig makes that bygone age come alive, as only he can. "Few, indeed," he writes in his matchless biography of Mesmer, "were the burghers of Vienna who owned so charming a residence as No. 261 Landstrasse. It was a veritable miniature Versailles on the banks of the Danube."[4] On the eve of the French Revolution and the new age it was to usher in, Mesmer thus lived the idyllic life of the gentleman-scholar. "He was a genial host, very learned, so that spiritual enjoyment, too, was not lacking. Here were to be heard, long before there was any thought of publishing them, not only the quartets, trios, arias, or sonatas of Haydn, Mozart, and Gluck, who were intimates of the house, but also the new compositions of Piccini and Righini. Those who preferred conversation to music found a ready listener and fertile talker in their host."[5]

What was such a fortunate man to do with his life? He could embrace a life of gambling, hunting, womanizing, and the pursuit of similar tangible pleasures; or he could pursue the spiritual pleasures of trying to satisfy his thirst for knowledge—and fame. Mesmer chose the latter course. The seed of the then-fashionable interest in magnetism and magnetic healing fell on fertile soil in Mesmer's mind. "As so frequently happens to slow-thinking individuals," writes Margaret Goldsmith in her biography of Mesmer, "it was an outward event which caused Mesmer . . . to take up the magnet seriously as a curative medium. In 1774 he heard that a Jesuit priest, Father Maximilian Hell, one of Maria Theresa's Court astrologers, was performing remarkable cures with the magnet."[6] In keeping with the temper of the times, Father Hell had switched from healing with water to healing with magnets. With the help of a technician, Hell was manufacturing multi-shaped magnets which he placed on the painful or affected parts of the patient's body. There is no evidence of the Vienna Medical Society lodging any complaints against him.

Zweig, too, credits Hell, whom he calls an astronomer rather than an astrologer, with arousing Mesmer's interest in magnetic healing. "In the summer of 1774, a distinguished foreigner and his wife were visiting Vienna," writes Zweig. "The lady was taken ill, and the husband asked the astronomer Maximilian Hell, of the Society of Jesus, to prepare a magnet suitable for application to the ailing part."[7] Magnetic treatment thus has a clearly religious origin. Mesmer's major additions to what he learned from Hell were, as we shall see, that he medicalized what had formerly been a religious form of therapy, and that he metaphorized the meaning of magnetism.

"Pater Hell, S.J., to whom the foreign gentleman turned in his trouble," Zweig continues, "was not a physician but an astronomer. He was not concerned to know whether indeed magnetic iron was efficacious in the treatment of stomach disorders. His job was merely to provide a client with a serviceable magnet. This he accordingly did. At the same time he informed his learned friend Dr. Mesmer of the unusual request, and of the purpose the magnet was to serve."[8] Zweig embellishes the facts here, as the request was hardly unusual. Hell was a professional magnetizer long before this particular couple sought him out. In any case, it was Hell who initiated Mesmer into the mysteries of mental healing. He also kept Mesmer informed of the progress of his case, which could not have been more gratifying. The patient was promptly cured. When Mesmer heard this, he went to the lady's house to verify the facts for himself. He too concluded that the patient was cured. Henceforth, Mesmer was hooked on magnetic healing.

Initially, Mesmer employed magnets in performing his magnetic treatments. We might call that period—from 1774 until 1776—the phase of literal magnetizations, in that actual magnets were placed on the patients or were waved over them in what were called "passes." The curative effects of the magnet fitted neatly into Mesmer's preconceived notion of a universal fluid responsive to magnetic manipulation. And yet, being a well-educated man, Mesmer was familiar with the verifiable properties of magnets. He thus knew that the demonstrable force of the magnets he possessed was limited to a few inches. This fact contradicted his theories. Accordingly, like all great religious and psychiatric leaders, he invented new facts to fit his theories. Then he invented new experiments to prove that his fictions were facts.

"His seer's vision," as Zweig puts it, "led him to the belief that the magnet possessed latent energies greatly in excess of those which so far had been demonstrable."[9] Mesmer then proceeded to prove the existence of the latent energies by producing "cures." His therapeutic successes were phenomenal, since Mesmer's practice, like that of all psychotherapists before and since him, was devoted exclusively to persons who pretended to be ill. Mesmer then quickly began to take his own metaphors more and more literally. Magnetism, originally a property of some ferrous metals, became, in Mesmer's mind, an omnipresent force. "He magnetized water," writes Zweig, "and caused his patients to bathe therein and to drink of it; he magnetized porcelain cups and plates, clothes, beds, and mirrors, in order that these objects might in their turn transfer the fluid."[10] His conviction that space was permeated by a magnetic fluid that, like electricity, could be stored and passed along conduits led to his invention of the contraption that became his trademark—the famous "baquet," a large oaken tub containing two rows of bottles filled with magnetized water. The lid was pierced with holes, and coming up through the holes were steel rods which the patients had to hold or apply to the ailing body parts. Finally, Mesmer created a sort of group therapy around the "baquet," making his patients sit around the tub in a circle holding hands, to create a more favorable circumstance for the passage of the magnetic fluid.

IV

As Mesmer's fame as a healer grew, and as he expanded his use of the term *magnetism,* he came to realize that he did not need a magnet to effect his cure. He would "magnetize" without magnets. Most contemporary commentators on Mesmer interpret this as a sign that Mesmer realized that his cures were due not to magnets but to his own personal influence—an interpretation for which there is absolutely no evidence. It seems much more likely, and more consistent with the facts, that as Mesmer literalized the metaphor of the magnet, he came to regard himself as a powerful magnet, and thus reasoned that he could dispense with the use of metallic magnets.

This important change in Mesmer's methods—that is, from magnetizing with magnets to magnetizing without them—occurred toward the end of 1775 and the beginning of 1776. It signaled the beginning of the second period of Mesmer's work, the phase of metaphoric magnetizations that lasted until his death. During this period he was consistently rejected as a quack by the scientists of his age: real scientists continued to use the term *magnetism* in the literal or restricted sense, as a measurable effect of a force, such as ferrous magnets exercise on iron filings; whereas Mesmer used it in a metaphorical or expanded sense, as the effect of a force "measurable" by the testimonials of his grateful patients. At the beginning of the age of science, Mesmer failed to fool his colleagues in the hard sciences; today, psychiatrists and psychotherapists have succeeded where he failed. Antoine Lavoisier and Benjamin Franklin knew that Mesmer's hands had no magnetic properties; yet most natural scientists now accept the psychiatric claims that mental diseases have anatomical and physiological causes and that mental treatments have medical properties.

Late in 1775, in a letter to a physician who had inquired about his method of magnetizing, Mesmer explains his new method of magnetic treatment without magnets: "The magnetic attraction of the spheres permeates all parts of our bodies and has a direct effect on our nerves; an active magnetic force must, therefore, be present in our bodies."[11] In that letter, Mesmer also uses the term *animal magnetism* for the first time, giving that name to the power of the animal organism to magnetize and be magnetized. In the same year, Mesmer writes: "I am now making experiments in curing epilepsy, melancholia, maniacal attacks, and ague."[12] Although Goldsmith seems unable to grasp that it is one thing to cure cancer and another to cure melancholia, and although she regards malingerers as if they were real patients, she does mention certain facts that are fatally damaging to the claim—whether Mesmer's or the modern psychotherapist's—that suggestion is a form of medical treatment. "One reason," remarks Goldsmith, "for the large proportion of recoveries in his clinic was his refusal to treat anyone whose ailments were organic rather than functional."[13] This is a remarkable admission and an important indication that already in Mesmer's day it was quite clear that not everyone who acted sick was in fact sick. "His consistent honesty," Goldsmith continues, "annoyed his confreres in Vienna quite as much as did his success. They could never accuse him of trying to hoodwink his patients, for he publicly declared that 'he could help only people suffering from nervous diseases and no others to recover.' "[14]

Mesmer's care in distinguishing between persons who acted as if they were ill and those who were actually ill is, I submit, the single most important and most instructive aspect of the whole fascinating story of Mesmerism. The facts are fully documented. In a recent biography of Mesmer, Vincent Buranelli writes: "When Mes-

mer took a patient, his first concern was to determine whether
the ailment was organic or functional. If it was organic, the result
of physical damage to the tissue, he considered it, following Proposition 23 [of the Mesmerian doctrine], beyond the aid of animal
magnetism."[15]

Mesmer's curing without magnets parallels exactly the situation
of the modern psychotherapist's curing without hypnosis, without
drugs, without even the couch! What sort of cure is that? Why
should it be considered a form of medical treatment? The fundamental epistemological and political problems that faced Mesmer
are still with us. And modern psychiatrists insist, exactly as
Mesmer did, that in the psychotherapeutic relationship rhetoric is
remedy, not rhetoric!

Zweig says that Mesmer "himself realized that he had made a
false start, that his cures were due not to the magnet he held in
his hand but to the hand itself . . . that not the magnet but the
magnetizer was the wizard who restored health."[16] Although that
is possible, we cannot be sure that Mesmer realized any such
thing. It seems more likely, given his fanatical obsession with an
omnipresent magnetic fluid, that instead of realizing that he could
cure without magnets, as Zweig suggests, Mesmer "realized" that
his hand was itself a magnet! Indeed, Mesmer's words and deeds
support my assumption.

In 1776, one of his patients gives the following account of
Mesmer's therapeutic method: "Dr. Mesmer performs most of his
cures today, not by the use of the magnet, but merely by directly
or indirectly touching the diseased part."[17] That is a long way
around, indeed, to the rediscovery of the laying on of hands. But,
of course, Mesmer claimed that his cure was not religious but
medical; more precisely still, he claimed that it was physical, that
is, magnetic. Zweig analyzes that crucial moment in the history of
Mesmerism with an astuteness few persons have displayed toward
it, and which in fact he himself fails to maintain regarding psychoanalysis. And yet his remarks about Mesmer apply, with only
slight modifications, to Freud as well. "Now was the moment,"
observes Zweig, "for Mesmer to admit candidly that he had erred,
that the magnet counted for nothing in the matter, and that he
himself was responsible for the phenomena he witnessed day by

day. . . . Henceforward he should have refused to call his curative method 'magnetic treatment,' and the whole grotesque apparatus of bottles charged with magnetism, of magnetized trees and
cups and water, should have been thrown overboard as so much
flummery and superstition."[18]

Here Zweig demands that a fake healer should act like a genuine healer; that a person whose influence depends on magic and
ritual should admit that fact, even though he has no scientific or
technical means with which to replace his loss; in short, that a
successful rhetorician should admit that he is an unsuccessful scientist. It would be nice if people were that honest; but people are
human beings, not angels. And human nature too often prompts
people to use language for promoting themselves rather than for
promoting the truth. Faced with the sort of dilemma Mesmer
faced when he discovered that he could cure without magnets, or
which Freud faced when he discovered that his female patients
who told him they were seduced by their fathers were lying, ambitious rhetoricians themselves become liars. Henceforth, they systematically deceive others—and themselves too, if that helps them
vis-à-vis their own consciences.

Zweig sadly concludes that Mesmer "had not the requisite
strength of mind."[19] But the matter at hand had nothing to do
with strength of mind. It was, I submit, ambition that prevented
Mesmer's rejecting as so much fakery the magnetic apparatus he
employed. But whatever the reason, Mesmer chose another
course. "Instead of publicly declaring that his theory was untena-
ble," Zweig continues, "Mesmer adopted a stratagem. He gave to
the concept of magnetism a twofold interpretation, saying that in
truth the mineral magnet had nothing to do with the cure, but
that, nevertheless, magnetism was responsible. The curative magnetism was, he said, 'animal' magnetism. Just as a mysterious
power resided in dead iron, so an analogous power was present in
the living human beings."[20]

Modern psychiatrists have employed exactly the same stratagem, but with this difference: whereas Mesmer's claims were
repudiated by the official science of his day, modern psychiatry's
claims are accepted by the official science of ours. Drugs cure infections, and that is called chemotherapy. Similarly, talking cures

mental illness, and that is called psychotherapy. The resemblance between chemotherapy and psychotherapy is, of course, purely analogic and verbal; and so is the resemblance between ferromagnetism and animal magnetism. Comments Zweig: "With every art and subtlety at his command, he [Mesmer] endeavored to make people believe that no essential change had been wrought in his system, whereas in reality the word 'animal,' *so cunningly introduced,* completely changed the whole aspect of the theory, and all but the shrewdest observers were likely to be led astray *by a mere verbal resemblance* [my emphasis]."[21]

But the analogy, the enthymeme, is, as I showed earlier, the stock in trade of the rhetorician. Hence, Zweig's plea that the Mesmerist eschew such analogical mislabeling is disingenuous. From 1776 onward, as Zweig correctly notes, "the term 'magnetization' when used by Mesmer no longer signified that the patient was touched or influenced by magnetic iron, but that a mysterious energy, an 'animal' energy, issued from the finger-tips of the operator and was capable of influencing persons exposed to it. It is, therefore, absolutely wrong-headed for practitioners of the art of 'sympathetic manipulative medicine' to call themselves 'magnetopaths.' Few, if any of them, possess a magnet at all."[22]

If we substitute electricity for magnetism, these passages apply perfectly to the contemporary scene in psychiatry. They also illustrate how well Zweig understood the extension of the magnetic analogy to nonmagnetic phenomena in Mesmerism, and yet failed to see the nature of the conceptual problem in mental healing. On the one hand, Zweig correctly notes that magnets have no healing power; on the other hand, he complains that magnetopaths possess no magnets, as if their possessing or not possessing magnets made any difference in how we judge, and ought to judge, the so-called magnetizers' curative powers. This last consideration is of paramount importance for our understanding of electroshock therapy. Conversation cannot cure sick people, say the organic psychiatrists. But instead of proving that their patients who pretend to be ill are really sick by demonstrating their lesions, they prove it by treating them with a real "physical" method—electrically induced convulsions. No contemporary observer of psychiatry can complain that the electroshockers have no electrical instruments! But does the fact that they use such instruments make their interventions vis-à-vis persons with pretended illnesses any less fake than were the interventions of Mesmerists using only themselves as magnets?

V

All faith healers share certain common characteristics and qualities, among which the most important are: first, the skillful use of rhetoric to support the claim that they perform marvelous feats of curing and to explain those feats with theories attractive to the popular mind; second, a collection of ceremonial garbs, ritual acts, and sacred places; and third, legendary cases of cures, exemplified by persons who achieve fame as patients "saved" by their therapist. I have already remarked on Mesmer's rhetorical skills, and will consider Freud's later. Their most famous ceremonial paraphernalia were the magnetic tub, in Mesmer's case, and in Freud's, the analytic couch. Their most famous patients were the Wolfman, in Freud's case, and in Mesmer's, Maria Theresa Paradies.

Fräulein Paradies, whose father was one of Empress Maria Theresa's private secretaries, was a normal little girl for the first three years of her life. On the morning of December 9, 1763, when she was not quite four years old, she suddenly became blind. Physicians diagnosed her condition as incurable, calling it a "paralysis of the optic nerve."[23]

Little Maria Theresa, named after the empress, was evidently a charming and talented child, who, together with her parents, made the most of her blindness. Not only did she become an accomplished pianist, but she excelled in many other ways as well: "Her memory was astonishing. She played cards, remembering the moves made by the other players. As a young girl, she occasionally took part in amateur theatricals. She moved about the house gracefully."[24] Moreover, the little girl's blindness literally paid off for the Paradies family. The empress made the child her protégée. She arranged and paid for her musical education, had the youngster perform at court, gave the parents a pension of two hundred gold ducats a year, and retained the best eye specialist in

Vienna to treat her eyes. For ten years the treatment went on without any success whatever.

As Fräulein Paradies reached her teens, the empress arranged for her first public appearance in Austria as a pianist and for her first continental concert tour. Soon she was performing in Paris and London and was an international celebrity as a blind woman pianist. "Now that she was so well known," writes Goldsmith, "Anton von Stoerk, the eye doctor, made a renewed effort to cure her: to have restored her sight would have increased his prestige enormously both at home and abroad. He was already greatly puzzled by her case, for he felt that her blindness must be due to some nervous disorder. The optic nerve itself, so he firmly believed, was healthy and intact. Despite this diagnosis, however, he was unable to restore her vision."[25]

Here, then, was a classic case of hysterical blindness; or, as I would put it, a case of imitated or pretended blindness. Fräulein Paradies was no more blind than an actor who plays Lincoln is Lincoln. Since acting blind was profitable for her and her family, existentially as well as financially, why should she cast off that role? How could she be more admired, famous, rich, and successful with sight than without it? Virtually the only way such a person can become motivated to recover is by becoming a famous patient.

The two celebrities, Dr. Mesmer and Fräulein Paradies, thus met —revealingly, the doctor seeking out the patient as a promising case on which to prove his powers. "Mesmer told the girl's parents," writes Goldsmith, "that no one could cure organic blindness, that no one could heal the optic nerve if it was seriously affected. His complete honesty impressed them, just as his calm manner had won for him the patient's confidence."[26] The parents agreed to place their daughter under Mesmer's care. Late in 1776, Mesmer gave Fräulein Paradies several treatments. Then, in January, 1777, she moved into Mesmer's private nursing home, which he had installed in one of the wings of his house. Within weeks, Fräulein Paradies' vision was partially restored. Her parents were exuberant. Frau Paradies "was almost hysterical with joy. She fluttered about Vienna praising Dr. Mesmer in extravagant terms."[27] The patient herself was, from the start, less than enthusiastic about her improving vision. Looking at Mesmer, the first person she saw—that is, after she was no longer officially blind—she significantly exclaimed: "What a terrible sight to behold. Is that the image of a human being?"[28]

That initial exclamation foreshadowed Fräulein Paradies' subsequent reaction to regaining her sight. She became depressed. She told a friend who came to see her: "Why is it that I am now less happy that I was when I was still afflicted? Everything that I now see gives me an unpleasant sensation. When I was blind I felt much calmer."[29] When she saw relatives or friends for the first time, she repeatedly fainted. She was critical of the appearance of most of the new persons or things she saw. "If the sight of new objects were to continue to make me so disturbed and restless," she threatened, "I should prefer to return to my blindness at once."[30] It would be difficult to imagine a more unequivocal admission by a hysterical patient that her disease is, in fact, a purposeful act. Moreover, Mesmer's colleagues also understood that hysteria was such an act.

VI

If the recovery of Fräulein Paradies' eyesight had been a fact, like a patient's recovery of the use of a limb after a healed fracture, Mesmer's medical enemies would not have launched the attack they did. The fact that they launched it proves that they understood that the state of Fräulein Paradies' vision depended on her personal relationship to Mesmer, the empress, and her parents, and was subject to influence through interpersonal, rather than medical, means. Seizing on the young patient's ambivalence about being cured by Mesmer—indeed, on her only thinly disguised preference for being blind—a group of leading Viennese physicians, under the leadership of Joseph Barth, started an ingenious campaign against Mesmer. First, the doctors declared that Fräulein Paradies was still blind because she could not correctly name objects placed before her. This upset Mesmer immensely, as his fame and self-esteem now rested increasingly on his ability to perform miraculous cures.

The doctors' next move was even more ingenious. "They called on the parents of the girl," writes Zweig, "and filled them with alarm by suggesting that the empress would withdraw the yearly pension of two hundred ducats if their daughter's sight were restored, and further, that the young pianist would lose half her attraction on the concert platform if she possessed normal vision."[31] These suggestions worked havoc on Mesmer's own suggestions. The young woman's parents turned bitterly against Mesmer and demanded that he give them back their daughter.

With Fräulein Paradies unable to play the piano with her eyes open, with her parents denouncing Mesmer as holding her against their will, and with the Viennese medical faculty openly calling Mesmer a quack, the Paradies affair was quickly transformed from what loomed as a glorious victory for Mesmer into a dismal defeat for him. Rumor now had it that not only did Mesmer fail to cure his patient, but that her seizures and other symptoms were worse than ever, and, moreover, that patient and doctor were lovers. Mesmer had miscalculated, as later on he would miscalculate repeatedly, the power-relations in the affair in which he embroiled himself. Herr Paradies was, after all, the empress' private secretary. For Mesmer to try to treat this man's eighteen-year-old daughter against his wishes was arrogant stupidity. With Vienna properly scandalized by the affair, Empress Maria Theresa commanded the president of the Vienna Medical Council, Anton von Stoerk—the man to whom she had earlier entrusted her protégée's eye-care—"to put a stop to this humbug."[32] On May 2, 1777, von Stoerk, writing from the Schönbrunn Palace, ordered Mesmer "to cease this imposture" and release the girl to her parents.[33] Mesmer was through in Vienna.

"Not surprisingly," comments Buranelli, Fräulein Paradies "lapsed back into blindness and never came out of it. . . . She no longer wished to have her sight restored, and returned with relief to the familiar, comfortable world of eternal darkness."[34]

What such a person with hysterical blindness actually sees or does not see is not for me to say; but surely it is absurd to characterize such a person's world as one of "eternal darkness." In any case, Maria Theresa Paradies' further career is of considerable interest. After her experience with Mesmer and her return home, she regained her musical abilities and went on to have a career as one of the outstanding musical personalities of her age. Nor was her success due solely to her self-enhancing stigma. She was a fine pianist: "She was so good that Mozart wrote a composition specially for her, the Concerto in B Flat Major, which made no concessions at all to her disability."[35] That piece, also known as the "Paradies Concerto," was first played by Fräulein Paradies in Paris in 1784, at the Tuileries, before Louis XVI and Marie Antoinette, who were charmed by both the composition and the performer. The queen of France was, of course, Empress Maria Theresa's daughter. And, ironically, in 1784, when all of Paris hailed Fräulein Paradies as a great pianist, Mesmer too, was there, once again in the role of the megalomaniacal but discredited quack.*

VII

Discredited in Vienna, Mesmer left for Paris in January, 1778. On arriving in Paris, Mesmer acted like reigning scientific royalty. He sought out Charles LeRoy, president of the Academy of Sciences, through whom he sought to gain the support of the academy for the validity of his theories. Mesmer's proposal was preposterous, but LeRoy took it seriously. To better present Mesmer's "discoveries" to the members of the academy, LeRoy asked Mesmer to prepare a summary of them, which Mesmer proceeded to do. Entitled *Mémoire de Monsieur Mesmer sur la*

---

* Mesmer's relationship with Maria Theresa Paradies calls to mind Breuer's (and Freud's) relationship with Anna O. Some of the similarities are arresting. Both patients were exceptionally talented young women; both had hysterical—that is, pretended—illnesses, the one faking blindness, the other pains, weakness, and seizures. Each was, initially, "cured" by a compassionate and greatly over-involved, male physician, only to suffer a total "relapse" after a brief therapeutic honeymoon. In each case, the therapy consisted of the physician gaining a certain kind of personal influence over the patient, which the therapists attributed, respectively, to "animal magnetism" and to "catharsis." Following the relapse, both patients went on to careers very exceptional in those days—indeed, careers that, in some ways, eclipsed those of their therapists. Finally, each former patient remained a lifelong enemy of the ideas and practices of her former therapist.[36] This brief summary of the parallels between Maria Theresa Paradies and Anna O. suggests that these women experienced their therapists' influence over them as profoundly intrusive and damaging to their self-esteem and needs for self-assertion.

découverte du magnetisme animal, the memorandum includes twenty-seven "propositions." It is a frightening document of personal megalomania and therapeutic totalitarianism. Mesmer's concluding claim illustrates the spirit and tone of his teachings: "This doctrine will, finally, enable the physician to decide upon the health of every individual, and upon the presence of the diseases to which he may be exposed. In this way the art of healing may be brought to absolute perfection."[37]

The intemperance of such a claim alone suffices to establish its author as a charlatan. What Mesmer proposes is the establishment of a state-controlled church to propagate his pseudoscientific religion. Small wonder that he is considered the founder of modern psychotherapy. But when Mesmer was writing, natural science—the free pursuit of knowledge independent of churches and governments—was just emerging from its Renaissance womb. Men like Lavoisier and Franklin did not look to the state to spread their ideas. Why, then, did Mesmer? And why have historians of science and psychiatry not paid more attention to Mesmer's unceasing efforts to convert heads of state, the nobility, and leading scientists of his day to his particular creed? From the moment of his own conversion from gentleman-scholar to magneto-therapist, Mesmer's whole life is the life of an evangelist laboring ceaselessly for his god—animal magnetism.

Indeed, Mesmer even contrived to establish a church for propagating his "faith." During his short-lived success in France, he formed, in 1782, a secret society to safeguard and merchandise his discovery. The origin and nature of this organization, called *Societé de l'Harmonie Universelle* (Society of Universal Harmony), has an uncanny resemblance to the committee that Freud organized in 1913 and to the subsequent history of the psychoanalytic movement.

Henri Ellenberger characterizes the society as "a strange mixture of business enterprise, private school, and masonic lodge."[38] For a few years, the society flourished, had branches in many French cities, and secured a large income for Mesmer. But despite its name, harmony did not reign long among the members. The main reason for dissension in Mesmer's society was the same as that for his success as a hypnotic therapist—namely, that he was a megalomaniacal despot. According to Buranelli, "Mesmer intended the society to be a benevolent despotism of which he would remain the despot. Animal magnetism was 'my discovery.' Therefore no one else fully understood it or had any right to contradict him on how it should be taught, used, or promoted."[39] Mesmer's idea of his movement, Buranelli continues, "was of willing, obedient subordinates accepting the doctrine as he was pleased to reveal it, transmitting it to the lower membership, and returning to him for enlightenment or direction when they ran into difficulties. He wanted no d'Eslons at the Hotel de Coigny."[40] Charles d'Eslon and Nicholas Bergasse were Mesmer's most successful pupils, as Adler and Jung were Freud's.

Since Mesmer, no less than his malingering patients, was in the last analysis caught up in a gigantic lie, both he and the patients were bound to be exposed, sooner or later, as fakers. Indeed, Mesmer's insistence that he be validated by contemporary men of science as a bona fide scientist duplicates the hypochondriac's insistence that he be validated by doctors as a bona fide patient.

Mesmer's wish to have his day in the court of science was finally granted in 1784. On March 12 of that year, Louis XVI appointed a commission to investigate animal magnetism on behalf of the Academy of Sciences. Perhaps because Mesmer's own clinic was overcrowded, perhaps because the commission wanted to avoid dealing with Mesmer, or perhaps because of other reasons still, the investigations were conducted at the special magnetic hospital established by Charles d'Eslon, Mesmer's leading pupil.

The members of the commission presented an impressive list of names. Among them were Antoine Lavoisier, the famous chemist who was to lose his head at the guillotine; Jean Sylvan Bailly, the mayor of Paris, an astronomer and statesman who was also destined to perish under the blade of that infernal machine; Joseph Ignace Guillotin, the physician immortalized by his great contributions to euthanasia and thanatology; and, last but not least, Benjamin Franklin, then aged seventy-eight, the United States ambassador to France who headed the commission.

What was the commission supposed to determine? How did its members see their own task? Bailly reminded his colleagues at the outset that they "must limit themselves to physical proofs."[41] They thus looked for magnetic influences in the Mesmerian treatment, and of course found none. But this view of the matter was too simple for those then enveloped in the Mesmerian craze, and it is too simple still for those now enveloped in the psychiatric craze. Thus, Goldsmith characteristically complains that "the Commission's investigation of animal magnetism was entirely materialistic. These scientists naturally failed, therefore, to become the discoverers of modern psychology."[42] Actually, it is the other way around. We could invert Goldsmith's misconstruction of what the commission did and say that Mesmer's scientific contemporaries succeeded in discovering that not only Mesmerism but modern psychology as well was fake science. The commissioners' task was to "find out whether or not Mesmer's 'universal fluid' existed; if so, could one feel it through the senses? Could one smell or taste it?"[43] Noting that that was the commissioners' task, Goldsmith nevertheless writes as if it should not have been their task, as if, on the contrary, their task should have been "to question—regardless of this *fluidum*—why, in practice, Mesmer and d'Eslon had been able to cure so many people."[44]

Actually, although that was not the question the commission sought to answer, the commissioners could not avoid addressing themselves to it. And they answered it, coolly and correctly, by noting that many of the patients cured by the Mesmerists were not really sick and that many were cured by faked magnetic treatments just as effectively as by real ones! Some of the commissioners' experiments are worth mentioning. In one experiment, they chose as patients persons who were "really diseased . . . [and] from the lower classes."[45] One patient was an asthmatic woman, "the widow Saint-Arman . . . having the belly, legs, and thighs swollen"; the other was the "dame Anseaume, who had swelling upon her thigh."[46] Both were totally unaffected by the Mesmeric treatment. A six-year-old child with tuberculosis also remained uncured. The commissioners performed the reverse experiment as well, curing the patients with a fake magnetizer. One of the commissioners impersonated d'Eslon to a woman who had her eyes bandaged. She fell immediately into a Mesmeric crisis.[47]

The commissioners had thus no difficulty concluding that Mesmer's scientific claims were nonsense. In their final report, dated August 11, 1784, they wrote: "The Commissioners have found that this fluid has no action, either on the Commissioners or on the patients subjected to it. . . . Finally, they have demonstrated by decisive experiments that imagination, apart from magnetism, produces convulsions, and that magnetism without imagination produces nothing."[48]

Surely that conclusion is in the best spirit of scientific empiricism. Insofar as modern psychotherapy traces its ancestry to Mesmerism, it traces it to a certified fakery. Indeed, the commissioners went so far as to declare, in a French at its aphoristic pithiest: *"L'imagination fait tout; le magnetisme nul"* ("Imagination is everything, magnetism nothing").[49]

It is ironic, indeed, that while the protagonists of Mesmeric treatment claimed falsely that it was a physical cure, its critics understood correctly that it was a psychological cure and did not dismiss its value as such. "As to animal magnetism so much talked of," observed Benjamin Franklin, "I must doubt its existence. . . . I cannot but fear that the expectation of great advantage from this new method of treating diseases will prove a delusion. That delusion, however, may in some cases be of use while it lasts."[50]

The disaster that befell Mesmer in 1784 when the commission appointed by the king condemned his method as fakery was then compounded, early in 1785, when Mesmer's trusted lieutenants rebelled against him. One of the things that precipitated the break was that Bergasse had given some public lectures on magnetic healing. Mesmer considered this a breach of the secrecy contract in the society's governing rules. His following scolding, addressed ostensibly to Bergasse but actually to the whole world, reveals these franchisers of folly, these sellers of indulgences against insanity, for the conceited charlatans they were:*

> I cannot remain silent, Monsieur. This pretension seems
> to me the height of injustice and blindness; and every
> honest man will think that same thing when he casts his
> eye over the engagements you have entered into, and
> when he reads there that I did not instruct you, any more

---

* For a survey of the cures of contemporary charlatans for the ills of mankind, see pp. 194–205, herein.

than any of my other students, except on the express and preliminary condition that he would not make, with any prince or foreign government, either a treaty, or an accord, or negotiations relating to animal magnetism, *this right being expressly and personally reserved to me*. Can the right to dispense my gift belong to anyone except myself [my emphasis]?[51]

Soon Mesmer gave up on Paris, as he had earlier given up on Vienna. He had popularized a new imagery and rhetoric, but he did not know that therein lay his only claim to fame. He thought he had discovered animal magnetism in the same sense in which we say that Lavoisier discovered oxygen. That confusion and disjunction—between fact and rhetoric—has characterized the history of psychiatry and psychotherapy ever since.

VIII

The drama of Mesmerism has two distinct sources: one is the sensational cures Mesmer seemed to have performed; the other is the even more sensational claims he propounded to explain them. The relationship between fact and explanation, observation and hypothesis is of course important not only in science but in every attempt to give a correct or rational account of events. However, in ordinary human affairs, especially in emotionally charged situations, people are often judged not so much by what they actually do as by what they, or others, claim that they do. Nowhere is this truer than in religion and psychotherapy. Mesmer's case is illustrative.

In 1799, Mesmer published a brief exposition of his doctrine, which was translated into English by Jerome Eden in 1957. Mesmer begins his treatise with a plaintive claim: "History offers few examples of a discovery which despite its importance has experienced more difficulty in establishing and confirming itself, than that of an agent acting upon nerves, an agent hitherto unknown, and which I call animal magnetism."[52] That statement must be interpreted in the context of the age in which it was made; an age in which a materialist natural science took its first halting steps forward, in which such things as electricity, oxygen, flights in balloons, and many other things were discovered. Mesmer wanted to be counted among the scientists who made such discoveries. Accordingly, we ought to view Mesmer not as a discoverer of hypnosis or suggestion or psychotherapy, but rather as the first physician to claim discovery of the material basis of mental illness. Subsequently, physicians would claim that infections, endocrine secretions, and molecular abnormalities caused mental disorders, and would be as unable to support their claims with scientific evidence as Mesmer had been. Except that they rely on different metaphors, contemporary claims concerning the material causes and cures of mental diseases are identical to Mesmer's claims concerning the magnetic causes and cures of the afflictions he treated.

Mesmer's fakery lay not in claiming that he helped certain persons to feel better, which indeed he did, but in claiming that he discovered new facts and principles of natural science, which he did not. "It pleases me," he writes in his memoir, "that the discoveries I made, which are the subject of this work, will extend the boundaries of our knowledge of physics, just as far as the invention of microscopes and telescopes have done. . . . They will make known . . . that man possesses properties analogous to those of the magnet."[53]

Then, man was analogized to the magnet. Now, the mind is analogized to the body. People then suffered from disorders in their "magnetic fluids" and were, accordingly, cured by being "magnetized." Now people suffer from disorders in their "mental apparatus" and are, accordingly, cured by being "psychoanalyzed."

Mesmer claimed that people and animals were species of magnets, that they were filled with the magnetic fluid he called *fluidum*. Mesmer's *fluidum*, like Freud's *libido*, was a creation of his imagination. It was precisely because these metaphoric abstractions, like the emperor's famous new clothes, could not be seen by others that they were so admirably suited to serve as the key term in the rhetoric of faith healing.

The univeral fluid became Mesmer's obsession. To him it was not an assumption, an idea, or a hypothesis, but an all-explaining fact. Having literalized the metaphor of the magnet, Mesmer was himself lost in a make-believe world of magnetic fluids—which is why all who knew him agreed that he was sincere. Yet his memoir reveals that he realized that his views were based on an analogy: "It is the magnet," he writes, "which offers us the model for the mechanism of the universe."[54] The magnet, the clock, infection by bacteria, computers—as science develops it generates its own metaphors whose literalization often leads to sudden fame and subsequent folly. In Mesmer's case, the fame and the folly were based on nothing less than a claim of being in possession of a complete explanation of the nature and causes of all diseases and all cures: "The immediate cause of all disease, internal or external, implies the defect or irregularity of the circulation of humors, or obstructions of different kinds of vessels: we shall finally understand, as I have stated, that such conditions arise as a result of a default of irritability. . . . It is thus, and by the same causes, that irritability is naturally increased or diminished; so that the course and development of diseases, and even their cure, which was vaguely attributed to nature, are regulated and determined by that influence, or by what I call *natural magnetism*."[55]

In the end, Mesmer's therapeutic claims were indeed indistinguishable from those of the faith healer or the quack. "Thus we have in a general and concise form," writes Mesmer, "the discovery of animal magnetism, which can be regarded as a means of preventing and curing disease."[56] Still, it was obvious that all ailing patients were not cured by animal magnetism. How did Mesmer account for that fact? The same way that other religions have: the person who has been properly exorcised, magnetized, analyzed—such a person would never fall ill. But not all individuals can live up to the ideal. Thus, Mesmer explains that while all diseases are curable not all patients are: "Because, although we might affirm that the application of magnetism suffices to effect the cure of *all species* of maladies, it would be senseless to pretend to cure *all* the individual cases."[57]

I have detailed Mesmer's explanations of his cures because they illustrate a recurrent phenomenon in the history of psychotherapy —namely, a healer altering the complaints and conduct of persons who claim to be ill or suffering, but who, in fact, display no objective evidence of illness. Like his patients who claim to be suffering from bona fide medical illnesses, such healers claim to be exerting their curative influence by means of bona fide medical treatments. It is, of course, precisely these claims that acclaim the sufferers as martyred patients or condemn them as malingering parasites; and that acclaim the healers as charismatic therapists or condemn them as clowning impostors. In fact, such sufferers and healers are, one and all, dramatis personae in the real life drama of illnesses and cures that are entirely imaginary and imitated— the successes and failures of the players depending on their abilities as actors and on the appetites of their audiences for such entertainments.

5

Johann Christian Heinroth:
Repression as Remedy

I

The psychotherapist's professional identity rests on that of the psychiatrist. And on what does the psychiatrist's professional identity rest? On the claim that he is an expert in the diagnosis and treatment of mental disorders. It is therefore logical to continue our scrutiny of the nature of psychotherapy with the work of Johann Christian Heinroth (1773–1843). Heinroth is a pivotal figure in the history of psychiatry: with his life and work modern psychiatry and psychotherapy are born. The title of the work that made Heinroth famous tells half the story: *Textbook of Disturbances of Mental Life, or Disturbances of the Soul and Their Treatment* (*Lehrbuch der Störungen des Seelenlebens*) (1818).[1] The German word *Seele* is, of course, best translated as *soul*. Thus, the birth of psychiatry occurs when the study of the human soul is transferred from religion to medicine, when the "cure of souls" becomes the "treatment of mental diseases," and, most importantly, when the repression of the heretic-madman ceases to be within the jurisdiction of the priest and becomes the province of the psychiatrist.

The distinction between bodily and mental diseases is, as we saw, Platonic in origin and has been a part of Western thought ever since then. However, this idea did not assume the modern,

scientific form in which we now know it until the end of the eighteenth and the beginning of the nineteenth century. It was clear
then, perhaps much more than it is now, that it was not necessary
for a person to be a physician in order to recognize a genuine
disease, especially if it was serious. Anyone could tell that a person wasting away with tuberculosis was sick, that his body was
disordered. Similarly, anyone could tell that a person in the grips
of maniacal frenzy was mad—that his soul, spirit, or mind was
disordered. In each case, the "expert" was confronted not so
much with a problem of identifying a disease or disorder—that
having been done for him, so to speak, by the obviousness of the
case in question—but rather with the task of explaining the causes
or nature of the problem and recommending appropriate measures
for its management.

Modern psychiatry thus developed in an historical and social
matrix in which madness was taken for granted. Hence, the questions to which the early psychiatrists addressed themselves were:
What is madness? What should we do to control or cure it?

II

What, in Heinroth's opinion, was wrong with madmen? Not
surprisingly, his explanations of the nature of madness supported
the then-popular notions and practices concerning madness. What
is surprising is the way Heinroth located, on the conceptual map
available to him, the place of madness: unlike most people today,
who locate it more or less concretely with misbehavior and
deviance, Heinroth placed it, abstractly, with "loss of freedom."
This notion, still pivotal to our understanding of mental illness,
helped to establish psychiatry as we now know it—that is, as the
medical discipline concerned with those who *act,* though they are
not considered genuine or full-fledged actors, and with their *actions* that, because they are not those of regular ("responsible")
actors, are called the manifestations, products, or symptoms of
madness, insanity, mental illness, or psychosis.

Heinroth's central definition of mental illness is that it is loss of
freedom. "The concept of mental disturbances," he declares, "is
now completely defined and separated from all other concepts.

The complete concept of mental disturbances includes permanent loss of freedom or loss of reason, independent and for itself, even when bodily health is apparently unimpaired, which manifests itself as a disease or a diseased condition, and which comprises the domains of temperament, diseases of the spirit, and will."[2]

Heinroth is tireless in explaining how the madman lacks freedom—not in a political sense, because someone has deprived him of it, but in a religious sense, because he has forfeited it, or in a biological sense, because he is incapable of exercising it. In mental disorders, Heinroth writes,

> The free will exists no more and is replaced by complete and permanent loss of freedom. This condition prevails in diseases commonly known as mental breakdown, aberration of reason, madness, diseases of temperament, mental diseases in general, etc. All these diseases, however, much as their external manifestations may differ, have this one feature in common, namely, that not only is there no freedom but not even the capacity to regain freedom. . . . Thus, individuals in this condition exist no longer in the human domain, which is the domain of freedom, but follow the coercion of internal and external natural necessity. Rather than resembling animals, which are led by a wholesome instinct, they resemble machines and are maintained by vital laws in bodily life alone.[3]

In his general classification of madness, Heinroth lists mental disturbance, or *vesania,* as his general "class concept," which, he says, is characterized by "permanent loss of freedom and loss of reason."[4] Heinroth does not tell us how he knows that persons suffering from *vesania* have lost their freedom. Perhaps he doesn't because it is too obvious or because it is axiomatic: madmen act wrongly—sinfully, according to Heinroth—and no one would act in such a way of his own free will. Under the genus *vesania,* Heinroth then distinguishes three species of madness: 1) "exaltations," for example, "insanity and mania"; 2) "depressions," for example, "melancholia and apathy"; and 3) "mixtures," for example, "insane melancholia and melancholic insanity."[5]

Heinroth goes to great pains to distinguish the mental disturbances secondary to identifiable injuries of the brain from what he considers to be true mental diseases: "Mechanical or chemical injuries as well as initially organic affectations, too, end in one of the two ways just described. We may consider a blow on the head as an example: the resulting delirium is either transient or lethal. For this reason, true dementia, melancholia, mania, etc., can never be the effect of such injuries. . . . We do not deny that weakness of memory or of reason are often the after effects of such injuries, but such states must not be reckoned to the soul disturbances since they do not display the essential character thereof, namely, loss of freedom."[6]

In short, for Heinroth it is not loss of reason, which psychiatrists would now call loss of the ability to test reality, that characterizes madness or "true insanity"; it is instead loss of freedom. What Heinroth meant by loss of freedom is exactly the same as what psychiatrists, and others, now mean by lack of rationality, competence, or responsibility—namely, that the "sick" person is not behaving properly, that he is not acting of his own free will, and that his conduct should, accordingly, be constrained and controlled by those who know better and can therefore safeguard his "best interests."

III

Still firmly planted in a religious conception of life, Heinroth understood more clearly than most contemporary psychiatrists that we call persons mad or mentally ill who behave badly—that is, whose conduct does not conform to social expectations but is, instead, "selfish" or under the sway of his "passions." The cause of all mental disease, according to Heinroth, is selfishness or sin, two terms he often uses synonymously.

"All passion," Heinroth asserts, "is truly a state of human disease. . . . Passions form a very complex tissue in the human soul. For they are as varied as the object of desire and fear and the forms of existence and possession can be. But all have in common that they rob the soul which panders to them of peace and freedom. . . . Anyone imprisoned by passion is unfree and unhappy."[7] Edmund Burke also said this; he said it earlier and without metaphorizing moral unfreedom as medical disease.

Heinroth and those who have followed him have insisted on such a medical metaphorization and on taking the metaphor literally. In Heinroth's writing, however, the metaphorical character of passion as tissue and of sin as disease is still undisguised enough to be easily visible. Henceforth, the smoke screen laid down by the dreadnoughts of medical metaphorization become thicker and more impenetrable, effectively concealing the true contours of "madness" from the eyes of modern man.

"The man who is fettered by passion deceives himself about external objects and about himself," declares Heinroth. "This illusion, and the consequent error, is called madness. Madness is a disease of the reason . . . [which] originated from the passions within the soul. . . . In madness the spirit is fettered and man, just as in passion (both being indissolubly linked), is unfree and unhappy."[8] It is this rhetoric that ushers in and justifies the psychiatric holy wars for making men free by constraint and happy by torture.

Although Heinroth sometimes designates the passions as the ultimate causes of mental diseases, more often he rails against "selfishness" as the veritable devil that unhinges men and women. It is of course impossible to know to what extent he believed in a reified version of his own account. The following passage conveys his essential views on the "etiology" of "mental diseases":

It [the stimulus to evil] strides through countries, it clings to objects and mutual relationships in the form of ideas which, when honestly but blindly believed in, were called spirits or demons and were said to possess the power of mischief, which is perfectly true. It is no mere image, and even less hyperbole, to say that these spirits have usurped control over the earth and that all those who are mentally disturbed have become so through their power. They all have a common starting point, a main principle to which they are subordinated: selfishness. This most evil of all evil ideas is present in the most remote and in the closest human relations; it is absorbed with the mother's milk and finds a fertile soil in the human heart. Selfishness . . . appears in a variety of guises to merge with the nature of man. The ideas of money, power, possession, pleasure, etc. are such guises and are subservient spirits of this great Beelzebub. They are all struggling against the good spirit.[9]

That is great rhetorical writing. Moreover, it contains the very same ideas that later Freud, Bleuler, and others used as weapons with which to conquer their own empires of mad-doctoring.[10] Heinroth's view of the nature of so-called mental illness is strikingly modern—resembling, save in its terminology, the contemporary existential or so-called psychosocial perspectives on it. "Briefly," he writes, "we believe that the quality of mental disturbances is the communion of the human soul with evil principles— this without entering here into the question whether individually this is a spiritual process or not—and not merely a communion with evil, because that is beyond doubt, but a total enslavement by it. This is the complete explanation for the lack of freedom or lack of reason in which all mentally ill are held captive."[11] Heinroth's view on the nature of mental illness thus neatly dovetails with his view on its management by depriving mental patients of their liberty and treating them as slaves.

In Heinroth's ideas we thus discern the dual origin and character of mental illness: it is defined in moral terms as an ethical defect, and yet it is classified as a medical disorder. "People work, speculate, and earn money," Heinroth explains, "for the sake of their bodies; and when we speak of life, we mean the body, while the soul, that is, the calculating intellect, is the servant of the body. Those who think in this way see no sense of considering human life from the point of view of good and evil; and our description of the nature of mental disturbances as originating from the Spirit of Evil will not be understood by these people and will be mocked by them; but it is nevertheless true, and it will be recognized when its day comes."[12]

But if mental illness is the name we give to conditions in which the "spirit is enslaved by evil," a view reminiscent of the idea of possession, then it would seem to follow that the enlightened clergyman, the successor of the priest-exorcist, ought to be the person most concerned with its diagnosis and treatment. Heinroth confronts this question candidly. His own answer to it—that is, to who should deal with madness?—reveals once more the blending, in his views and work, of the religious and medical metaphors and roles.

"If we assume"—writes Heinroth introducing us to the problem of what he calls the "concept of the doctor of the psyche"—"that it is at all possible to cure mental disturbances . . . there arises the following question. Since it is the degenerate mental life which must be led back to normal, since it is the humanly healthy condition which must be restored, would this be the task of a doctor? or perhaps of a cleric? or of a philosopher? or of an educator? There are arguments which speak in favor of each of these four viewpoints, and each of these professions is at least apparently entitled to take possession of this curative task."[13]

Heinroth's open-mindedness, however, is more apparent than real. In fact he has decided in advance both on the nature of the problem and on the proper solution for it: the problem is moral; the solution is medical. He revealingly continues: "We must inquire to which of these professions (or perhaps to none of them), in their conventional and customary meaning, we are to entrust this branch of medical art and science."[14] By calling mad-doctoring a branch of medical art and science, Heinroth has in effect decided how to classify it: the "cure of souls," a term he assiduously avoids, is thus clearly a matter not for the cleric, the philosopher, or the educator, but for the doctor. That is indeed what Heinroth concludes. However, since he knows and candidly acknowledges that there is little if anything in medical tradition to enable physicians to deal with mental disturbances, he proposes the creation of a new branch of medical science and practice, namely psychiatry: "Since we are speaking of medical art and science, we should think that nobody but a doctor should have a right to make mental disturbance the object of his studies and treatment."[15] Thus does the practice of mental healing as a medical specialty come into being.

IV

What qualifies the early nineteenth-century doctor for claiming sole and supreme jurisdiction over the mind of the madman and the treatment of his "mental disease"? First, it is the self-serving

analogy between mind and brain, soul and body, and the literalization of the medical metaphor of mental illness embodying
it; second, it is the doctor's assumption of authority over the patient. By becoming the mental patient's master and treating him as
a slave, and by securing society's sanction for this arrangement, the
psychiatrist authenticates his special competence in the art of
"psychotherapy."

"The doctor of the soul (or psyche)," declares Heinroth, "is a
true man of reason. He has overcome selfish interests and treats
for purely humanitarian reasons. He considers his patients only as
sufferers and not in relation to his own personality."[16] Heinroth
thus succeeds in dispelling one of the most disquieting differences
between what he and his colleagues did and what ordinary physicians did—namely, that while regular doctors treated sufferers
who wanted to be treated for their suffering, mad-doctors treated
persons who did not want to be treated for theirs. At the same
time, Heinroth here articulates the detachment of the psychiatrist
from the person of the mental patient, a condition that has characterized psychiatry throughout its history.

Being the "man of reason" opposing the "man of unreason,"
the psychiatrist must have unrestrained power over the patient:
"From the very outset he [the psychiatrist] influences the patient
by virtue of his, one may be permitted to say, holy presence, by
the sheer strength of his being, his glance, and his will."[17] That is
a remarkable opinion indeed: as we witness the decline in the belief that popes and monarchs rule by virtue of being divinely dep-
utized, Heinroth actually proposes that psychiatrists should rule
because they are—because their very presence is—holy. It is impossible to overemphasize how strongly, and evidently how sin-
cerely, Heinroth and his followers believed that, perhaps because
of his "holy" calling, the psychiatrist had an unqualified right to
do anything to mental patients—short of murdering them in cold
blood.[18]

"What is needed in such cases," writes Heinroth in reference to
patients for whom there is still hope of recovery, "is constraint,
which is in no way cruelty or inhumanity, but is necessary for the
reeducation of such patients to the norm of reason. . . . It is
those least deserving of freedom, namely *maniaci,* who love free-

dom best; and as long as they are left to themselves and to their perverted activity, even if only in an Autenrieth chamber, no recovery is thinkable. . . . For as long as such and similar patients have their will, nothing can be done with them."[19]

Heinroth imputes suffering to all so-called mental patients to justify psychiatrically enslaving them. For example, he acknowledges that "maniacs" love freedom and therefore enjoy it, failing to note that such "patients" do not suffer, but make others suffer. The Autenrieth chamber, to which he here refers, was a contemporary device for torturing mental patients, one which Heinroth fully approved of. It was a movable cell or stockade, named after its inventor, the German psychiatrist Ferdinand Autenrieth (1772–1835), and was used to isolate, restrain, and move patients who were considered dangerous.

When Heinroth turns to presenting his specific recommendations for various psychiatric treatments, he rests them on a flamboyant metaphorization of (mis)behavior as mental disease: "Patients with a sick disposition must be treated differently from those with a sick spirit, and patients with a sick will, again differently, since it is the disposition, the spirit, and the will, respectively, which are sick, and their diseases are specifically different."[20] That assertion—couched in a terminology which, though quaint in its choice of terms, is as modern as the contemporary psychiatric practice of classifying alcoholism as a mental illness—is then followed by a transparent metaphorization of torture as treatment, of coercion as cure. Under the heading "Means of Gradual Treatment," Heinroth lists "Medicaments Which Depress Excessive Excitement—First Genus: Means of Restraint."[21] This arrangement of words comes so close to the American slang expression of "giving someone the treatment" that it would be pointless to say more about it. Under the "first genus" of restraints, Heinroth lists—that is, recommends—cold, darkness, and silence. Next, he recommends—and it is difficult to see how he could be any more modern, considering that he had no phenothiazines to dispense—"pharmaceutical means of restraint," under which heading he lists camphor, musk, naphthene, atropine, stramonium, hyosciamus niger, opium, and the cinchona bark.[22]

Nor does this exhaust Heinroth's therapeutic armamentarium.

He next turns to "surgical means of restraint," under which heading, he explains, "we shall discuss only the second type of surgical
means, namely, the mechanical apparatus which, according to the
circumstances, can keep the patient still or make him move in
order to cure his disease."[23] How did Heinroth justify such
brutalities? By disregarding the patient's will and analogizing the
restraint of his person to the immobilization of certain parts of his
body. "This," he writes in the next sentence, "is not unlike the setting of broken limbs in a mechanical device in the proper position,
or the adjustment of strained joints by mechanical countermotion.
Many such devices are available, according to the degree of restraint to be imposed on the patient."[24]

Among the devices Heinroth recommends are: the strait-
jacket, the sack, the confining belt, the confining chair, Cox's
swing, Autenrieth's mask, the pear, the box, Autenrieth's chamber, and lacing.[25] It seems worthwhile to reproduce Heinroth's
own description of some of these truly remarkable devices. The
sack, we learn, is an "ordinary sack made of ordinary material,
with a length and circumference suited to the height and girth of
the patient, fitted with straps at its open end, and completely or
partly covered with wax cloth to prevent the entry of light. Experience has shown that the patient in the sack is in danger of
asphyxiation and of falling victim to convulsions."[26] That, of
course, was before doctors used electrically induced convulsions
to treat mental patients.

The confining chair is "an armchair . . . comfortable to sit
in. . . . The seat has an opening for the buttocks of the patient.
The back of the chair has straps for the neck, the chest, and the
body. . . . It is not at all easy to bind the patient so as not to
cause him pain and at the same time make it impossible for him to
slip out. . . . Extensive observations made by the author led him
to the conclusion that the chair is completely harmless; the patient
can remain bound in the chair for weeks on end without incurring
the slightest bodily harm."[27]

The pear, named more metaphorically than the confining chair,
is a "piece of hard wood, with the shape and dimensions of a
medium-sized pear, has a cross-bar fitted with straps which can be
tied at the back of the neck of the patient. Since the oral cavity of

the patient is more or less filled by this instrument, the patient can obviously utter no articulate sounds, but he can still utter stifled screams, which is the more undesirable as the patient has to make a greater effort to do so; except that he might grow tired of this effort and become quiet. This is actually the purpose of this device, which must not be condemned as cruel, since its aim is to produce one of the most healing restrictions."[28]

It must not be thought, however, that amidst all these grisly devices for torturing so-called mental patients, the psychiatrists had completely lost their sense of humor. They had not. Indeed, they deployed it, too, in the interests of mental healings. Thus Heinroth informs us that "the box" is a "device that resembles the casing of a grandfather clock, such as may still be found in the halls or rooms of old families. It is as tall as a man, and it has an empty space in the place of the clock face. The patient is put inside, and his face is then displayed in the place of the dial. The patient is thus rendered ridiculous, which is the purpose of the device."[29]

Heinroth describes several dozen more "treatments" for mental illness, among them starving the patient, making him work, and many others, but surely the interventions I have remarked on suffice to show what he and the psychiatry of his day were all about. Toward the end of his discussion of psychiatric treatment methods, Heinroth himself summarizes the "rules" to which his seemingly endless variety of procedures may be reduced. They are: "first, be master of the situation; second, be master of the patient."[30] Psychiatric therapy is here seen nakedly for what it basically always was and still is: the psychiatrist dominating, subjugating, and enslaving the patient. Heinroth elaborates at length on this principle. For example, he emphasizes that "no special treatment should be attempted unless the physician can control the external surroundings, relationships, and influences on the patient. . . . The third rule is: the physician must not apply any specific treatment unless he is master of the patient, and this he can only become if he is spiritually superior to him. Unless this superiority is established, all treatment will be in vain."[31]

Perhaps because he was a pioneer—or perhaps because he wrote in an age when people were ready to replace priests with physicians as the benevolent authorities who, in conjunction with the state, ensured their domestic tranquillity—Heinroth could express the essence of psychiatric treatment with less stealth than do psychiatrists today. The elements of religion, rhetoric, and repression are thus instructively evident in his writing. "Since the physician of the psyche," declares Heinroth, "appears to the patient as helper and savior, as father and benefactor, as a sympathetic friend, as friendly teacher, but also as a judge who weighs the evidence, passes judgment, and executes the sentence, and at the same time seems to be the visible God to the patient, it follows that the component parts of the procedure he adopts must be, according to conditions, mildness and friendliness, gentleness, calmness, patience, consideration, sympathy, and a measure of condescension, but also earnestness, firmness, impressive though restrained authority, and the exercise of a just, consistent, firm discipline."[32]

How could the psychiatrist be all the things Heinroth said he ought to be? As if anticipating such a question, Heinroth answers it: "Like the monarch, the physician does not do all this directly by himself. He must accordingly find suitable assistants . . . faithful, honest, humane, hard-working, skillful individuals, such as may be found among the servant class."[33] When the madman says he is the emperor, he has delusions; when Heinroth says the mad-doctor is like a monarch, he explains the nature of psychotherapy.

V

In view of what the psychiatrist did to his patient, it must have been obvious, to Heinroth or to anyone else, that the relationship between mental patients and mental healers was fundamentally different from that between ordinary patients and regular physicians. Although Heinroth is not nearly as direct about this subject as he is about others, he is still explicit enough to make what he tells us instructive.

Heinroth never actually raises the question of who pays the psychiatrist. Instead, toward the end of his book, under the marvelously revealing Latin heading of *"Medicina Psychica Politica* (Psycho-Political Medicine)," he declares, "It is the duty of the state to care for mentally disturbed persons whenever they are a burden to the community or present a public danger; and the accommodation, cure, and care of such individuals is the duty of the police."[34] Although much of Heinroth's thesis rests on his claim that mental diseases are similar to bodily diseases, here he departs from his analogy in a way characteristic of mad-doctors both before and since him: that is, Heinroth does not assert that it is the duty of the state to care for bodily ill persons who are a burden to the community or a public danger. The fact that today ever-increasing numbers of people believe that it is the duty of the state to cure and care for *all* "sick persons"—regardless of the nature of their illness and their ability to care for themselves—testifies once more to our progress in the quest for a Therapeutic State.

In his recommendations for the proper organization of "lunatic asylums," we see, at last, the practical thrust behind Heinroth's rhetoric. "Since the purpose of the lunatic asylum is evident from the name itself," he writes, "it follows that it would be contrary to its purpose to connect it in any form or manner with any other kinds of institutions, such as prisons, institutions for the care of the infirm, juvenile disciplinary institutions. . . . While all efforts must be made to have perfect security, all impression of a prison must be avoided."[35] A crucial element of psychiatric treatment is here exposed in its naked reality: namely repression concealed as treatment. In this respect, almost nothing has changed since Heinroth's day. "The doors"—he earnestly recommends, foreshadowing the spirit of the not-quite-open-door-policy of modern institutional psychiatry—"must not have bolts or chains, but should have spring locks which cannot be opened by the patients. . . . A special building must be set aside for the physical treatment of the mentally disturbed. This building should have a special bathing section, with all kinds of baths, showers, douches, and immersion vessels. It must also have a special correction and punishment room with all the necessary equipment, including a Cox swing (or, better, rotating machine), Reils's fly-wheel, pulleys, punishment chair, Langermann's cell, etc."[36]

After describing the various structural parts and social makeup of the insane asylum, Heinroth reemphasizes the role of the psychiatrist as medical superintendent in it. "But the most important teacher and master is the physician. . . . His instructions are binding on everyone. He is the life and soul of the lunatic asylum."[37] Curiously, perhaps because he was aware that private medical practice would place practice in the madhouse in a peculiarly unfavorable perspective, Heinroth recommends that the madhouse doctor not have any other employment: "The task of the physician of the psyche is too great, too comprehensive, and too demanding on his forces, solicitude, and powers of observation to admit the practice of any other occupation as a sideline. The physician in a mental hospital must devote himself exclusively to the hospital and to his art; external practice and distracting, diverting hobbies must not be tolerated."[38] Heinroth here envisions, indeed demands, that, like slave and master, patient and psychiatrist unite in a mutually confining embrace. The results of this psychiatric matrimony are, as I tried to show elsewhere, schizophrenia and modern institutional psychiatry.[39]

VI

How do contemporary psychiatrists view Heinroth's work? Zilboorg acknowledges Heinroth as one of the founders of modern psychiatry and attributes his use of religious terms to the alleged nonexistence in the German language of his day of other terms suitable for the purpose. "He [Heinroth] used the word 'soul,'" writes Zilboorg, "merely because there was no other word in the German language of the time to denote that complex phenomenon called 'human mind' or our present-day 'sense of guilt.' This was a definite step toward a general psychopathology, because it went beyond the purely formal considerations of the patient's mode of reasoning."[40] Zilboorg remains silent about Heinroth's psychotherapeutic methods.

Alexander and Selesnick give Heinroth even more credit—as a founder not only of modern psychiatry but also as a "forerunner of psychoanalysis." They write: "He expresses in religious-moralistic terminology the central concept of modern psychiatry, that of inner conflict. If Heinroth would have used the modern expression, 'sense of guilt' for sin, he would have been more readily recognized as a forerunner of psychoanalysis. . . . Stated in modern terms, the source of mental disturbances is the conflict between the unacceptable impulses (the id) and the conscience (the superego)."[41] Alexander and Selesnick here try to say, and I assume think they say, that Heinroth was a good man because he had the same ideas about mental illness as Freud did and they do. In fact, what they are saying, albeit unwittingly and only implicitly, is that the change from Heinroth to Freud is only a matter of translation—that is, from old-fashioned terms to contemporary ones, from one language to another.

Alexander and Selesnick also remark approvingly on Heinroth's psychotherapeutic work and go so far as to praise him for his "opposition to routine treatment [which] marks a most significant step toward individualized psychotherapy."[42] Ellenberger is even more laudatory. After describing Heinroth's ideas about psychopathology, he praises him as a foremost psychotherapist because he "describes in a detailed and practical manner the various treatments that should be given to the excited and depressed patients as well as to patients of all conditions. Once again, the reader marvels at the modern character of many of these concepts."[43]

I can only marvel at how shamelessly contemporary psychiatrists continue to endorse the brutalities that Heinroth called "psychotherapy"; at how Ellenberger even claims that "one of Heinroth's main concerns [was] to abstain from any unnecessary or dangerous treatment";[44] at how repression by naked force, religion disguised as therapy, and rhetoric concealed as medical jargon continue to be extolled by modern psychiatrists as humanitarian treatments for mental diseases.

6

Wilhelm Erb, Julius Wagner-Jauregg, and Sigmund Freud: Electrical Treatment

I

In the nineteenth century, the leading treatment of nervous diseases was electrotherapy. Freud himself began his practice as a nerve doctor by employing that procedure. Nevertheless, few contemporary psychiatrists, and even fewer lay persons, know what this therapy consisted of or why and how it was used. The subject of electrical treatment is, in effect, expurgated from modern psychiatric texts. For example, in the index to Zilboorg's standard *History of Medical Psychology,* there is no entry for either "electrical treatment" or "electrotherapy."[1] Nor is there any in *The American Handbook of Psychiatry,* edited by Silvano Arieti.[2] The reason for this must remain a matter of conjecture. My assumption is that it is because, in the encounter between neurotic and electrotherapist, the mutual faking and pretending are too obvious and too embarrassing.

The leading electrotherapist of his age was a German physician named Wilhelm Erb (1840–1921). Erb was a famous and deservedly respected neurologist. A professor at the University of Leipzig, he was the discoverer of the absent knee-jerk reflex in tabes dorsalis, or syphilis of the spinal cord, an important objective sign of this then quite common illness. Erb had also contributed to the clinical description and identification of muscular dystrophy, as well as to the understanding of the pathology of peripheral nerves, the spinal cord, and the brain stem. He was, in short, an accomplished neurologist and neuropathologist. But perhaps that was all he was. In keeping with the adage that a workman who can use only a hammer treats everything as if it were a nail, Erb treated every patient with complaints referable to the nervous system as if he or she had a neurological disease. Moreover, since physicians in those days were powerless to really help patients suffering from bona fide neurological diseases, and since it was known that nerves exhibit electrical activity, it was logical, however fruitless, to treat so-called nervous patients by means of electricity.

Erb was the author of *Handbuch der Elektrotherapie,* the most famous and influential textbook of "modern" electrotherapy. Published in Leipzig in 1881, it was translated into English in 1883, and into French in 1884. The English edition, titled *Handbook of Electro-Therapeutics,* runs to 336 pages and contains detailed descriptions of the methods of electrotherapy Erb recommends, the indications for them, and accounts of cures achieved by means of them.[3] Reading this book, one is astonished to discover that though Erb realized that many of his patients were not demonstrably ill, perhaps not ill at all, he nevertheless behaved as though they were ill, because it was generally acknowledged—and this he neither scrutinized nor challenged—that they "suffered" from a "nervous disease" or "neurosis." The following passage is illustrative:

> Of the diseases of the nervous system in the strictest sense it now remains to discuss a large group of frequent, severe, and important affections. These morbid processes vary greatly in character, but a feature common to all is that they must be regarded as so-called "functional neuroses," i.e., diseases in which a gross anatomical lesion is not demonstrable by our present means of investi-

gation. Not even the exact localization of these affec-
tions in the nervous system—whether in the peripheral
nerves, spinal cord, brain, or sympathetic system—is always known, or several localizations must be assumed at
the same time; indeed, in certain forms of the neuroses, a
general diffuse affection of the entire nervous system is
assumed, and they are called "general neuroses."[4]

Erb, it should be noted, says that in such cases a disease of the
nervous system is *assumed*. But is not this asumption simply a
euphemism for the neurologist's desire to accept the patient's
claim that he is sick as sufficient evidence of the fact that he is?
This assumption then justifies accepting the physician's claim that
his use of so-called electrical treatment on the patient is sufficient
evidence of the fact that he is, actually, treating a sick person.
"We are apt to believe," he writes, "that purely functional, molecular and finer nutritive disturbances will be relieved more readily
than grosser anatomical lesions by the action of electricity."[5] We
now know—and most psychiatrists would even admit it—that electrical treatment was pure fakery. It had no more therapeutic
value—in a physicochemical rather than ceremonial-ritual sense
—than did aspersion with holy water.

Erb's description of the neuroses not only supports my contention that these are not diseases, but even suggests that Erb and his
contemporaries knew that they were not. Concerning "neurasthenia or nervous exhaustion," Erb remarks, "this is the most fashionable neurosis at the present time, and appears in a thousand remarkable forms. It may be best described as a marked degree of
irritable weakness of the nervous system, accompanied by the
most varied functional disturbances, although we are not justified
in assuming an anatomical foundation."[6]

Not only does Erb call neurasthenia "fashionable," he also
describes it in such a way as to leave no doubt that he understands
that it is not a disease. Nevertheless, he calls it a disease and treats
it as one! "In making the diagnosis [of neurasthenia]," Erb explains, "you should always remember that, despite the innumer-
able complaints of the patient, the most careful examination always affords an absolutely negative result. . . . Every objective
change, however slight, of sensation, motion, the reflexes, pupils,

etc., must cast a doubt upon the accuracy of the diagnosis. Electrical examination offers no assistance, since it reveals, as a rule, absolutely normal conditions."[7] Erb's description of neurasthenia could not be more clear: it is the portrait of a person who claims to be sick but is not. And yet, in the next sentence, Erb turns to the "treatment" of neurasthenia, justifying it in terms of the classical brain-mythology of pre-Freudian psychiatry.

"With regard to treatment," he writes, "it is advisable to differentiate various forms of the disease: one in which the cerebral functions are mainly affected (cerebral neurasthenia) . . . another which affects mainly the spinal functions (spinal neurasthenia and spinal irritation) . . . and, finally, a not infrequent combination of both . . . (general neurasthenia)."[8] The nervous patient's fraudulent claims about being ill are thus validated by the nerve doctor's fraudulent claims about the nature of his illness. The following medical mythologizing is illustrative: "In the large majority of cases, however, we must assume a finer nutritive disturbance of the implicated nervous apparatus."[9] How little has psychiatry changed during the past century! Then psychiatrists deceived the public, and perhaps themselves, by pontificating about "the finer nutritive disturbance of the nervous apparatus"; now they do so by pontificating about "cathecholamine metabolism." In the end, of course, all the rhetoric about the symptoms and causes of neurasthenia serves only to justify the use of electricity as a mode of therapy: "Electricity often produces admirable results in this neurosis. Its office consists in the removal of the nutritive disorder of the nervous system."[10]

It may be worthwhile here to reproduce the exact method of that treatment, to see actual examples of the fakery that passed, and still passes, for psychiatric treatment. For enuresis, Erb writes, "I apply usually the An [anode] to the lumbar cord, the Ca [cathode] at first above the symphysis, then upon the perineum, with a tolerably strong current for one to two minutes; at the close, a wire electrode is introduced about two centimeters into the urethra—in girls I apply 'small' sponge electrode between the labia close to the meatus urethrae—and the faradic current passed for one to two minutes with such a strength that a distinct, somewhat painful sensation is produced."[11]

Since in neurasthenic patients the sexual function was often impaired, Erb offered all sorts of practical advice for treatment by means of electricity. For example, he explains that "the majority of cases also require direct electrical treatment of the genitals, and this may constitute the main feature of the treatment if the sexual disorder is the sole or predominant symptom."[12] There then follows a detailed description of the electrical stimulation of the genitals:

> The following is the method which I consider most serviceable: the An ("large" electrode) is placed upon the spinal cord, the Ca ("medium" electrode) stabile and labile along the seminal canal. . . . Then follows vigorous labile application of the Ca (about one minute) to the upper and lower surfaces of the penis as far as the glans; finally the Ca may be applied labile and stabile upon the perineum as far forward as the root of the penis (one to two minutes). . . . If the penis, especially the glans, is anesthetic, the Ca may be applied in this position for a longer period. . . . This method of application is suitable especially in impotence: if pollutions or spermatorrhea are present, the irritant procedures should be avoided, and stabile currents should be employed, in great part, perhaps also the An upon the perineum.[13]

The treatments that modern sex therapists offer for these "diseases" are, no doubt, more pleasant. But are they any more medical or scientific than were these Victorian electrical massages of the genitals? In the century that has elapsed since Erb, psychiatry has progressed only in the sense that the patients' claims to the sick role and the psychiatrists' claims to the therapist's role have grown steadily more brazen and strident, and each group has managed to gain ever more popular and political acceptance for its legitimacy.[14]

II

During the First World War, among the persons responsible for torturing soldiers with painful electric shocks and disguising the brutality as therapy was the foremost neuropsychiatrist of Austria-

Hungary and perhaps of Europe, Julius Wagner-Jauregg (1857–1940). From 1893 to 1928, Wagner-Jauregg was professor of psychiatry at the University of Vienna Medical School. He was famed for his discovery of the fever treatment of neurosyphilis, for which he received the Nobel prize in 1927. It was this lofty medical personage who had used electrotherapy as a form of medically concealed torture, and whose use of it Sigmund Freud defended.

When the war was over, relates Ernest Jones in his biography of Freud, "there were many bitter complaints about the harsh, or even cruel, way in which the Austrian military doctors had treated the war neurotics, notably in the Psychiatric Division of the Vienna General Hospital of which Professor Julius Wagner-Jauregg was the Director."[15] These complaints led, in 1920, to the appointment by the Austrian War Ministry of a special commission to investigate the charges. The commission asked Freud to submit a memorandum of his expert opinion on this matter. In it, as well as in his personal appearance before the commission, Freud defended Wagner-Jauregg's use of this method of medical torture.

There were many complex reasons for Freud's defense of Wagner-Jauregg, only one of which need concern us here—that is, Freud's view of the war neuroses, which, as we shall see, conflicts with Wagner-Jauregg's view of them. In his "Memorandum," Freud offers a conception of the so-called war neuroses that obscures their true nature, helps to protect Wagner-Jauregg, and extols psychoanalysis as the only psychiatric theory able to account for the etiology and nature of these alleged diseases. In contrast, in his autobiography, Wagner-Jauregg asserts that the war neurotics were "malingerers" and acknowledges that his treatments of them were "harsh measures."

In his "Memorandum," Freud briefly reviews the traumatic origin of the "war neuroses" and then launches into an advertising of psychoanalysis. "What is known as the psychoanalytic school of psychiatry, which was brought into being by me," he writes, "had taught for the last twenty-five years that the neuroses of peace could be traced back to disturbances of emotional life. This explanation was now applied quite generally to war neurotics. . . . It was therefore easy to infer that the immediate cause of all war neuroses was an unconscious inclination in the soldier to withdraw from the demands, dangerous and outrageous to his feelings, made upon him by active service."[16] Freud here claims as his personal discovery what is actually a platitude: surely, except for qualifying the soldier's inclinations to quit the service as unconscious, Freud's foregoing formulation has nothing whatever to do with psychoanalysis, or even with psychiatry. It is, and was, plain common sense and general knowledge. Nevertheless, as a skilled rhetorician—base, to be sure, as these passages so dramatically demonstrate—Freud seizes upon the war neuroses to impute unconscious motives to soldiers, the better to inflate his own importance. Moreover, the way Freud does this is important, as his method has remained the key rhetorical device of psychoanalysis in its ceaseless efforts to justify classifying all sorts of behaviors as mental illnesses by imputing "unconsciousness" to the actor's motives. Noting the rather obvious motive that presumably animates the war neurotic, namely, the desire to absent himself from the war, Freud writes:

> A soldier in whom these affective motives were very powerful and clearly conscious would, if he was a healthy man, have been obliged to desert or pretend to be ill. Only the smallest proportion of war neurotics, however, were malingerers; the emotional impulses which rebelled in them against active service and drove them into illness were operative in them without becoming conscious to them. They remained unconscious because other motives, such as ambition, self-esteem, patriotism, the habit of obedience, and the example of others, were to start with more powerful until, on some appropriate occasion, they were overwhelmed by the other, unconsciously-operating motives.[17]

This is pure psychoanalytic mythology, the direct descendant of the brain mythology that Freud contemptuously dismissed as "fantasy." The mythology of subtle neurological disturbances flattered the neurologists: that is why they invented it and claimed scientific status for it. Similarly, the mythology of unconscious motives flattered Freud: that is why he invented it and claimed scientific status for it. But the distinction Freud here proposed between malingering and neurosis is worse than false.[18] It is arrogantly capricious, as it places oracular powers into the hands of the psychoanalyst, the sole arbiter of whether an actor's motives are conscious or unconscious.

What has all this to do with Wagner-Jauregg's guilt or innocence for using painful electric shocks in treating war neurotics? Actually, Freud is well past the halfway mark in his "Memorandum" before he even mentions that issue or Wagner-Jauregg. He works his way to the ostensible point of the document, after two pages of self-glorification, by noting that "this insight [*i.e.,* Freud's insight] into the causation of the war neuroses led to a method of treatment which seemed to be well grounded and also proved highly effective in the first instance. It seemed expedient to treat the neurotic as a malingerer and to disregard the psychological distinction between conscious and unconscious intentions, although he was known not to be a malingerer."[19] I submit that Freud was here "consciously" lying. In fact, he himself had used painful electric shocks in treating Fräulein Elisabeth von R., before he developed any psychoanalytic theories at all. Hence, the claim that the use of electricity in the treatment of nervous disorders was in any way related to this "insight" is plainly false and self-serving.

Still, Freud's skill as a rhetorician is evident here. He confuses us with his discussion of the similarities and differences between malingerers and neurotics, with his use of the polarity between conscious and unconscious motives, and with his careful avoidance of giving so much as a hint about how an impartial observer might judge behavior motives in terms of these concepts. He perseveres in the traditional psychiatric practice of calling all soldiers implicated as war neurotics "patients," their avoidance of service "illness," and the physicians' interventions "treatments." And he concludes with a purely personal plea for exonerating Wagner-Jauregg, unsupported by a shred of actual evidence for or against him. "Since his [the war neurotic's] illness," Freud declares, "served the purpose of withdrawing him from an intolerable situation, the roots of the illness would clearly be undermined if it was made even more intolerable to him than active service. Just as he had fled from the war into illness, means were now adopted which compelled him to flee back from illness into health, that is to say, into fitness for active service. For this purpose, painful electrical treatment was employed, and with success."[20]

What more is there to say? Freud acknowledges here that soldiers were "compelled" to submit to the so-called treatment—in short, that electrotherapy was employed as a means of repression. But psychiatry had always relied primarily on force or repression; there was nothing new about that. The only new thing in this episode is Freud's blatant use of the rhetoric of health, illness, and treatment in the service of patently moral, political, and social— rather than medical—interests.

As to Freud's specific defense of Wagner-Jauregg, it is all contained in a single sentence. "This painful form of treatment," writes Freud, "introduced in the German army for therapeutic purposes could no doubt also be employed in more moderate fashion. If it was used in the Vienna Clinics, I am personally convinced that it was never intensified to a cruel pitch by the initiative of Professor Wagner-Jauregg. I cannot vouch for other physicians whom I did not know."[21]

In his autobiography, however, Wagner-Jauregg admits to doing exactly what Freud denied him capable of doing: "If all the malingerers I cured at the Clinic, often by harsh enough measures, had appeared as my accusers, it would have made an impressive trial."[22] Comments Jones: "Fortunately for him, as he remarked, most of them were scattered over the former Austro-Hungarian Empire and were not available, so the Commission ultimately decided in his favor."[23]

Actually, at least one of Wagner-Jauregg's accusers did appear before the commission, a fact we learn from the stenographic transcript of Freud's direct testimony before the commission, which has been preserved in the archives of the Austrian Ministry of War. In his oral testimony Freud speaks of having "listened to Mr. Kauders and to the history of his illness" and of Kauders' claim that he "has been wronged" by Wagner-Jauregg. Freud refutes that claim by flatly asserting, "I know that the motivating force in his [Wagner-Jauregg's] treatment of patients is his humaneness." But Freud does not stop there:

PROF. FREUD: I also believe that Hofrat Wagner caused this [the patient's antagonism toward himself], in part, by reason of the fact that he did not avail himself of my therapy. I don't demand of him that he do so; I cannot possibly demand it of him; even my own students cannot do it.

PROF. WAGNER: I used disciplinary treatment, which was very much recommended, instead of persuading him that he is not ill.

PROF. FREUD: Your treatment had no success here; it only brought him to misunderstand the doctor's intentions. Well, I have overstepped my duty as an expert witness, but I have stated the impressions I gained from the deliberations.

CHAIRMAN: The expert expresses the point of view that he would have found it correct to give psychoanalytic treatment.

PROF. FREUD: In this case, yes.[24]

But the efficacy of the psychoanalytic treatment of the war neuroses was completely irrelevant to the charges brought against Wagner-Jauregg! That Freud was able to so alter the commission's agenda is further evidence of his powers as a rhetorician, as well as of his boundless egotism.

Wagner-Jauregg was at least honest in retrospect; he called the so-called war neurotics "malingerers." But if these men who assumed the patient role to avoid danger or death were not sick, what was he "treating" them for? Although Wagner-Jauregg calls the persons who abused the sick role "malingerers," he stops short of calling the doctors who abused the therapist role "torturers" or "medical criminals." In this vignette we can thus see war neurosis unconcealed as malingering, but electrical torture remains concealed as medical treatment.

III

Because of Freud's dominant role in the history of modern psychotherapy, his extensive involvement with electrotherapy deserves further consideration and comment. When Freud was a young doctor trying to make a career out of treating patients suffering from "nervous diseases," his situation was remarkably similar to that of a young doctor trying to make a career out of treating patients suffering from "mental diseases" today. There were then, as there are now, two types of such patients: those who sought help more or less voluntarily, and those upon whom help was imposed. The former patients exhibited mainly symptoms that mimicked those of neurological diseases; they were, accordingly, treated in their homes and in their physicians' offices by neurologists or "nerve doctors." The latter, about whom I shall say no more in this chapter, exhibited mainly the symptoms of what was then considered to be "insanity"; they were treated in insane asylums by alienists or psychiatrists.

Just as in Freud's youth nervous patients were treated with electrotherapy, so mental patients are now treated with chemotherapy. The fakery of these officially accepted methods was and is rendered well-nigh impenetrable for the average young doctor by the language in which these "treatments" were and are couched; by their authoritative espousal by all the leading scientific, medical, and legal authorities; and, last but not least, by their avid acceptance by the patients and their families.

What was wrong with these "nervous patients"? Many things. None of which, as I showed elsewhere, had anything to do with medicine or illness.[25] Why, then, did they and those about them think that they were ill? The answer is terrifyingly simple: because the "patients" pretended that they were ill, because they malingered or faked illness. Clarity is vital here. Without blaming the so-called neurotic for malingering or praising him for the excellence of his performance, we must look without prejudice at what these "nervous patients" did in order to understand what their "nerve doctors" did with, for, and to them.

Freud's first significant reference to electrotherapy (which he and others used synonymously with electrical treatment) is in his contribution to *Studies on Hysteria* (1893–95), in connection with the case of Fräulein Elisabeth von R. As will be recalled, this was one of the first hysterical patients whom Freud himself had treated.

What was wrong with Fräulein von R.? Freud tells us "that she complained of great pain in walking and of being quickly overcome by fatigue both in walking and in standing, and that after a short time she had to rest, which lessened the pains but did not do away with them altogether."[26] The patient had no demonstrable bodily illness and had been referred to Freud as a case of hysteria. "I did not find it easy to arrive at a diagnosis," Freud writes, "but I decided for two reasons to assent to the one proposed by my colleague, viz., that it was a case of hysteria."[27] The treatment, Freud then relates in a passage that has received much too little attention, "proceeded on the assumption that the disorder was of this mixed kind [*i.e.,* that the patient suffered from a combination of hysteria and an 'organic change in the muscles']. We recommended the continuation of systematic kneading and faradization of the sensitive muscles, regardless of resulting pain, and I reserved to myself treatment of her legs with high tension electric currents, in order to be able to keep in touch with her."[28]

Here, then, in one of his earliest references to electrotherapy, Freud casually acknowledges that the use of electricity was simply a gimmick or fraud—an *imitation of treatment* that allowed him "to keep in touch with" the patient. We learn, too, that the patient liked the treatment, and that the more it hurt, the more she liked it. "In this way," Freud continues, "we brought about a slight improvement. In particular, she seemed to take quite a liking to the painful shocks produced by the high tension apparatus, and the stronger these were the more they seemed to push her own pains into the background."[29]

Freud's next sentence in this account is so important that it deserves to stand alone. In it, Freud explicitly calls the use of electric shocks a pretense treatment. "In the meantime," he writes in this key sentence, "my colleague was preparing the ground for psychical treatment, and when, after four weeks of my pretence treatment, I proposed. . . ."[30]

By calling electrotherapy a pretended or fake treatment, Freud implies that he considers some other treatments genuine. What were these real, genuine, or literal treatments? Freud must have regarded certain medical or surgical interventions—for example, giving drugs or performing operations—as real treatments. In addition, he considered his own "analytic" interventions real treatments. The reason for this judgment—besides his desire to aggrandize himself and be accepted as a healer of mental diseases—was, I assume, his sincerity. When Freud used electrotherapy or hypnosis, he realized, and admitted, that he was "acting," whereas when he used psychoanalysis, he believed, and we have no reason to doubt him, that he was "being himself." But whereas sincerity may or may not be a virtue, depending on circumstances, the sincerity of a physician's belief that what he is doing is "therapy" has, assuredly, no relevance at all for ascertaining whether his act constitutes a bona fide treatment.

IV

The development of psychoanalysis, first out of electrotherapy, and then out of hypnosis, has been responsible for one of the most persistent and pernicious claims of psychoanalysts—namely, that whereas such standard pre-Freudian methods of psychotherapy as electricity, hydrotherapy, and hypnosis work by "suggestion," psychoanalysis does not, its beneficial effect resulting from "interpretation" or "analysis." Despite its persuasiveness, this argument is completely false. To be sure, there are important differences, as well as similarities, among these diverse methods of personal influence. However, each method constitutes a rhetorical address by the therapist to the patient; in each case, "suggestive" influence is exerted on the patient. Moreover, the process is reciprocal: the patient "suggests" certain messages to the doctor by means of "symptoms" (hysteria, neurosis), and the therapist "suggests" certain other messages to the patient by means of "treatments" (hypnosis, psychoanalysis). The essential distinction, from the point of view of suggestion—or, better, rhetoric—between electrotherapy and hypnosis on the one hand, and psychoanalysis on the other, is that the former methods are crudely suggestive, whereas the latter is more subtly so.

This is a familiar distinction. As in merchandising we distinguish between the "hard sell" and the "soft sell," so in psychotherapy we ought to distinguish between overt or unconcealed suggestion and covert or concealed suggestion. The psychoanalytic claim that the analyst exerts no suggestive influence on his patient is as fraudulent as would be the claim that the merchant who uses the "soft sell" exerts no suggestive influence on his customer. Nevertheless, much of the prestige of psychoanalysis rests on this brazenly self-serving claim which—largely because of Freud's unceasing effort to conceal suggestion as interpretation and his success in selling this myth—has been widely accepted.[31] For example, in 1910 he makes just this claim in comparing psychoanalysis to electrotherapy:

> I trust you will not say that the fact of the authority of society coming to our aid and increasing our successes so greatly would do nothing to prove the validity of our hypotheses—arguing as you might that, since suggestion is supposed to be able to do anything, our successes would then be successes of suggestion and not of psychoanalysis. Social suggestion is at present favourable to treating nervous patients by hydropathy, dieting, and electrotherapy, but that does not enable such measures to get the better of the neuroses. Time will show whether psychoanalytic treatment can accomplish more.[32]

This argument, as well as the importance of electrotherapy in Freud's own professional development, is set forth more fully in Freud's essay, "On the History of the Psycho-Analytic Movement":

> I myself had only unwillingly taken up the profession of medicine, but I had at that time a strong motive for helping people suffering from nervous affections or at least wishing to understand something about their states. I had embarked upon physical therapy, and had felt absolutely helpless after the disappointing results from my study of Erb's *Elektrotherapie* (1882), which put forward such a number of indications and recommendations. If I did not at the time arrive on my own account at the conclusion which Möbius established later, that the successes of electrical treatment in nervous patients are the effects of suggestion, there is no doubt that only the total absence of these promised successes was to blame. Treatment by suggestion during deep hypnosis, which I learned from Liébault's and Bernheim's highly impressive demonstrations, then seemed to offer a satisfactory substitute for the failure of electrical treatment.[33]

In addition to alluding to the extremely important role that electrotherapy played in Freud's day and in the development of his own personal career, Freud here again divides the field of psychotherapy into two parts: one, comprising what others do, consisting of therapies by "suggestion"; and another, comprising what he does, consisting of "analysis." But the difference between these two classes, as I noted earlier, is one of degree, not kind: it is a difference between crude and subtle rhetoric. Indeed, it was because Freud was a consummate artist in refining his rhetoric that he became so outstanding a rhetorician. And he used the oldest rhetorical trick in history—the claim that he had no desire to persuade people of anything at all, but wanted only to bring them the truth.

V

Whenever Freud remarked on the origin of psychoanalysis, he always linked it to electrotherapy, and always so as to claim for psychoanalysis an empirical and logical status separate from and superior to all other psychotherapeutic methods: that is, all past, present, and future treatments of the neuroses, other than his own, are based on "suggestion"; only his treatment is not. "Psychoanalysis," writes Freud in 1919, "was born out of medical necessity. It sprang from the need for bringing help to neurotic patients, who had found no relief through rest-cures, through the arts of hydropathy, or through electricity."[34]

In 1923, Freud characterizes electrotherapy with another significantly revealing term. In "A Short Account of Psycho-Analysis," he writes: "Electrical treatment was given out [when he was a young physician] as being a specific cure for nervous conditions; but anyone who has endeavored to carry out Erb's (1882) detailed instructions must marvel at the space that phantasy can occupy even in what professes to be an exact science."[35] If Freud really believed that Erb's electrical treatment was a "phantasy," then he would have had to classify it as a "psychopathological symptom" or "illness" rather than as a form of "psychotherapy" or "treatment." In fact, "psychopathology" and "psychotherapy" belong in the same logical class: both are rhetorical forms. Their names depend on who is doing what, where, when, and to whom.

Freud's most extensive reference to electrical treatment is in his *Autobiographical Study:*

> Anyone who wants to make a living from the treatment of nervous patients must be clearly able to do something to help them. My therapeutic arsenal contained only two weapons, electrotherapy and hypnotism. . . . My knowledge of electrotherapy was derived from W. Erb's textbook (1882), which provided detailed instructions for the treatment of all the symptoms of nervous diseases. Unluckily I was soon driven to see that following these instructions was of no help whatever and that what I had taken as the epitome of exact observations was merely the construction of a phantasy. The realization that the work of the greatest name in German neuropathology had no more relation to reality than some 'Egyptian' dream-book, such as is sold in cheap bookshops, was painful, but it helped to rid me of another shred of the innocent faith in authority from which I was not yet free. So I put my electrical apparatus aside, even before Möbius had saved the situation by explaining that the successes of electric treatment in nervous disorders (in so far as there were any) were the effects of suggestion on the part of the physician.[36]

Freud began his practice as a nerve doctor by using electrotherapy. He switched to the ritualized repression called hypnosis, and then to the ceremonial conversation which he called "psychoanalysis," because he believed that electrotherapy and hypnosis were pretenses. We can thus see in, and can infer from, Freud's own remarks about hysteria and electrotherapy that the neuroses are, in fact, pretenses of illness, and that their cure, whether by electricity, hypnosis, or psychoanalysis, are pretenses of treatment.

III

The Paradigm
of Psychotherapy

7

The Psychoanalytic Movement: Franchising the Freudian Faith

I

Sigmund Freud's (1856–1939) claims about psychoanalysis were fundamentally false and fraudulent. He did not discover a new science, a science of the unconscious; nor did he develop a new method of treating illness, based on free association, transference, and resistance. His science is a system of inspired invectives concealed in medical metaphors; and his treatment is a contrived and controlled conversation relabeled with the technicized terminology of his self-styled science. In short, Freud devised a new rhetoric which he represented as a scientific theory and a medical therapy.

The contemporary reader cannot be attentive enough to the historical changes that have occurred in the practice of psychiatry since Freud was a young man. Just as there was no automobile, radio, or television in those days, there was also no psychotherapy. (To be sure, there were activities that we now call by this name but that is another matter.) One could therefore not practice psychotherapy. The fact that today one can is, perhaps, Freud's most significant achievement. Whether this is a laudable or a lamentable development is a question all too little examined by modern thinkers.

After Freud received his M.D. degree from the University of Vienna in 1881, he worked for two years in the Vienna General Hospital. His position there could be best compared to that of an intern. In those years Freud evidently did not plan to do the sort of work he ended up doing. "In his first hospital year," writes Jones, "Freud gave no indications of a wish to specialize. . . . When he thought of the future it was more of settling in a provincial town or abroad than of a career in Vienna."[1] After 1883 Freud drifted, partly influenced by his own interests and partly through accidental circumstances, into becoming a neurologist. In 1884, he writes in a letter: "I am gradually marking myself off as a neuropathologist to my Chief in the hope of its furthering my prospects."[2] From October, 1885, until February, 1886, Freud was in Paris, for the four and a half months of his famous study under Jean-Martin Charcot. In 1887 and 1888, he was working on a book on the anatomy of the brain, a project that was never finished. In 1891, Freud published his first book, a study of aphasia, which is still considered a neurological classic. Jones categorizes the fourteen years in Freud's life from 1883 until 1897 as his neurological period.

How, then, did Freud come to "discover" psychoanalysis? Or, more precisely, how did he come to invent, borrow, or develop it after catharsis? The word one uses here is terribly important, as it preforms and prejudges one's whole attitude toward Freud's work.

II

Freud became interested in psychotherapy through Josef Breuer (1842–1925), who was a prominent medical practitioner in Vienna. Breuer was appointed a *Privatdozent* in 1868, when he was only twenty-six years old; he was one of the most sought-after physicians in Vienna when Freud was a young man. As a practicing physician, Breuer had, of course, his share of patients who complained of a variety of bodily symptoms but who were not demonstrably ill. These patients, many of them young women, were then usually called "hysterics." Between 1880 and 1882, one of Breuer's hysterical patients was a twenty-one-year-old woman who has since become known as Anna O. It was she who discovered—or, better, rediscovered for herself—that telling Breuer, in considerable detail, the disagreeable events of her present and past life helped to relieve, at least temporarily, many of her symptoms. Gradually Anna O. and Breuer fell into the habit of spending an hour or more a day engaged in this sort of "therapy." Revealingly, the patient herself named the treatment "the talking cure" or "chimney sweeping." Breuer and Freud later renamed it "catharsis." Freud defined catharsis as a technically undeveloped form, a therapeutic precursor, of psychoanalysis. We can thus trace, step-by-step from the very beginnings of modern psychotherapy, the pretentious and self-serving use of medical jargon— by Freud and by most of those who came after him. The talking cure—or "just talking," as psychotherapy is sometimes described nowadays, with a contempt that is in fact a compliment—was thus immediately concealed behind the facade of the Greek word *catharsis*.

That the term *catharsis* should be attached to an activity that was then defined as medical and therapeutic is especially ironic, since the procedure originated with the sufferer or patient rather than with the scientist or physician, as is usually the case in regular medicine. The patient, an exceptionally intelligent and ambitious young woman who became a devout feminist and pioneer social worker,[3] not only learned to produce her own "illness" by imitating the symptoms of neurological disease, she also learned to "cure" it by imitating the ideas and interventions of classical Greek religion and drama.* That an educated young woman living in Vienna should have had no difficulty in familiarizing herself with this notion was demonstrated convincingly by Ellenberger and Lain Entralgo in their reconstruction of the cultural setting in which Breuer's treatment of Anna O. took place. From Ellenberger we learn that, in 1880, Jacob Bernays—the uncle of Freud's future

---

* There is no evidence to suggest that Breuer's "treatment" helped Anna O. There is some evidence to suggest that it harmed her. In any case, presumably as a result of her "treatment," she became an uncompromising, lifelong enemy of psychoanalysis.[4]

wife—published a book on Aristotle's concept of theatrical catharsis and that this idea "was at the time one of the current topics of conversation in the Viennese salons. . . . No wonder a young lady of high society adopted it as a device for her self-directed cure."[5] Lain Entralgo also notes that Jacob Bernays had written on Aristotle's use of the concept of catharsis. "The study of Bernays," he states, "appeared for the first time in the *Mémoires* of the Academy of Breslau in 1857 and was subsequently reprinted in . . . Berlin in 1880."[6] These important observations indicate that the "therapy" for mental illness, no less than its pathogenesis, is largely a matter of imitation.[7] Anna O. imitates illness and becomes a patient; she then imitates being cured, and becomes well again. The view thus generated is consistent with the fact that in the self-produced illnesses we now call "mental" every intervention has been both successful and unsuccessful. That is to be expected in a situation in which "therapeutic" success and failure depend, ultimately, on the "patient's" decision to "recover" or remain "ill."

Another reason that the modern medicalization and mystification of catharsis as psychotherapy is bitterly ironic is the original historical context and meaning of the term. That context is ancient Greek religion. In it, as in most early religions, the central image of misfortune and malady of every kind is pollution; and the corresponding image of recovery from misfortune and malady is purification.[8] The process of purification or cleansing—which was a religious and ritual activity even if it involved purgation or fasting—the ancient Greeks called catharsis. Subsequently, the Greeks themselves used the term more broadly and metaphorically, a usage typified by Aristotle's calling the effect of tragedy on the audience an emotional catharsis, especially of fear and pity. The spiritual needs of man were thus well understood in Greek antiquity; and they were well articulated in the religious and artistic images and terms appropriate to them. Educated in the classics, Freud and the early Freudians remolded these images into, and renamed them as, medical diseases and treatments. This metamorphosis has been widely acclaimed in the modern world as an epoch-making scientific discovery. Alas, it is, in fact, only the clever and cynical destruction of the spirituality of man, and its replacement by a positivistic "science of the mind."

The ideas I articulate here are, of course, timeless truths that have been voiced before, especially by artists. For example, in his following observation about psychoanalysis, Franz Kafka makes the same point that I have made about mental illness and treatment in general:

> You say you do not understand it. Try to understand it by calling it illness. It is one of the many manifestations of illness that psychoanalysis believes it has revealed. I do not call it illness, and I regard the therapeutic claims of psychoanalysis as an impotent error [*hilfloser Irrtum*]. All these so-called illnesses, however sad they may look, are facts of belief, the distressed human being's anchorages in some maternal ground or other; thus it is not surprising that psychoanalysis finds the primal ground of all religions to be precisely the same thing as what causes the individual's "illnesses." . . . And does anyone really think this is a subject for treatment?[9]

These ideas of Kafka's resemble those of Carl Jung, of which, according to Max Brod, the editor of the volume in which this posthumously published passage appears, Kafka had no knowledge;[10] they also resemble the views of Karl Kraus, with whose writings Kafka must have been familiar.[11]

III

In 1886, in his thirtieth year, Freud began private practice. When he first opened his office in Vienna, he did so as a specialist. The term used to describe his specialty—neurology—is important. That term is accurate, so far as it goes, since Freud's training was in neuropathology and neurology. In German, such a physician was then called a *Nervenarzt;* his English or American counterpart was called a specialist in diseases of the nervous system or in nervous diseases.

What did Freud, as a beginning practitioner, do? He did what was expected of any young specialist in nervous diseases. Here is the way Jones describes it: "In the summer of 1886, his life was confined to the work at the Kassowitz Institute [an institution for pediatric neurology] three times a week, to his translations and book-reviewing work, and to his private practice. The latter naturally consisted mainly of neurotic patients, so that the question of therapeutics arose with an urgency."12

Patients came to Freud for the diagnosis and treatment of their alleged or actual nervous diseases, and he had to do something to justify charging them a fee. Charcot and other institutional specialists in nervous diseases had it easy: they received salaries from universities or hospitals, their institutional patients were mainly indigent, and they could therefore simply study their patients as "cases" and wait for them to die so that they could dissect their bodies and examine their brains. However, that approach could not be applied to patients who had money and who often were of a higher social rank than their doctors. Confronted with such cases, the physician had to offer the patient treatment, and if he did not know how to cure the illness he at least had to pretend that he did—to survive as a professional. That is how the complementary pretendings of patient and physician were built into the social situation in which modern psychotherapy originated.

Since psychotherapy did not exist at that time, how did Freud treat his neurotic patients? Freud's first therapeutic attempts, Jones relates, "were made by the orthodox electrotherapy as described in Erb's textbook. It seems odd that he should thus bow to authority when he was already acquainted with Breuer's more promising cathartic method; Charcot's derogatory attitude had certainly influenced him in putting it aside in his mind."13 These remarks betray Jones's lack of understanding of psychoanalysis and its development. Electrotherapy was the name of an accepted method of treating nervous diseases,14 whereas catharsis was the name of a particular encounter between Breuer and one of his patients. Thus, a physician in those days could choose to be an electrotherapist, but he could not choose to be a catharsist.

For nearly two years, Freud confined himself to electrotherapy, accompanied by adjuvants such as baths and massages; and he continued to use these methods for at least five or six years. Then, as he lost interest in electrotherapy, Freud switched to hypnosis, which he practiced until 1889. Regardless of how valuable or worthless hypnosis might have been as a treatment, it was then an accepted therapeutic method for physicians, and especially for specialists in nervous diseases. Moreover, it was hypnosis which, through hypnocatharsis, Freud reshaped into psychoanalysis. What all these methods had in common, and what is most important about them, is that each was at bottom a conversation between patient and doctor, and that this simple fact was disguised by a scientific-sounding Greek term that legitimized them as therapeutic interventions.

Because the hypnotized patient was supposed to be in a "trance," a state somehow resembling sleep, such patients were placed in a supine position, on a bed or couch. That arrangement —the patient lying on a couch, the physician sitting on a chair— Freud retained throughout his practice. It, too, helped to make it appear that what patient and doctor were doing was not just talking: the analyst's couch thus became the leading symbol—rivaled only by the cigar—of the psychoanalytic method.

Here is the way Jones describes the crucial steps in Freud's reshaping of hypnosis into psychoanalysis. In 1892, with a young woman who was refractory to hypnosis, Freud tried what he called the "concentration technique." Placed on the couch, the patient was asked to close her eyes as if to be hypnotized and "to concentrate her attention on a particular symptom and to try to recall any memories that might throw light on its origin. When no progress was being made Freud would press her forehead with his hand and assure her that then some thoughts or memories would indubitably come to her. . . . This was the first step towards the later free association method."[15]

What Jones describes here is Freud's attempt to encourage a person who is reluctant to talk to him to do so. As late as 1895, in *Studies on Hysteria,* Freud still calls his method of psychotherapy "Breuer's cathartic method."[16] In 1896 he uses the term *psychoanalysis* for the first time, and of course he never lets go of it.* At

---

* The sentence in which Freud first uses the term *psychoanalysis* reads: "I owe my results to a new method of psycho-analysis, Josef Breuer's exploratory procedure; it is a little intricate, but it is irreplaceable, so fertile has it shown itself to be in throwing light upon the obscure paths of unconscious ideation."[17] Freud here identifies psychoanalysis itself as Breuer's creation.

the age of forty, Freud thus invents the trademark with which to identify talking as treatment; with its aid he can separate his method from—and place it above—those of his competitors.

IV

Let us now turn to Freud's concept of neurosis. If our present ideas about the nature of mental disorders are confused, the ideas that prevailed around the turn of the last century were even more so. Now people try to understand what sorts of mental diseases neurotic disorders are; then they tried to understand what sorts of bodily disorders caused or constituted the neuroses. After all, the name of the disease itself implied that it was a disease of neurones, or nerves. Thus, the nerve doctors tried to explain what sort of bodily illness this or that neurosis was. That is the stage upon which Freud entered in the late 1880s. It was a stage whose props, theatrical and technological, he never completely relinquished.

Freud differed from many of his colleagues who practiced nerve doctoring in that he was never satisfied with merely treating his patients, but always wanted to know what was wrong with them. The two most important early sources of Freud's views on the nature of neurosis are his *Project for a Scientific Psychology* and his correspondence with Wilhelm Fliess. In the first sentence of the *Project,* Freud announces his devout commitment to a materialist and reductionist psychology, from which he never wavered. "The intention of this project," he writes, "is to furnish a psychology which shall be a natural science: its aim, that is, is to represent psychical processes as quantitatively determined states of specifiable material particles."[18] Because that proposition of Freud's is epistemological nonsense, and because Freud must have gradually realized that it was, he had only two choices: he could abandon it and admit that human affairs belonged in the realm of morals rather than medicine; or he could redouble his efforts and insist ever more stubbornly that in psychoanalysis he had created a science of "mental life," a science that is "like any other" in its power to offer causal explanations for what it observes and influences. Freud chose the latter path.

The *Project* is, of course, pure science fiction. Its linguistic form is characterized by a multitude of Greek words and symbols and by statements such as the following: "Thus there are *permeable* neurones (offering no resistance and retaining nothing) which serve the function of perception, and *impermeable* neurones (offering resistance and retaining quantity [Qn]) which are the vehicles of memory and presumably, therefore, of psychical processes in general. Henceforward, therefore, I shall call the former system of neurones O and the latter Y."[19] Here, from as early as 1895, we glimpse a sample of what became Freud's characteristic method: the offering of scientific-sounding metaphors as the accounts of actual phenomena in the brains or minds of persons. The fact that Freud succeeded in establishing these metaphors widely as accounts of what really happens in the world is, of course, testimony to his powers as rhetorician, rather than to the "scientific validity" of his neurological and chemical fantasies.

Let us now pursue the path of Freud's metaphorizings through his famous correspondence with Wilhelm Fliess (1858–1928). During the crucial years when Freud was close to Fliess and engaged in an intimate correspondence with him (1887–1902), Fliess was living in Berlin and had a successful practice as an ear and nose specialist. Through his respect for Fliess, Freud gave himself an infusion of the self-respect he lacked. For example, he called their personal meetings during vacations and other visits "Congresses," exhibiting the same inflation of language that characterizes so much of his work.

Facts are, of course, stubborn. Freud knew perfectly well that his actual "medical" work was only "talking." Thus, just as the hysteric concealed her marital unhappiness behind a veil of neurological symptoms, so Freud concealed his medical unhappiness behind a veil of neurological symbols. All of this is undeniably clear from a close and careful reading of his letters to Fliess. On February 4, 1888, Freud writes: "My practice, which, as you know, is not very considerable, has recently benefited somewhat because of the name of Charcot. The carriage is expensive, and visiting, and talking people into and out of things, which is what my work consists of, robs me of the best time for work."[20]

Here, plainly stated, is what few in psychiatry want to see: ". . . talking people into and out of things"!

In August of the same year, Freud tells Fliess that he chose neuropathology not because he was interested in it, but because he was unqualified for general practice. The two men were evidently discussing the idea of Freud doing medical work, for Freud answers: "I admit unreservedly that you are right in what you say, and yet I cannot do as you suggest. To go into general practice instead of specializing, to use all the resources of general medicine and treat the patient as a whole, is certainly the only way which promises real satisfaction and material success; but for me it is too late for that now. I have not learned enough for that kind of practice; there is a gap in my medical equipment which it would be hard to close. I was able to learn just enough to become a neuropathologist."[21]

Freud's acknowledgment of his incompetence as a physician is important. It helps to explain not only his ambivalent identification with the role of the medical doctor, but also his insistence that neuroses were bona fide medical diseases: by "discovering" their etiology and treatment, he proved not only that they were real diseases, but also that he was a real doctor.

What, according to Freud's earliest views, was a neurosis? It was simply an illness, which differed from other illnesses in that its cause, or "ætiology" as he liked to put it, was "sexual"—an idea he borrowed from Charcot, Breuer, and Fliess. Fliess had a large practice in which he encountered many neurotic patients. In the early 1890s he developed a theory about the "reflex" connections between the nasal mucous membrane and the genitals; he named the alleged clinical entity the "nasal reflex neurosis." The fact that he had good success in curing it by applying cocaine to the nasal mucosa convinced him—and Freud—that Fliess was right about why "neurasthenic complaints, in other words, the neuroses with a sexual ætiology, so frequently assume the form of the nasal reflex neurosis."[22]

The notion that something sexual causes something they called a neurosis was an idea that Fliess and Freud shared. Freud then proceeded to elaborate upon it. In his introduction to "The Aetiology of the Neuroses," Freud cautions Fliess—in a manner that may well have struck Fliess as condescending and that now strikes us as prissy even for those times—"You will of course keep the draft away from your young wife."[23] The speculations Freud then advances are the medical prejudices of his day. "It may be taken as common knowledge," he writes, as indeed it was, "that neurasthenia is a frequent result of an abnormal sexual life. The contention which I am putting forward and desire to test by observation is that neurasthenia is always *only* a sexual neurosis."[24] The phrasing suggests that Freud also recognized nonsexual neuroses, but he mentions none. Metaphorization again displaces description; Freud's metaphorization, moreover, mystifies with the imagery of the medical wages of a sexual sin.

"Neurasthenia in males," Freud continues, "is acquired at the age of puberty and becomes manifest in the patient's twenties. Its source is masturbation, the frequency of which runs completely parallel with the frequency of neurasthenia in men. One can regularly observe in the circle of one's acquaintances that (at least in urban populations) men who have been seduced by women at an early age escape neurasthenia."[25] These few lines contain astonishing revelations.

First, Freud asserts that masturbation causes neurasthenia in such a way as to suggest that he was not familiar with the then well-established psychiatric theory that masturbation causes insanity.[26] Actually, the masturbatory theory of insanity was then more than one hundred years old, and Freud must have been made aware of it at least through the cautionary tales of the nursery if not through the clinical teachings of the medical school.

Second, Freud asserts that "sexual seduction at an early age" protects men from neurasthenia. This is a startling idea, in view of his theory that precisely the same act causes, rather than prevents, mental illness in women. In short, Freud claims that "sexual seduction at an early age" causes hysteria in women and prevents neurasthenia in men!

Finally, in alluding to observations of his own acquaintances, Freud suggests that he is alluding to himself and his own experiences; that is, to his own sexual fears, sexual abstinence, and the neurasthenia which he attributed to it. The suspicion that Freud's sexual theories were in fact his speculations about his own sexual predicaments is borne out by his subsequent remarks in "The Aetiology of the Neuroses" and in his letters to Fliess.*

In addition to masturbation, he identifies as a second "sexual noxa" what he calls *"onanismus conjugalis*—incomplete copulation to prevent conception."[29] He concludes: "It follows from what I have said that the neuroses can be completely prevented but are completely incurable."[30] It seems more than likely that Freud was here thinking of syphilis, and applying what was a medical banality for that disease to the "neuroses" (which remained conveniently undefined, except that they, too, had something to do with sex). Freud's remarks following immediately after his foregoing speculation support my suggestion:

> The physician's task is thus wholly concentrated on prophylaxis. The first part of this task, the prevention of the sexual noxa of the first period, coincides with prophylaxis against syphilis and gonorrhea, for these are the noxae which threaten anyone who gives up masturbation. The only alternatives would be free sexual intercourse between young males and respectable girls; but this could only be resorted to if there were innocuous preventive methods. Otherwise, the alternatives are: masturbation, with neurasthenia in males and hysteroneurasthenia in females, or syphilis in males, with syphilis in the next generation, or gonorrhea in males, with gonorrhea and sterility in females.[31]

Freud's own fears of venereal disease are here elevated to the rank of a comprehensive theory of mental diseases, a theory all-too-apparently absurd today. What may not be so apparent, however, is Freud's twofold use of the idea of sexual noxa or harm: he used it to refer to literal sexual dangers, such as syphilis and

---

* It is also borne out by his lifelong preoccupation with the twin specters of masturbation and the "castration" of women. Freud's distorted ideas on sex, deriving wholly from his cultural milieu and the personal adjustment he made to it, recur unceasingly in his writings and he revealingly returns to them in the last disconnected paragraphs he commits to paper, in London, at the end of his life. On July 12, 1938, he writes: "As a substitute for penis-envy, identification with the clitoris: neatest expression of inferiority, source of all inhibitions."[27] And on August 3, 1938, he adds: "The ultimate ground of all intellectual inhibitions and all inhibitions of work seems to be the inhibition of masturbation in childhood."[28]

gonorrhea, and to metaphorical sexual dangers, such as masturbation and other "perversions." The microorganisms of syphilis and gonorrhea cause diseases; masturbatory and homosexual acts do not. Nevertheless, Freud never stopped insisting that masturbation causes neurasthenia and that (repressed) homosexuality causes paranoia.

Did Freud know that he was using a metaphor, a figure of speech, when he referred to neuroses as diseases caused by sexual noxae? Evidently he did not. On May 30, 1893, Freud writes to Fliess: "I am curious to know whether you will accept my diagnosis of the cases I have sent you. I make it often now, and entirely agree with you that the reflex neurosis is one of the commonest disorders."[32] Later he adds: "I hope that the nasal reflex neurosis will soon be generally known as Fliess's disease."[33] What happened to that disease? It disappeared. Why? Because Freud's own products took it off the market. The neuroses, and especially the transference neurosis, were the follies that Freud finally successfully franchised.

V

The basic "discoveries" of psychoanalysis were all made and published before 1906. In the course of about ten years, Freud placed before the scientific world, as well as the general public, the classic psychoanalytic ideas on hysteria, repression, dreams, infantile sexuality, and the unconscious. Other impressions to the contrary notwithstanding, Freud encountered no difficulties in publishing and popularizing any of these ideas. Most of his writings were favorably received, though they evoked indignation and opposition as well. What happened next in the history of psychoanalysis was of fateful consequence.

During the first decade of the twentieth century, Freud abandoned the kind of leadership we associate with the progress of science and adopted instead the kind of leadership typical of big business. In effect, he founded a cartel that was to have a monopoly over psychoanalysis. In the language of commerce, the first phase of psychoanalysis, the period prior to 1906, may thus be regarded as the period of product development. It is as if Freud had developed the formula for, say, Coca-Cola and found that, within a narrow circle, there was considerable interest in and demand for it. He then decided that his next move ought to be to sell his product to a wider range of customers than he could reach with the simple methods of advertising that he had been using—that is, by merely publishing his observations and ideas. In 1910, Freud formed a stock company, the International Psychoanalytic Association, for the purpose of promoting and distributing psychoanalysis.

Freud, of course, was the majority stockholder, with Sándor Ferenczi, Adler, Jung, Karl Abraham, and Wilhelm Stekel being the other principal stockholders. The first order of business was to give the firm a pleasing public image. This was crucial, because Freud and most of the pioneer psychoanalysts were Jews and because psychoanalysis had to do with sex. In the Central Europe of those days, neither Jewishness nor sexuality was considered attractive.

How did Freud proceed to create a more winning corporate image for organized psychoanalysis? He did it by setting up a dummy corporation headed by a front-man chosen especially to inspire confidence and respectability. Such a public-relations maneuver was intended to camouflage both the Jewishness and the socially subversive qualities of the organization.

Freud himself acknowledged some of these motives for acting as he did, and they are not difficult to understand. Here was a Jewish firm, psychoanalysis, that wanted to do business with anti-Semitic customers—that is, the German-speaking world. Obviously, in such a circumstance the thing to do was to set up a dummy corporation headed by a non-Jew. Thus was Carl Gustav Jung chosen to be the first president of the International Psychoanalytic Association.

When Freud announced his plan to make Jung president, his Viennese colleagues bitterly disagreed. Perhaps they had in mind a scientific organization, headed by a person most expressive of the group's scientific ideals. But Freud was organizing a movement, and he frankly said so. Before the issue came to a vote, the Viennese group held a protest meeting to prevent Jung's election to the presidency. When Freud heard of this, he rushed to Stekel's hotel room, where the group had congregated, and, according to Jones, "made an impassioned appeal for their adherence. He laid stress on the virulent hostility that surrounded them and the need for outside support to counter it. Then dramatically throwing back his coat, he declared: 'My enemies would be willing to see me starve; they would tear my very coat off my back.' "³⁴ Freud appealed to economic rather than to scientific considerations. Jung was needed for business, not for professional, reasons.

In order to appreciate the sort of leadership Freud exercised vis-à-vis his colleagues, it is necessary to examine his own version of the foregoing events. In "On the History of the Psycho-Analytic Movement," he writes: "What I had in mind was to organize the psycho-analytic movement, to transfer its center to Zürich and to give it a chief who would look after its future career. As this scheme has met with much opposition among the adherents of psychoanalysis, I will set out my reasons for it in some detail. I hope that these will justify me, even though it turns out that what I did was in fact not very wise."³⁵ He then describes Jung's qualifications for the post—such as his proven contributions, his talent, his energy. "In addition to this," adds Freud, "he seemed ready to enter into a friendly relationship with me and for my sake to give up certain racial prejudices which he had previously permitted himself."³⁶

Could Freud have had such a naïve view of religious or racial prejudice? In the passage quoted, Freud refers to Jung's anti-Semitism as if it were an old piece of furniture that Jung had promised to discard. But the self-proclaimed discoverer of the unconscious must have known better. If Jung was indeed anti-Semitic, that was not something he could promise to give up, just like that.

VI

The International Psychoanalytic Association having been established, and branch societies having been formed, the widespread promotion of psychoanalysis seemed well under way. But no sooner was the venture incorporated than it ran into trouble. As official psychoanalytic history has it, the difficulty was that

Adler and Jung developed ideas too radically divergent from those considered characteristic of psychoanalysis. Thus, in the interests of the "purity" of psychoanalysis, a separation had to be made between genuine Freudian psychoanalysis and modifications of it.

Such an interpretation presupposes, however, certain distinctions between psychoanalysis proper and variations of it. In this connection, our commercial model of product-development, promotion, distribution, and so forth, will prove illuminating. In terms of it, we could say that what really happened was that as soon as the psychoanalytic business was launched, the distributors —Adler, Jung, Stekel, and the others—refused to abide by the franchiser's demands. Freud treated psychoanalysis as if it were an invention that the inventor could patent, thus restricting the rights of others in its use. Accordingly, Freud insisted that psychoanalysis was to be dispensed only in accordance with his specifications. But he went even further—declaring that he, and he only, could change the original formula.

Most of Freud's colleagues, whom he appointed as distributors of psychoanalysis, had loftier aspirations. They were all intelligent and ambitious men, and most of them were heretical characters to boot. Once the distributors established themselves as franchised psychoanalysts, they began to tamper with their merchandise. Soon they announced that they had modified the formula, making it superior to the original. In that way, one franchised distributor of psychoanalysis after another went into "research and development work," and then set up manufacturing facilities for his own particular brand of improved psychoanalysis.

Had Freud been satisfied with being a scientific investigator of human behavior, this would have been no cause for objection. Indeed, he would have rejoiced that his ideas proved so fertile, that they stimulated so much interest and investigation in areas hitherto neglected by scientists. Gerhard Domagk, the discoverer of Prontosil, the first of the sulfonamide drugs, ushered in a new era of chemotherapy. As a result of the work he stimulated, the patent rights on Prontosil resulted in only limited revenues for the chemical firm that held them. Yet, no chemist or medical man would have dreamed of complaining that sulfanilamide, the original sulfone drug, was being ruined; or of claiming that only Domagk had a right to change its formula!

The fact that certain scientific discoveries and technological inventions can be patented means only that the revenues from them shall accrue primarily to those who discovered or developed them. As ideas, as contributions to human knowledge, the fruits of science and technology cannot be patented; nor can the noncommercial uses of discoveries and inventions—for example, learning or teaching new information or new skills. In short, scientific theories and therapeutic techniques—the major "products" to which Freud laid claim as an inventor—cannot be patented. That fact must have caused Freud much unhappiness, for he adopted a highly monopolistic attitude toward psychoanalysis and tried to restrict its use to those he considered loyal disciples. In effect, Freud acted as if he were trying to patent psychoanalysis. Naturally, he failed to accomplish that. However, he did succeed in setting an example, as a result of which many of his followers have also acted as if they were trying to patent their ideas. After Freud's death, controversy over patent-rights erupted between the principal new patent-holder, the American Psychoanalytic Association, and the leading post-Freudian revisionists, such as Karen Horney, Harry Stack Sullivan, and Erich Fromm.

But to return to Freud's own efforts at patenting psychoanalysis: Illustrative of them is his controversy with Adler. Exactly why did Freud object to Adler? The facts are simply that Adler had somewhat different ideas about psychology and psychotherapy than Freud. That, of course, explains nothing. They could still have proceeded with their work, as other scientists do. J. Robert Oppenheimer and Edward Teller differed on the feasibility of the hydrogen bomb, but that did not mean that one or the other man had to cease being a nuclear physicist.

Freud and Adler fought over fame and money. Freud was like an early American business tycoon. Here is his own explanation of his objection to Adler: "I wish merely to show that these theories controvert the fundamental principles of analysis (and on what points they controvert them) and that for this reason they should not be known by the name of analysis."[37] The issue, then, was not whether Adler was right or wrong, but what should be called psychoanalysis. It was as if, after patenting Coca-Cola, Freud did not really care whether Pepsi-Cola was just as good or better. He merely wanted to make sure that only his product carried the original label. The following passage, in which Freud contrasts the differences between Freudian and Adlerian psychoanalysis, amply supports my interpretation:

> The first task confronting psycho-analysis was to explain the neuroses; it used the two facts of resistance and transference as starting-points, and taking into consideration the third fact of amnesia, accounted for them with its theories of repression, of the sexual motive forces in neurosis, and of the unconscious. Psychoanalysis has never claimed to provide a complete theory of human mentality in general, but only expected that what it offered should be applied to supplement and correct the knowledge acquired by other means. Adler's theory, however, goes far beyond this point, it seeks at one stroke to explain the behavior and character of human beings as well as their neurotic and psychotic illnesses.[38]

Here is Freud, in 1914, criticizing Adler for failing to confine himself to explanations of the neuroses, and for offering a general theory of human behavior. But did Freud limit himself to explaining the neuroses? Did he not also try to develop a general theory of human behavior? In 1904, ten years before his foregoing criticism of Adler's work, Freud published *The Psychopathology of Everyday Life;* in 1911, the Schreber case; in 1912–1913, *Totem and Taboo;* and in 1914, a short paper on "The Moses of Michelangelo." Are these contributions to our understanding of neurosis or to our understanding of human behavior generally?

How was the patent-infringement suit against Adler decided? It could not be settled legally, as literal patent-infringement suits are. Nor could it be settled by the presiding officers of the leading psychoanalytic societies: Jung was then president of the International Psychoanalytic Association, and Adler was president of the Vienna Psychoanalytic Society. In 1911, at the height of the conflict with Adler, Freud held no official position in psychoanalysis. Adler and Jung, the two official leaders, were, as I suggested, merely franchised dealers, the representatives of the powerful owner and behind-the-scenes board chairman of the corporation. If the dealers misbehaved, Freud could withdraw their franchises. That is exactly what he did. As a member of the Vienna Psychoanalytic Society, Freud had several choices once he found himself in serious disagreement with Adler. He could have waited until Adler's term as president expired and then brought pressure on the membership to prevent his reelection. Or he could have resigned. Had he taken Adler's presidency seriously, he would have been honor bound to take one of these steps. But Freud preferred an open showdown; he forced Adler's resignation in order to discredit Adler as a representative of psychoanalysis. Only in that light—namely, as a symbolic act of discrediting—does Freud's forcing Adler's resignation make sense.

Controversy over patent-rights like this one with Adler continued throughout Freud's life. Virtually the same conflict was repeated later with Jung, with Stekel, with Rank, and finally with Ferenczi.

Despite these facts, Jones interprets Freud's attitude toward leadership in the following way: "Freud greatly disliked occupying any prominent position, especially if it might bring with it any duties that implied the ruling of other people. . . . But as the founder of his new methods and theories, and with his wealth of experience and knowledge behind him, his position in the little circle of Viennese followers could not fail to be an exceptionally dominating one."[39]

Although Freud's tendency to autocratic leadership has often been commented on, not enough light has been cast on the way in which Freud exercised leadership. The problem was not so much that he was autocratic or tyrannical; overt tyranny can be appraised for what it is, and there are many ways of resisting it. But Freud's leadership was deceitful. He created a pseudodemocratic, pseudoscientific organization, taking care to retain for himself the power to decide all important issues. Freud thus managed the affairs of the psychoanalytic movement much as a Caribbean dictator, called upon to democratize his regime, might conduct his government. Such a dictator might appoint a president and a cabinet; he might even appoint a person to be leader of an opposition party. In the resulting mock parliamentary system, the dictator, retaining all the real power, operates from behind the scenes rather than openly. Freud's own account of how Jung became president, quoted earlier, supports such an interpretation: "What I had in mind was to organize the psychoanalytic movement, to transfer its center to Zürich and to *give it* a chief . . . [my emphasis]."[40]

But how can one person appoint another as chief, unless he is himself the chief? And what sort of chief is he who, should he displease a member of the group, can be forced by that member to resign? What Freud really did was to bestow tokens of power on his competitors, only to discredit them if they dared to use it. Thus, about Adler he writes: "As an instance of the 'persecution' to which he asserts he has been subjected by me, I can point out the fact that after the Association was founded *I made over to him the leadership of the Vienna group*. It was not until urgent demands were put forward by all the members of the society that *I let myself be persuaded* to take the chair again at its scientific meetings [my emphasis]."[41]

VII

Freud's reaction to the outbreak of the First World War and his claims concerning the usefulness of psychoanalysis for waging it are consistent with his militant style as the organizer and leader of his own gnostic-messianic movement. After Germany declared war, Freud said, "All my libido is given to Austria-Hungary."[42] Before the war was over, he sought to further his own fame by claiming that psychoanalysis had demonstrated its usefulness, both to medicine and to the military, by its alleged effectiveness in explaining and curing the so-called war neuroses. It was a preposterous claim, but it was, and still is, widely accepted as valid.

Moreover, Freud, the great moralist of our day, had even expressed regret—perhaps half-jestingly, but surely also half-seriously—that the war had ended too soon, just when psychoanalysis was beginning to prove its usefulness to it! The Fifth International Psycho-Analytic Congress was held in Budapest on September 28 and 29, 1918. The war had not yet ended. Budapest was still a glittering city. Sándor Loránd offers this recollection of the event: "For in friendly, pleasure-loving Budapest he [Freud] was being recognized officially for the first time as a scientist outside of any exclusively psychiatric or psychoanalytic institution. Budapest took him to its heart with much warmth. . . . What made the Congress so extraordinary in my memory was the presence of a number of high-ranking army officers, including representatives from other Central European nations."[43] Instead of hiding this curious collaboration between psychoanalysis and warfare for the shameful thing it was, Loránd celebrates it as a glorious event. "The highlight of this remarkable event, the reason for the presence of top Hungarian military officers and some from other nations," he writes, "was the impressive insights and approach to the understanding and therapy of combat-induced emotional trauma. The lectures on the problems of war neuroses attracted large crowds."[44] The affair was "a marvellous occasion for Freud,"[45] the more so because a wealthy Hungarian former patient of Freud's donated $250,000, a huge sum at that time, to the psychoanalytic movement.

These happy developments prompted Freud to write to Ferenczi, still in the midst of war: "I am revelling in satisfaction and my heart is light, since I know that my 'Sorgenkind' (worrisome child), my life's work, is protected by your and others' cooperating, and its future is taken care of."[46]

Loránd is candid enough to acknowledge that he and his psychoanalytic colleagues were, to put it charitably, politically stupid. "At the time, in the early autumn of 1918," he remarks, "we had no notion that the world as we knew it had already come to an end. In retrospect, it seems amazing that hardly anyone at the Congress, least of all the military men, seemed to be very concerned that the utter defeat of the Central Powers was a matter of mere weeks away. . . . Hungary was no longer in the war; the military situation seemed far off and stabilized, with Germany occupying territories that ranged from France to the Crimea. The imminent capitulation and collapse were unexpected."[47]

However unexpected the Austro-Hungarian defeat in the First World War might have seemed to the self-centered soul-doctors, it was not only imminent, it was devastating. In 1919, Freud writes to Ferenczi: "Our psychoanalysis has also had bad luck. No sooner had it begun to interest the world because of the war neuroses than the war comes to an end."[48] So wrote the man idolized as the greatest mental healer of our age.

8

Psychoanalysis as Base Rhetoric: Oedipus, from Rex to Complex

I

I have argued that psychotherapy is not treatment but talking. However, as there are many types of talkings, we must identify more narrowly what type psychotherapy is. In the relationship we now call psychotherapy, there are two persons, patient and therapist, both of whom talk. The patient talks mainly in the language of symptom and illness; the therapist, in that of treatment and cure.[1] Accordingly, I shall use the term *psychotherapy* to refer to the verbal (and sometimes nonverbal) activities of the person formally identified as a psychotherapist, and particularly a psychoanalyst. I shall view Freud as a great rhetorician rather than a great scientist, and will examine his writings not for what they tell us about mental diseases or psychoanalytic cures, but for what they tell us about Freud and the language of psychoanalysis.

II

In Freud's view, persons do not act; they are moved by impulses that are largely unconscious. They are moved, moreover, in directions that are generally venal and vile.

Freud's contention that man has no free will is pivotal to the rest of his theory. In *The Psychopathology of Everyday Life*—the title itself is revealing of his penchant for pathologizing human behavior—he shows, quite cogently, that everyday parapraxes are influenced or shaped by the experiences and information of the person who commits them. Freud then uses that evidence to try to prove the absence of free will. "Many people," he remarks, "contest the assumption of complete psychical determinism by appealing to a special feeling of conviction that there is a free will. This feeling of conviction does exist. . . . But so far as I can observe, it does not manifest itself in the great and important decisions of the will: on these occasions the feeling that we have is rather one of psychical compulsion, and we are glad to invoke it on our behalf."[2] Freud then cites Martin Luther's immortal exclamation: "Here I stand, I can do no other!" to prove his point.[3] Freud here argues either from bad thinking or bad faith or both. For it is clear that Luther's statement was a figure of speech: it was precisely because he could have acted otherwise but did not that his decision had the irresistible moral force it had. Freud either misunderstands this or denies it; it is difficult to know which would put him in worse light.

Freud's subsequent comments strongly suggest that he was advancing the theory of psychic determination to establish not how the human mind works, but what a great scientist he is. He thus continues: "If the distinction between conscious and unconscious motivation is taken into account, our feeling of conviction [of a free will] informs us that conscious motivation does not extend to all our motor decisions. . . . What is thus left free by the one side receives its motivation from the other side, from the unconscious; and in this way determination in the psychical sphere is still carried out without any gap."[4]

Freud never tired of praising and preaching this doctrine. In a footnote added in 1907, he writes: "These conceptions of the strict determination of . . . psychical acts have already borne rich fruit in psychology, and perhaps also in the juridical field." He cites two pupils "of Hans Gross, the Professor of Criminal Law in Prague, [who] have developed out of these [word association] experiments a technique for the establishment of the facts in criminal proceedings."[5] These pronouncements do not reflect the sort of picture the eulogists of Freud like to paint of him.

Freud's essay on Leonardo da Vinci—that pioneer exercise in psychoanalytic character assassination which has become the model for modern psychohistorians—displays even more clearly Freud's "dirty hands." In introducing his paper, Freud cites Schiller's words about not wanting to "blacken the radiant and drag the sublime into the dust" as a disclaimer of any intention on his part to sully Leonardo's shining image.[6] He then proceeds to characterize Leonardo as a neurotic and a homosexual.

Freud notes that Leonardo worked slowly; and without any other evidence he calls this trait a "symptom": "The slowness which had all along been conspicuous in Leonardo's work is seen to be a symptom of this inhibition."[7] Seen to be by whom? Note the impartial, passive voice, followed by the "scientific" term *symptom*, both feigning objectivity. The next sentence reveals Freud's feelings about Leonardo: "It was this too which determined the fate of the Last Supper—a fate that was not undeserved."[8] Freud even explains to the reader unfamiliar with the techniques of painting characteristic of that age why Leonardo's work "deserved" to be destroyed: "Leonardo could not become reconciled to fresco painting which demands rapid work while the ground is still moist, and this was the reason why he chose oil colors, the drying of which permitted him to protract the completion of the painting to suit his mood and leisure. These pigments however detached themselves from the ground on which they were applied and which separated them from the wall. Added to this, the defects in the wall, and the later fortunes of the building itself, determined what seems to be the inevitable ruin of the picture."[9]

Page after page in this essay reveals Freud as the destroyer of a great artist's good name and character, concealed behind the mask of the serious student of the "science" of psychoanalysis. Leonardo, Freud observes, "was gentle and kindly to everyone; he declined, it is said, to eat meat, since he did not think it justifiable to deprive animals of their lives; and he took particular pleasure in buying birds in the market and setting them free."[10] Do these qualities evoke Freud's approval and admiration? On the contrary: they signify Leonardo's "feminine delicacy"![11] Freud continues: "It is doubtful whether Leonardo ever embraced a woman in passion . . . a charge of forbidden homosexual practices was brought against him, along with some other young people, which ended in his acquittal."[12]

Leonardo may have been acquitted by the court that tried him, but he was not acquitted by Freud or the science of psychoanalysis. Moreover, Freud's proof of Leonardo's homosexuality and the status of that "proof" in the official history of psychoanalysis constitute one of the most curious episodes in the curious history of this cult. Freud's psychoanalytic proof of Leonardo's homosexuality rests squarely on a vivid childhood memory that the artist himself recorded. According to that memory, as Freud understood it, a vulture came down to Leonardo's cradle and struck him in the mouth with its tail. Freud interpreted this as an expression of Leonardo's "passive homosexuality": "This reminiscence, which has the same importance for both sexes, has been transformed by the man Leonardo into a passive homosexual fantasy."[13]

Let us suppose that Leonardo had never imagined seeing a vulture. Would that make any difference for this psychoanalytic construction, based as it is on the symbolism of that animal and its tail? In fact, Leonardo never imagined seeing a vulture. Freud based his work on a German text in which the Italian word for *kite* was mistakenly rendered as *vulture!* That error is duly noted in a footnote to this essay in the *Standard Edition*.[14] However, in psychoanalytic circles, none of this has had the least effect on the "validity" of Freud's views on Leonardo and his homosexuality.

III

The single most important term in the Freudian vocabulary is the *Oedipus complex*. It is the Rosetta stone of the language of psychoanalysis. It is also the Rosetta stone of that language as base rhetoric.

Freud first uses the term *Oedipus complex* in 1910,[15] and thereafter places increasing emphasis on its importance in psychoanalytic theory. Soon it rivals in importance the libido and the unconscious. Ten years later, the Oedipus complex overshadows them and becomes the supreme sacred symbol in the religion of psychoanalysis. Illustrative is the footnote Freud adds, in 1920, to a new edition of *Three Essays on the Theory of Sexuality,* in which he declares:

> It has been justly said that the Oedipus complex is the nuclear complex of the neuroses and constitutes the essential part of their content. It represents the peak of infantile sexuality, which, through its after-effects, exercises a decisive influence on the sexuality of adults. Every new arrival on this planet is faced by the task of mastering the Oedipus complex: anyone who fails to do so falls victim to neurosis. With the progress of psychoanalytic studies the importance of the Oedipus complex has become more and more clearly evident; its recognition has become the shibboleth that distinguishes the adherents of psychoanalysis from its opponents.[16]

Despite writings like this, Freud became and remains widely accepted as a scientist. Here he claims to have discovered a "law" that governs the "psychosexual development" of every individual on earth, the violation of which unfailingly causes the development of the disease he calls "neurosis." At the same time, he refers to the Oedipus complex as a "shibboleth," and to psychoanalysis as having "adherents" and "opponents," thus adopting the terminology of religious dogma and organization to characterize his views and work.

The Oedipus complex plays the same sort of role in the beliefs and practices of the faithful psychoanalyst as the Eucharist played in those of the faithful Medieval Catholic. What is perhaps most significant about Freud's use of the term *Oedipus complex* is his insistence that it refers to something factual and that it must be taken literally rather than figuratively. In this respect, his use of that image and the Medieval Church's use of the image of the Eucharist are identical. As in the latter view, sacramental bread and wine took on the substance of the body and blood of Jesus, so in the former, the male infant desires to kill his father and have genital intercourse with his mother. But even the Medieval Church acknowledged this change in the Eucharistic elements as a supernatural event that occurred with the consecration of the host, and asked that it be taken on faith. Not so with the Freudian literalization. Freud offered his Oedipus complex as *fact*.

Just when does the infant want to kill one parent and have sex with the other? Very early, indeed. "Later, but still in the first year of infancy," Freud declares, "the relation known as the *Oedipus complex* becomes established: boys concentrate their sexual wishes upon their mother and develop hostile impulses against their father as being a rival, while girls adopt an analogous attitude."[17] Although such a proposition can hardly be taken literally, Freud insists that interpreting the Oedipus complex metaphorically is heresy against psychoanalysis.

In "On the History of the Psycho-Analytic Movement," Freud denounces Jung specifically for suggesting such a metaphorical or, as Freud puts it, "symbolic" interpretation of the Oedipus complex. For Jung, writes Freud, "The Oedipus complex has merely 'symbolic' meaning: the mother in it means the unattainable, which must be renounced in the interests of civilization; the father who is killed in the Oedipus myth is the 'inner' father, from whom one must set oneself free in order to become independent."[18]

Jung, who is here clearly right and innocent, is declared wrong and guilty, his views are labeled "mystifying and incomprehensible." But Jung's judge is not impartial. Freud is very much a party to this conflict, and it is in his interest to insist on his sole authority to determine how the Oedipus complex—and other psychoanalytic metaphors—may or may not be interpreted.

To be sure, Jung was guilty in his attitude toward psychoanalytic mythology. He committed the gravest sin possible against the theology of positivistic psychoanalysis—that is, he acknowledged that psychoanalysis is not a science but a religion. "In this way," Freud summarizes his charge against Jung, "a new religio-ethical system has been created, which, just like the Adlerian system, was bound to reinterpret, distort, or jettison the factual findings of analysis."[19]

Freud was right in asserting that Jung and Adler had created new religio-ethical systems. They had, indeed. Jung made this increasingly explicit in his later work. Freud's error was in claiming that his own fantasies were factual findings. In trying to refute Jung's objection to the Oedipus complex as the cause of all neuroses, Freud again reveals himself as the base rhetorician. "Occasionally," he writes, "enthusiasm for the cause even permitted a disregard of scientific logic—as when Jung finds that the Oedipus complex is not 'specific' enough for the etiology of the neuroses."[20] Although Freud never defines what constitutes a neurosis, he insists that the Oedipus complex is its etiology, and dismisses objections against his theory as contrary to scientific logic.

At this point, let us interrupt our inquiry into Freud's concept and use of the Oedipus complex and violate another unwritten psychiatric taboo—namely, against examining Freud's original invention of the Oedipus complex. To do this, we must first review the Oedipus legend itself.

IV

Grieved by his childlessness, King Laius of Thebes consults the Delphic Oracle, only to learn that his apparent misfortune is a blessing, as any child born to him and his wife Jocasta would become his murderer.[21] He therefore puts her away. Angered, Jocasta makes Laius drunk and seduces him. Nine months later, a son is born. Laius snatches the infant from his nurse's arms, pierces his feet with a nail, and, binding them together, exposes him on Mount Cithaeron.

The child does not perish, however. A Corinthian shepherd finds him, names him Oedipus (because his feet are deformed by the nail wound), and brings him to Corinth, where he is reared as the son of King Polybus and Queen Periboaea, who had been childless. One day, Oedipus, now a young man, is taunted by one of his friends for not resembling his parents. He thereupon goes to ask the Delphic Oracle what future lies in store for him. "Away from the shrine, wretch," she cries in disgust. "You will kill your father and marry your mother!"

Since Oedipus loved Polybus and Periboaea, he decides against returning to Corinth. On the road to Daulis, in a narrow passage, he meets Laius traveling in a chariot. There is not enough room for the chariot to pass. Laius roughly orders Oedipus to step off the road and make way for his betters. Oedipus defiantly retorts that the only betters he knows are the gods and his parents. Laius orders his charioteer to drive on. He complies, and the chariot's wheels bruise Oedipus' foot. Enraged, Oedipus kills the charioteer and then kills Laius by flinging him to the ground and making the horses drag him to his death.

Oedipus proceeds to Thebes. There he solves the riddle of the Sphynx, ridding the city of the monster. The grateful Thebans acclaim him king. He marries the newly widowed Jocasta, unaware that she is his mother. Plague then descends on Thebes. The Delphic Oracle is consulted once more. "Expel the murderer of Laius!" she advises. Oedipus, still not knowing whom he had killed on the road to Daulis, pronounces a curse on Laius' murderer and sentences him to exile.

Blind Teiresias, the most renowned seer in Greece at that time, now demands an audience with Oedipus. He declares that the plague will cease only if a Sown Man dies for the sake of the city. Jocasta's father, Menoeceus—one of those who had risen out of the earth when Cadmus sowed serpents' teeth—at once leaps from the walls and all Thebes praises his civic devotion. Teiresias then reveals the secret. "Menoeceus did well, and the plague will now cease. Yet the gods had another of the Sown Men in mind, one of the third generation: for he has killed his father and married his mother. Know, Queen Jocasta, that it is your husband, Oedipus!" Disbelief greets Teiresias' words. But they are soon confirmed by a letter from Periboaea, revealing the circumstances of Oedipus' adoption. Jocasta, thereupon, hangs herself. Oedipus blinds himself with a pin taken from her garment.

That, in brief, is the Oedipus legend. How did Freud derive the complex from the legend? And how justifiable are his claims for it?

Actually, Freud constructed the Oedipus complex by seizing upon some parts of the story, ignoring others, and reinterpreting quite arbitrarily the features he retained. The idea of incest—of sexual attraction and activity between mother and son or father and daughter—is, after all, ubiquitous. Freud probably thought of it and of its relation to neurosis long before he invented the Oedipus complex. However, since sex was to be the foundation of his empire, he needed impressive and yet catchy phrases to describe certain patterns of sexual conflict, in particular that deriving from the relationship between mother and son. To that end, he made use of the Oedipus legend as follows.

He reinterpreted the fact that Oedipus did not want to kill his father and marry his mother. Actually, Oedipus did all he could to avoid doing so. That circumstance Freud transformed into his famous formula that denial is a type of affirmation. In other words, had Oedipus deliberately set out to do what he did, this would have proved that he wanted to kill his father and marry his mother; and had he set out to avoid doing so, that also would have proved that he wanted to do so.

According to the "manifest content" of the legend, Oedipus did not know that the man he killed was his father or that the woman he married was his mother. Freud accounted for that too, by postulating that "unconsciously" Oedipus did know who they were. If he had not, of course, his act would have been a tragic mistake rather than true patricide and incest.

The most damaging evidence against Freud's case, however, is the fact that he never considered Laius' role in the Oedipus legend. If it is psychologically legitimate to interpret all of Oedipus' actions as intentional, is it not just as legitimate to interpret Laius' actions in the same way? If so, we should have to conclude that the original motive in this legend is Laius' desire to kill his son— that is, filicide. But Freud never suggested that fathers had a "Laius complex," consisting of a desire to kill their sons and keep their wives solely to themselves, and that such a "complex" is a universal trait of the human psyche. Such an interpretation of the Greek legend—more clearly implicit in the story than Freud's interpretation of it—would suggest, further, that Oedipus' act was in fact a sort of self-defense. After all, Laius tries to kill Oedipus not only when he is an infant, but also when they meet again on the road between Delphi and Daulis. In fact, Laius injures Oedipus a second time before Oedipus strikes back. Since none of this fits into Freud's thesis, he conveniently ignores it.

Freud's case is weak from an anthropological point of view as well. We know that the ancient Greeks were not at all reluctant to express themselves in direct language about such things as patricide and incest. This weakens the Freudian argument that Oedipus' alleged motives had to be disguised and are therefore presented in the legend in a concealed form. "Oedipus' remorseful self-blinding has been interpreted by psychologists to mean castration," writes Robert Graves. "But though the blindness of Achilles's tutor Phoenix was said by Greek grammarians to be a euphemism for impotence, primitive myth is always downright, and the castration of Uranus and Attis continued to be recorded unblushingly in classical textbooks. Oedipus's blinding, therefore, reads like a theatrical invention, rather than original myth."[22] Understandably contemptuous of the liberties Freud took with the Oedipus legend, Graves remarks that "while Plutarch records (*On Iris and Osiris*) that the hippopotamus 'murdered his sire and forced his dam,' he would never have suggested that every man has a hippopotamus complex."[23]

Writing in the *Encyclopaedia Britannica,* Donald Wormell also notes that the Freudian Oedipus complex bears not the slightest similarity to the facts of the Oedipus legend: "While it is easy to understand how Freud chose the term 'Oedipus complex' to designate a son's feeling of love toward his mother and hate toward his father, it must be observed that these are not emotions that motivated Oedipus' actions or determined his character in any ancient version of the story."[24]

But if that is so, why did Freud never allude to or acknowledge it? Why do the psychoanalysts never admit it? Because the Oedipus complex is the paradigm of their right to reinterpret mythology, religion, history, and personal conduct in such a way as to debase others, elevate themselves, and make their defamatory "interpretations" seem factual because they are "scientific" and acceptable because they are "therapeutic."

This arbitrary, but rhetorically inspired, conversion of Oedipus from king to complex was Freud's foot in the door. Encountering no resistance—indeed, finding enthusiastic acceptance for the Oedipus complex in many quarters—Freud was ready to penetrate deeper into enemy territory. In other words, he now had a license to reinterpret all manner of behavior. And because of his immense rhetorical skill and increasingly large following, he was now able to gain acceptance for his "psychoanalyses" of historical figures and hysterical patients.

V

By dint of his rhetorical skill and persistence, Freud managed to transform an Athenian myth into an Austrian madness, a tragic hero into a trifling patient. Freud's transformation of the saga of Oedipus from legend into lunacy is at once the paradigm and the epitome of his approach to psychopathology, to people as patients. Hamlet, Leonardo da Vinci, Woodrow Wilson, his "disloyal" disciples—Freud converted the deeds and the character of each from noble to ignoble, from admirable to abhorrent.

The Oedipus complex was, of course, one of Freud's favorite inventions. Toward it he displayed his characteristically contradictory attitude: his discoveries were a part of "science," but they were nevertheless his personal property. Paul Roazen has also remarked on this aspect of Freud's attitude: "Freud thought he had special property rights to his field, and at the same time wanted to think of psychoanalysis as independent of human will and a part of Western science."[25]

An example of this posture toward the Oedipus complex can be discerned in the *Introductory Lectures on Psycho-Analysis*. With unconcealed arrogance, Freud remarks: "It cannot be said that the world has shown much gratitude to psycho-analytic research for its revelation of the Oedipus complex."[26] But there is no ground for Freud's conceited peevishness, save his own hunger for fame. How could he regard the Oedipus complex as a fresh discovery if, as he admitted, it had been familiar to artists since ancient days? And since Freud had not shown how his "discovery" of the Oedipus complex helped the world, why or for what should the world be grateful to him?

Throughout his life, Freud held to the idea of the Oedipus complex with the fervor of a religious zealot. It was the *fons et origo* of everything that happened to people in life and determined their mental diseases. Moreover, he was free to interpret it literally or figuratively, strictly or loosely, as the occasion demanded—while others could interpret it only as he allowed them to.

In *An Outline of Psycho-Analysis,* written at the end of his life, Freud repeats his belief in the centrality and universality of the Oedipus complex in mental development and psychopathology. He seeks to prove the universality of the Oedipus complex, not by appealing to empirical evidence but by interpreting the original myth so as to support this idea. "The coercive power of the oracle"—he intones, as if that were still another of his "discoveries" —"which makes, or should make, the hero innocent, is a recognition of the inevitability of the fate which has condemned every son to live through the Oedipus complex."[27] That is patent nonsense. Indeed, a few paragraphs earlier, in describing the development of the Oedipus complex, Freud himself remarks that "his father has hitherto in any case been an envied model to the boy, owing to the physical strength he perceives in him and the authority with which he finds him clothed."[28] But these remarks support the Jungian, not the Freudian, interpretation of this "complex." Freud acknowledges here that what the little boy responds to "Oedipally" is the person in the home whom he recognizes as someone to reckon with. But suppose the father is emotionally weak, physically crippled, or dead; or that the little boy is brought up by a lesbian couple. How could he, in such a family, be impressed by the strength of the father? Freud does not deal with such practical contingencies and their bearing on his grand scheme of life and lunacy. Instead, he seeks to dispel doubts by redoubling his rhetoric: "Again it was pointed out from psycho-analytic quarters [referring to himself and his lackeys] how easily the riddle of another dramatic hero, Shakespeare's procrastinator, Hamlet, can be solved by reference to the Oedipus complex, since the prince came to grief over the task of punishing someone else for what coincided with the substance of his own Oedipus wish—whereupon the general lack of understanding on the part of the literary world showed how ready is the mass of mankind to hold fast to its infantile repressions."[29]

Here is Freud at the end of his life but still at the top of his form as a base rhetorician. It is not he who demeans Hamlet as a pervert and mankind as repressed and infantile; it is he who is demeaned by a world refusing to honor him as the Einstein of Human Behavior. That is Freud's most characteristic tactic. We can watch it unfold throughout his life and writings: he belittles, demeans, and attacks others—only to claim that he is belittled, demeaned, and attacked by them. His patients, dominated and exploited by his demands for "free association," are "resistant"; his colleagues, pressed into the service of his "cause," are "disloyal"; the Viennese, and mankind in general, whom he castigates and scorns as unlovable and unworthy, refuse to honor him.

VI

In Freud's smithy of self-aggrandizement, everything he grasps is reshaped—by a process of relabeling—into evidence of his own genius. The mind, for example, becomes the "psychic apparatus," the passions the "id," the self the "ego," and the conscience the "superego." One could easily construct an entire glossary of the equivalents in ordinary language of the Freudian semantic masquerading as science. A few more examples must suffice here.

In Freud's new language, people have no conflicts and conflicting desires; instead, they have "complexes" and "ambivalences," terms he appropriated from Jung and Bleuler, respectively. Sexual appetite and interest, indeed interest of any kind, becomes "libido," a metaphysical entity of which one may have more or less and which is the product or manifestation of "eros" or the "life instinct." Talking—by Freud or according to his rules—is "psychoanalysis"; but similar talking—by dissidents or by rules of which Freud disapproves—is a "regression into suggestive psychotherapy" or worse.

Freud's linguistic treatment of women is perhaps the most damaging example of all. He casually characterizes half of the human race as "castrated," portraying the biologically given constitution of women in the metaphor of the mutilated male genital. "The discovery," he writes, in the *New Introductory Lectures on Psycho-Analysis,* "that she is castrated is a turning point in a girl's growth."[30] This metaphor dominates his whole discussion of femininity. Women, Freud explains, have an "inferior clitoris";[31] and "shame . . . has as its purpose, we believe, concealment of genital deficiency."[32] Worse still, he chivalrously cautions his audience: "Do not overlook the fact that an individual woman may be a human being in other respects as well."[33]

When such an argument is made by Jacobins against clerics, we recognize it as anticlericalism. When it is made by Nazis against Jews, we recognize it as anti-Semitism. But when it is made by Freud against women, we do not recognize it as antifeminism. On the contrary, we hail Freud not only as a great humanist, but also as an expert on the relations between the sexes and on sexuality in general. Actually, Freud had an extremely limited grasp of the subject. He viewed sex in the same antierotic way the Church Fathers had before him—that is, as either procreation or pathology. Freud looked at sex, and saw only venereal disease, masturbation, perversion; the Church Fathers looked at it, and saw only temptation, weakness, sin. Freud had not the slightest understanding of sex as legitimate lust, as personal adventure, and as the potential locus for the highest degree of intimacy and respect between a man and a woman.

But Freud was not content with categorizing half of the human race as psychosexual cripples, reviling them as castrates. He insisted on categorizing the entire human race as psychopathic cripples, reviling them as neurotics. Consider his famous "discovery" that religion is "the universal obsessional neurosis of humanity,"[34] a diagnostic opinion he really loved to toss around.

Late in life, in a letter to Ludwig Binswanger, Freud returns to this theme. "I have always lived," he writes, using the house of science as his metaphor, "on the ground floor and in the basement of the building—you maintain that on changing one's viewpoint one can also see an upper floor housing such distinguished guests as religion, art, and others. . . . In this respect you are the conservative, I the revolutionary. If I had another life of work ahead of me, I would dare to offer even those high-born people a home in my lowly hut. I already found one for religion when I stumbled on the category 'neurosis of mankind.' "[35]

Freud's meaning here could not be clearer. His life work, he says, has been devoted to lowering religion from the "upper floor" into the "basement"—that is, from inspiration to insanity. If he only had more time left in his life—says the base rhetorician posing as scientific revolutionary—he would similarly degrade art and the other lofty accomplishments of the human spirit.

9

Sigmund Freud:
The Jewish Avenger

I

Because I regard psychotherapy as a moral rather than a medical enterprise, it is reasonable to inquire into the religious origin, development, and self-identification of the founder of psychoanalysis. Heretofore, such an inquiry was considered relevant, if at all, only as background material, a part of the cultural history of individuals and ideas. I consider it relevant as foreground material, a part of the ethical systems that psychotherapists and their works constitute, conceal, and convey.

Freud's great-grandfather was Rabbi Ephraim Freud, and his grandfather was Rabbi Schlomo Freud. It is not known whether these men were rabbis in the religious sense or whether their titles merely connoted respect. Freud himself was born a Jew, was given the Jewish name Schlomo after his grandfather, and remained a Jew.[1]

II

The inconsistency between Freud's passionate antireligious tirades and his profound commitment to Jewishness significantly highlights an important aspect of Freud's personality and productions, namely his anti-Gentilism. The popular image of Freud as an enlightened, emancipated, irreligious person who, with the aid of psychoanalysis, "discovered" that religion is a mental illness is pure fiction. Freud was extremely fond of this image of himself, and he did all he could to cultivate it. Subsequently, Jones successfully merchandised it, with the result that, although the facts of Freud's personal sense of Jewishness and his anti-Gentilism are duly recorded, mainly in his letters, the significance of these facts somehow disappears in Jones's treatment of them.

Freud was, throughout his life, *a proud, chauvinistic,* even *vengeful* Jew. David Bakan offers the following evidence to support his contention regarding Freud's positive self-identification as a Jew:

> Freud believed that anti-Semitism was practically ubiqui-
> tous in either latent or manifest form; the broad masses
> in England were anti-Semitic, "as everywhere"; he was
> of the opinion that the book on Moses would anger the
> Jews; he expressed a love of Hebrew and Yiddish, ac-
> cording to Freud's son; he refused to accept royalties on
> Hebrew and Yiddish translations of his works; he was
> sympathetic to Zionism from the first days of the move-
> ment and was acquainted with and respected Herzl; he
> had once sent Herzl a copy of one of his works with a
> personal dedication; Freud's son was a member of the
> Kadimah, a Zionist organization, and Freud himself was
> an honorary member of it.[2]

Bakan also notes that on "Freud's thirty-fifth birthday, his father gave him the Bible which he had read as a boy, inscribed in Hebrew,"[3] and that when "he was in America he sent greetings by cablegram to his family on the High Holidays."[4] In addition, Freud displayed his devotion to Judaism in the letters he wrote, in the friends and enemies he made, in the way he lived, and, last but not least, in his anti-Gentilism.

III

Intensely interested in religion and religious history, Freud indulged in countless speculations on these subjects. In many of these he simply followed his central formula—which was to become the trick of the psychoanalytic trade—namely, that everything is something other than what it seems to be or than what the authorities say it is. Oedipus was not a king but a complex; Leonardo was not a heroic painter but a homosexual pervert; Moses was not a Jew, but an Egyptian. It is significant, in this connection, that Freud was satisfied with transforming the founder of his own religion from a Jew into an Egyptian; he did not suggest that Moses was mad. That was an "interpretation" Freud reserved for patients, dissident colleagues, and Jesus. "Once in a conversation on the topic [of religion]," Jones relates, "Freud remarked to me that Jesus could even have been 'an ordinary deluded creature.' "[5]

One of Freud's many pronouncements on religion is recorded in his *The Future of an Illusion:*

> We call a belief an illusion when a wish-fulfillment is a prominent factor in its motivation, and in doing so we disregard its relation to reality, just as the illusion itself sets no store by verification. Having thus taken our bearings, let us return once more to the question of religious doctrines. We can now repeat that all of them are illusions. . . . Some of them are so improbable, so incompatible with everything we have laboriously discovered about the reality of the world, that we may compare them . . . to delusions.[6]

Voltaire, Nietzsche, and many other thinkers since the Enlightenment have noted that religious doctrines are not empirically verifiable observations. What does Freud add to such positivistic antireligiosity? Only the assertion that religious belief and conduct belong in the same class as mental disorders; they are madnesses, medical disorders, matters on which Freud is, or claims to be, an expert.

There is, in short, nothing scientific about Freud's hostility to established religion, though he tries hard to pretend that there is. The same sort of antireligiosity that Freud preached was rampant in ancient Greece: its character was identified by Plato, and its

significance for the modern age has been reidentified by Eric
Voegelin. Plato's particular wrath, notes Voegelin,

> is aroused by the type which combines agnosticism with
> rascality. . . . [Most] dangerous is the agnostic who is at
> the same time possessed by incontinent ambition, by a
> taste for luxuries, who is subtle, intelligent, and persua-
> sive; for this is the class of men who furnish the prophets
> and fanatics, the men who are half sincere and half in-
> sincere, the dictators, demagogues, and ambitious gen-
> erals, the founders of new associations of initiates and
> scheming sophists (908d–e). In order to designate these
> evils of the age appropriately and comprehensively, Plato
> now uses the category of *nosos,* a disease of the soul
> (888b).*[7]

The terms—diviner, fanatic for all kinds of imposture, and con-
triver of private Mysteries—fit Freud perfectly. Plato's foregoing
observations are important because they provide some of the
basis for Voegelin's, and Karl Popper's, classification of psychoanalysis as a modern gnostic movement and for their bracketing it,
as such, with Communism and Nazism.[9]

It is ironic that Plato diagnoses as a "disease of the soul" precisely that mental state which Freud claims characterizes the ideally mature, psychoanalytically imbued person; and that Freud
diagnoses as a "disease of the mind" precisely that mental state
which Plato claims characterizes the ideally moral, ethically imbued person. In both cases, of course, mental health and mental

---

* Voegelin's reference here is to Plato's *Laws,* Book X:
  But those in whom the conviction that the world has no place in
  it for gods is conjoined with incontinence of pleasure and pain
  and the possession of a vigorous memory and a keen intelligence
  share the malady of atheism with the other sort, but are sure to
  work more harm, where the former do less, in the way of mischief
  to their fellows. The first man may be free-spoken enough about
  gods, sacrifices, and oaths, and perhaps, if he does not meet with
  his deserts, his mockery may make converts of others. But the
  second, who holds the same creed as the other, but is what is pop-
  ularly called a "man of parts," a fellow of plentiful subtlety and
  guile—that is the type which furnishes our swarms of diviners and
  fanatics for all kinds of imposture; on occasion also it produces
  dictators, demagogues, generals, contrivers of private Mysteries,
  and the arts and tricks of the so-called Sophists.[8]

disease are defined in moral terms and reflect the ethical standards of the definer.*

IV

One might think that a man who writes about religion as Freud
did in *The Future of an Illusion* and elsewhere would declare
himself an atheist or agnostic. Not so. In his *Autobiographical
Study,* Freud declares: "My parents were Jews, and I have
remained a Jew myself."[11] It will repay us to look closely at what
Freud himself meant by that affirmation. Obviously, he did not
mean that he abstained from eating pork or from working on Saturday. What he meant, he tells us, is this: "When, in 1873, I first
joined the University, I experienced some appreciable disap-
pointments. Above all, I found that I was expected to feel myself
inferior and alien because I was a Jew. I refused absolutely to do
the first of these things. I have never been able to see why I
should feel ashamed of my descent or, as people were beginning to
say, of my 'race.' "[12] In short, Freud decided that "Jewish is beautiful!"

It is open to question whether Freud's assessment of the nature
of anti-Semitism in Central Europe before the First World War
was accurate. Karl Popper offers a quite different view of that
cultural scene:

> I believe that before the First World War Austria, and
> even Germany, treated the Jews quite well. They were
> given almost all rights, although there were some barriers
> established by tradition, especially in the army. In a per-
> fect society, no doubt, they would have been treated in
> every respect as equals. . . . The proportion of Jews or
> men of Jewish origin among university professors, med-
> ical men, and lawyers was very high, and open resentment
> was aroused by this only after the First World War. . . .
> Admittedly, it is understandable that people who were

---

* The fundamental similarities between Plato's and Freud's concepts of
mental functioning have been noted by others, for example by A. J. P.
Kenny, who observes that "Both Freud and Plato regard mental health as
harmony between the parts of the soul, and mental illness as unresolved
conflict between them."[10]

despised for their racial origin should react by saying that
they were proud of it. But racial pride is not only stupid
but wrong, even if provoked by racial hatred.[13]

Popper's concluding remark, with which I agree, raises another
question, namely: Does deciding that "Jewish is beautiful" imply
that "Gentile is ugly?" As we shall see, it did indeed for Freud.

In 1882, when Freud is twenty-six, he reaffirms his religious
ties. "And as for us," he writes to his fiancée, "this is what I believe: even if the form wherein the old Jews were happy no longer
offers us any shelter, something of the core, of this meaningful and
life-affirming Judaism will not be absent from our home."[14] From
his youth onward, Freud sought strength from his identification
with Judaism. In it, he found not only strength but also solace
from solitude and a historical-religious transcendence. For example, when in 1895 he felt increasingly isolated from his medical
colleagues, he joined the B'nai B'rith Society, a Jewish fraternal
organization, to which he belonged for the rest of his life. Every
other week he attended social gatherings, and occasionally lectured there himself. "I gave a lecture on dreams to my Jewish society last Tuesday," he writes to Fliess on December 12, 1897,
"and it had an enthusiastic reception. I shall continue it next
Tuesday."[15] On March 11, 1900, he writes: "I spend every other
Tuesday evening among my Jewish brethren, to whom I recently
gave another lecture."[16]

Freud's proud self-identification as a Jew is also well displayed
in his letters, especially to Abraham and Ferenczi. For example,
on December 26, 1908, Freud encourages Abraham with his appeal to their common faith: "Do not lose heart. Our ancient Jewish toughness will prove itself in the end."[17] He ends the letter
with this frank revelation: "Our Aryan comrades are really completely indispensable to us, otherwise psycho-analysis would suc-
cumb to anti-Semitism."[18]

On July 20, 1908, Freud writes to Abraham: "On the whole it
is easier for us Jews, as we lack the mystical element."[19] Three
days later, he writes: "May I say that it is consanguineous Jewish
traits that attract me to you? We understand each other. . . . I
nurse a suspicion that the suppressed anti-Semitism of the Swiss

that spares me is deflected in reinforced form upon you."[20] On October 11, he picks up the same theme: "Just because I get on most easily with you (and also with our colleague Ferenczi of Budapest), I feel it incumbent upon me not to concede too much to racial preference and therefore neglect that more alien Aryan [Jung]."[21]

After sustaining a psychiatric attack on psychoanalysis in Germany, Freud writes to Ferenczi in a similar vein. In the midst of the First World War, a Professor Franz von Luschan declares that "Such absolute nonsense [as psychoanalysis] should be countered ruthlessly and with an iron broom. In the Great Times in which we live, such old wives' psychiatry is doubly repulsive."[22] Freud's reaction to this, in a letter to Ferenczi, on April 4, 1916, is: "Now we know what we have to expect from the Great Times. No Matter! An old Jew is tougher than a Royal Prussian Teuton."[23]

Freud's references to Jewishness, his own or his interlocutor's, figure prominently in much of his correspondence. An often-quoted example of it is his famous letter to the Protestant pastor Oskar Pfister, in which Freud writes proudly, "Incidentally, why was it that none of all the pious ever discovered psychoanalysis? Why did it have to wait for a completely godless Jew?"[24] To which Pfister offers the incredibly inane answer that Freud is not a bad Jew but a good Christian!

In a letter to Barbara Low, written in English in 1936, Freud remarks: "I know that you have not thought that the death of your brother-in-law David [Eder, a psychoanalyst] had left me untroubled, because I had not written at once. . . . Eder belonged to the people one loves without having to trouble about them. . . . We were both Jews and knew of each other that we carried that miraculous thing in common, which—inaccessible to any analysis so far—makes the Jew."[25] As we saw earlier—in his letter to Abraham in 1908—when Freud wants to extol Jews as better fitted for science than Christians, he boasts that "we [Jews] lack the mystical element." In this letter to Barbara Low, however, he boasts that being a Jew is something "miraculous." The phrase "inaccessible to analysis" is also worth remarking on. It was one of Freud's favorite terminological inventions, dividing the world into two classes in terms of his own "science"—things accessible to analysis and things inaccessible to analysis. Into the latter category he placed not only his own and Eder's "miraculous" Jewishness, but also the "genius" of those he respected (the genius of those he didn't respect being reduced, by "analysis," to its psychopathological roots).

Freud's letter to Enrico Morselli, an Italian author who had sent him a book critical of psychoanalysis, is also of interest in this connection. "I noticed with regret," writes Freud, "that you cannot accept our youthful science without great reservations. . . . But your brief pro-Zionist pamphlet on the Zionist question I was able to read without any mixed feelings, with unreserved approval. . . . I am not sure that your opinion which looks upon psychoanalysis as a direct product of the Jewish mind is correct, but if it is, I wouldn't be ashamed. Although I have been alienated from the religion of my forebears for a long time, I have never lost the feeling of solidarity with my people and realize with satisfaction that you call yourself a pupil of a man of my race —the great Lombroso."[26] There are at least two things in this letter that deserve special attention. In the first place, Freud's assertion that he was alienated from the Jewish religion was simply not true; as we saw, his alienation from it was limited simply to his not practicing most of its rituals—a very different thing. In the second place, why was Freud so proud of Lombroso's Jewishness? Was Lombroso a good man? Cesare Lombroso (1836–1909) was a pioneer forensic psychiatrist whose claim to fame rested on his supposedly scientific psychiatric-genetic "discovery" that criminals were "degenerates" who could be identified by certain physical stigmata of "atavism." His views thus presaged those of Nazi geneticists and Soviet psychiatrists, hardly something to be proud of.*

Besides testifying to Freud's pride in his Jewishness—and to his essential, however unformalistic, religiosity—these examples, of which many more could be cited, also illustrate his consistent

---

* Karl Kraus, another Viennese Jew—but one who was quite free of the venomous anti-Gentilism that suffused Freud—recognized the evil character of Lombroso's "genius." In 1903, at the height of Lombroso's fame, Kraus called him a "charlatan" and ridiculed him for having made "his own scientific stature impregnable by demonstrating that anti-Semitism is a mental illness."[27]

duplicity with respect to the relations between psychoanalysis and Judaism. In print and in public, Freud insists, with the voice of the wounded savant, that psychoanalysis is a science like any other and has nothing to do with Jewishness. In person and in private, however, he identifies psychoanalysis, with the voice of the prophet militant, as a Jewish creation and possession.

V

One of Freud's most powerful motives in life was the desire to inflict vengeance on Christianity for its traditional anti-Semitism. This idea has been suggested by Freud himself, and has been alluded to by others. In *The Interpretation of Dreams,* where Freud tells us so much about himself, he relates one of his dreams in which he is in Rome. To explain it, he offers the following episode about his childhood:

> I had actually been following in Hannibal's footsteps. Like him, I had been fated not to see Rome; and he too had moved into the Campagna when everyone had expected him in Rome. But Hannibal, whom I had come to resemble in these respects, had been the favourite hero of my later school days. Like so many boys of that age, I had sympathized in the Punic Wars not with the Romans but with the Carthaginians. And when in the higher classes I began to understand for the first time what it meant to belong to an alien race, and anti-Semitic feelings among the other boys warned me that I must take up a definite position, the figure of the Semitic general rose still higher in my esteem. To my youthful mind Hannibal and Rome symbolized the conflict between the tenacity of Jewry and the organization of the Catholic church. And the increasing importance of the effects of the anti-Semitic movement upon our emotional life helped to fix the thoughts and feelings of those early days. . . . At that point I was brought up against the event in my youth whose power was still being shown in all these emotions and dreams. I may have been ten or twelve years old, when my father began to take me with him on his walks and reveal to me in his talk his views

upon things in the world we live in. Thus, it was on one such occasion that he told me a story to show me how much better things were now than they had been in his days. 'When I was a young man,' he said, 'I went for a walk one Saturday in the streets of your birthplace; I was well dressed, and had a new fur cap on my head. A Christian came up to me and with a single blow knocked off my cap into the mud and shouted: "Jew! get off the pavement!" ' 'And what did you do?' I asked. 'I went into the roadway and picked up my cap,' was his quiet reply. This struck me as unheroic conduct on the part of the big, strong man who was holding the little boy by the hand. I contrasted this situation with another which fitted my feelings better: the scene in which Hannibal's father, Hamilcar Barca, made his boy swear before the household altar to take vengeance on the Romans. Ever since that time, Hannibal had had a place in my phantasies.[28]

Hannibal, the African—whom Freud calls a "Semite"—takes vengeance on the Romans who conquered and humiliated the Carthaginians. Freud, the Semite, takes vengeance on the Christians who conquered and humiliated the Jews. Hannibal was tenacious and had a secret weapon: elephants. Freud, too, was tenacious, and he, too, had a secret weapon: psychoanalysis. Hannibal's elephants terrorized his enemies whom the animals then trampled to death. Freud's psychoanalysis terrorized his enemies whom his "interpretations" then degraded into the carriers of despicable diseases. The story of Freud's life and the story of psychoanalysis in his lifetime are variations on the theme of justified vengeance in the pattern not only of the legendary Hannibal but also of the literary Count of Monte Cristo: the humiliated but morally superior victim escapes from dependence on his morally inferior victimizers; he hides, schemes, and grows powerful; he returns to the scene of his defeat, and there remorselessly humiliates and subjugates his erstwhile victimizers as they had humiliated and subjugated him.

Carl Schorske also finds the dream I have cited and the events surrounding it of the greatest significance for understanding Freud's work. However, he interprets Freud's desire "to take vengeance on the Romans" as a "project [that] was at once political and filial."[29] In most other great creative Viennese who were Freud's contemporaries, observes Schorske, "the generational revolt against the fathers took the specific historical form of rejection of their fathers' liberal creed. Thus Gustav Mahler and Hugo von Hofmannsthal both turned back to the baroque Catholic tradition. Not so Freud, at least not consciously. He defined his oedipal stance in such a way as to overcome his father by realizing the liberal creed his father professed but failed to defend. Freud-Hannibal as 'Semitic general' would avenge his feeble father against Rome, a Rome that symbolized 'the organization of the Catholic Church' and the Habsburg régime that supported it."[30] This is an extremely persuasive interpretation which, although it deflects some of Freud's animus against the Gentiles to his father, does not negate the pervasive anti-Christian animus behind much of the Freudian opus.

Stanley Rothman and Phillip Isenberg adopt and adumbrate Schorske's foregoing hypothesis. "It does not seem far-fetched to suggest," they write, "that with the publication of *The Interpretation of Dreams* Freud felt that he had weakened if not fully conquered the Catholic Church and had thus succeeded in doing what his father had feared to do."[31] Rothman and Isenberg adduce much additional evidence to support their thesis concerning Freud's "Jewish marginality" as the reason for his disaffection with the Christian world in which he lived. "Is it possible, then," they ask, "that some of the motives associated with Freud's discovery of psychoanalysis had their sources in the same drives which led other Jews to Marxism, i.e., the desire to end marginality by undermining the bases of the dominant culture?"[32] They answer this somewhat rhetorical question affirmatively, though cautiously: "There is at least some evidence that it is and that Freud was at least partially motivated by an animus towards the Catholic Church which informed and profoundly influenced his initial discoveries."[33] I differ from this view only by holding that Freud was more than partially influenced by such an animus and that it influenced not only his earlier writings but all of his work.

Rothman and Isenberg note that "Freud's successful (if symbolic) conquest of Rome"—in *The Interpretation of Dreams*—did not "lessen his dislike for the Catholic Church. . . . It was in Rome, too, that Freud, some years later, put the finishing touches on *Totem and Taboo,* which he always regarded as one of the most important and satisfying things he had written. The volume ostensibly deals with the origins of religion. Yet it is Christian practice and ritual that are examined in terms of primitive drives and defence mechanisms."[34]

Finally, Rothman and Isenberg cite another item from Freud's correspondence that supports quite decisively the view that Freud's anti-Gentilism was a leading motive in his life. "In 1938," they write, "while waiting to leave Austria for England to escape from the Nazis, he wrote to his son Ernst: 'It is high time that Ahasuerus came to rest somewhere.' He was, of course, identifying with Ahasuerus, the wandering Jew, who was compelled to wander, because he would not allow Christ to rest while the latter was carrying the cross to Calvary. It is difficult to believe that the choice of this allusion was purely accidental."[35]

That Freud had identified himself, and privately thought of himself, as a Jewish warrior, fighting against a hostile Christian world, has thus been amply documented.[36] What has received less attention, however, is the way Freud always portrayed his Jewish militancy, his anti-Gentilism, as a self-defense, a necessary and legitimate protection against attacks on him, as a Jew and a psychoanalyst. While such self-defensive claims are sometimes factually justifiable, they must always be evaluated cautiously: most aggressors, especially most modern ones, have claimed merely to be defending or protecting what was rightly theirs. In the case of Freud qua psychoanalyst, the claim is patently fraudulent: after all, he had to invent psychoanalysis before he could defend it. Although he was proud to assert that he created psychoanalysis when it came to claiming priority for it, he acted as if psychoanalysis had somehow always existed, as if it were merely a collection of "facts," when it came to responding to those who regarded its very creation as an act of aggression against their own interests and values. Jung's impression of Freud's seemingly defensive vengefulness is pertinent in this connection. According to Ellenberger, Jung felt that Freud's main characteristic was bitterness, "every word being loaded with it . . . his attitude was the bitterness of the person who is entirely misunderstood, and his manners always seemed to say: 'If they do not understand, they must be stamped into hell.' "[37]

VI

In the early days of psychoanalysis, many of the persons interested in it were Jewish, and the intellectual life of Central Europe was then heavily influenced by Jewish journalists, writers, physicians, and scientists. Thus, Freud's vengefulness toward personal enemies in particular and Gentiles in general, as well as the potential destructiveness of psychoanalysis as a rhetoric of execration and invalidation, found a secure sanctuary behind the walls of the unwritten rule: "If it is Jewish, it is liberal, progressive, scientific, humane, and helpful." The writings of many contemporary authors on Freud and on the Vienna of his time support this assertion—which, moreover, is familiar to many who, like myself, still possess some memories of an era only one generation away from my own. Indeed, the above maxim is still operative, as the following example illustrates.

In his book on the Viennese writer Karl Kraus, Frank Field considers Kraus's criticism of psychoanalysis. Kraus not only saw through psychoanalysis, but also had the courage to identify what he saw—namely, base rhetoric. After presenting a rather unimaginative review of Kraus's criticisms of Freud's work, Field quotes Kraus's famous aphorism in which he declares, "Psychoanalysis is the disease of which it pretends to be the cure."[38] "Of course, this was unfair," is Field's comment on that aphorism.[39] He then tries to obscure Kraus's insight and to counteract the force of his attack:

> It was indeed from the position of an artist, anxious to preserve the wholeness of human experience in an age of increasing specialization, that much of the satire of Kraus was directed. But the distinction between satire

and polemic was often obscured in his work by a marked element of personal and social animosity. It has already been seen that one of the reasons for Kraus's attack on psychoanalysis was the analysis of his own personality that was performed by a member of Freud's circle. When the satirist expressed his fear that, in the hands of men less devoted to the integrity of their profession as Freud himself, psychoanalysis might become merely a lucrative source of income derived from the unhappiness of mankind, he was certainly maliciously underlining the fact that the overwhelming majority of the practitioners of psychoanalysis were Jewish. The incident might seem trivial if it were not part of a pattern. Kraus's position over the Dreyfus Affair has already been noted. [He allowed the publication of anti-Dreyfusard opinion in the *Fackel*.] So have his attacks on the Jewish press of Vienna. Now he is making remarks about Freud's circle which, if they came from a non-Jew, would be regarded as anti-Semitic.[40]

This passage appears in a book about Kraus written by an author sympathetic to his subject. Yet, when it comes to Freud's Jewishness, Field acts as if Kraus had simply gone too far: one does not say such things about psychoanalysis, even if they are true! Actually, Field's attribution of Kraus's animosity toward psychoanalysis to his being "analyzed" by Fritz Wittels is, as I have shown in my book on Kraus, demonstrably false.[41] And, while belaboring Kraus's "animosities" in this passage, Field quite forgets Freud's, and simply ends up dismissing Kraus's profound critique of pychoanalysis by tarring Kraus with the feather of anti-Semitism.

Field's remarks epitomize an intellectual-scientific attitude toward Freud and his work that developed in the early days of psychoanalysis, before the First World War, and one which Freud did everything he could to cultivate. I refer here to the view that it was in bad taste to point out that psychoanalysis was not a matter of science but of Jewishness, or that it was, especially in its actual use by Freud and his lackeys, an immoral and ugly enterprise. If such a charge was made by a Christian—so held the supporters of this position—it revealed the critic's anti-Semitism; and if it was made by a Jew, it revealed a lapse in his judgment, or grew out of his self-hatred as a Jew. Since there were few Mohammedans in Freud's Vienna, and fewer still who cared a whit about psychoanalysis, this attitude in effect exempted psychoanalysis from effective intellectual or scientific criticism. One more example of this phenomenon—from among countless similar accounts—should suffice here.

Remarking on the persons Freud hated the most, Kurt Eissler —secretary of the Freud Archives—identifies among them Theodor Lessing (1872–1933), a philosopher of history killed by the Nazis.[42] Lessing had called psychoanalysis "a monstrosity of the Jewish spirit." Thinking that the author was a descendant of Gotthold Ephraim Lessing (1719–1781), the famous exponent of Central European enlightenment, Freud wrote him and reminded him of the memory of his great ancestor. When Lessing replied that he himself was a Jew, Freud "turned away from him in disgust."[43] "It is significant," comments Eissler, "that Freud remained comparatively unruffled, as long as he thought that psychoanalysis was being reviled by a Christian because of the Jewishness of its founder and of most of its adherents (as was the case at that time), yet could not tolerate the same type of defamation coming from a Jew."[44] Probably unwittingly, Eissler here highlights Freud's double standard in judging critics of psychoanalysis—a double standard that has become the stock-in-trade of the loyal analysts: if the critic was Jewish, he owed loyalty to the Freudian religion just as he did to the Mosaic one; if he was not Jewish, his opposition to psychoanalysis was just another manifestation of his anti-Semitism.

The result of such efforts to dismiss or repress criticisms of psychoanalysis as the symptom either of Christian anti-Semitism or of Jewish "self-hatred" is the stubborn persistence of a set of false images about Freud and his doctrine. I refer in particular to the tendency to see Freud as a humane and forgiving therapist, even when he uses psychoanalysis not to heal but to harm; and the refusal to see him as a vengeful enemy of non-Jews and non-believers in psychoanalysis, even when he uses psychoanalysis not to understand but to undermine.

VII

Vengeance and forgiveness are important themes in all religions, especially in Judaism and Christianity. Jahweh is a vengeful god, punishing remorselessly through the third generation. Jesus is a forgiving god, redeeming mankind through His own martyrdom. It would be foolish, however, to conclude simply that Jews are vengeful and Christians forgiving. In fact, one of the sad facts of history has been the remorseless vindictiveness of Christians toward Jews, avenging the death of the God of Forgiveness by never forgiving the Jews for His fate and by persecuting them as "Christ-killers," not through three generations but through two thousand years. Freud lived, of course, in a society imbued with the spirit of such Christian anti-Semitism. Hence, there was nothing particularly novel either about Freud's resolution to revenge himself on his enemies, religious or personal, or about his method of using words to accomplish this goal. In fact, both Christianity, the culture in which he lived, and psychoanalysis, the sphere of activity in which he prospered, made extensive use of the rhetoric of rejection for attacking and annihilating their enemies. As these two wars with words, and with the acts those words were used to justify, constitute an immense historical panorama, I shall confine myself here to a brief illustration of each.

No sooner did Christianity cease to be the despised religion of a minority, and become instead the dominant religion of the majority, than it decreed that non-Christians were insane, that their places of worship could not be called churches, and that they were fit subjects for the penalty of death. The *Codex Theodosianus* or *Theodosian Code,* issued in the fourth century A.D., contains these astonishing, but sobering, words:

> Emperors Gratian, Valentinian, and Theodosius Augustuses: It is Our will that all the peoples who are ruled by the administration of Our Clemency shall practice that religion which the divine Peter The Apostle transmitted to the Romans. . . . We command that those persons who follow this rule shall embrace the name of Catholic Christians. The rest, however, whom We adjudge de-

mented and insane, shall sustain the infamy of heretical
dogmas, their meeting places shall not receive the name
of churches, and they shall be smitten first by divine
vengeance and secondly by the retribution of Our own
initiative, which We shall assume in accordance with the
divine judgment.[45]

Here, 1,300 years before the birth of institutional psychiatry,
and 1,500 years before the birth of psychoanalysis (and only 400
years after the death of Christ), we encounter the theological version of the war with words which, after the decline of Christianity,
became the stock-in-trade of the psychopathologist. The deviant is
branded as "demented" and is deprived first of his language, then
of his life.

Psychiatry—the specialty out of which psychoanalysis grew,
which it never abandoned, and which, since Freud's death and especially in the United States, it has decisively reembraced—is, of
course, largely an ideology and rhetoric of rejection, albeit one
disguised, in the vocabulary of medicine, as diagnosis and treatment. This pseudomedical ideology and rhetoric is closely related
to the theological ideology and rhetoric it displaced.[46] Thus, as
words of execration were implemented by acts of execution in the
Church, demeaning diagnoses were implemented, in psychiatry,
by acts of imprisonment and torture called "certification," "hospitalization," and "treatment."

Revealingly, no sooner did psychoanalysis become a source of
psychiatric influence to be reckoned with, and hence a threat
to the hegemony of established psychiatric power, than it too
became a target for diagnostic derogation by establishment psychiatry. Illustrative of this sort of attack is a paper delivered
by a German psychiatrist in Baden-Baden on May 28, 1910.
At the Congress of South-West German psychiatrists held in
that resort, Alfred E. Hoche (1865–1943), a professor of psychiatry in Freiburg, read a paper with the dramatic title, "An Epidemic of Insanity Among Doctors." In a letter to Freud dated
June 2, 1910, Jung gives the following account of that occasion:
"Hoche did indeed declare us ripe for the madhouse. Stockmayer
was there and has told me about it. The lecture fell into the well-
known pattern: charges of mysticism, sectarianism, arcane jargon,

epidemic of hysteria, dangerousness, etc. Isolated clapping. Nobody protested. Stockmayer was quite alone and hadn't the gumption."[47] According to Jones's account of it, Hoche declared that "Psychoanalysts were ripe for certification in a lunatic asylum."[48] Ironically, many of the criticisms that Hoche leveled against psychoanalysts were well founded, but he overplayed his hand: he was not content to dispute with psychoanalysts in the free marketplace of ideas, but wanted to dispose of them by demeaning them as mad and locking them up in madhouses. Clearly, the idea that disagreement is a disease, and that he who defies authority is deranged and should be disposed of by the methods of social repression then in vogue, is very old indeed.

Thus, when Freud developed his own lexicon of loathing, called it psychoanalysis, and used it to smite his enemies, he did nothing new, either historically or morally. It would, therefore, be as inaccurate and unfair to blame Freud for inventing a wholly novel method of assassinating characters as it would be to praise him for inventing a wholly novel method of curing souls. Psychoanalysis has been credited with, and discredited for, far too many virtues and sins—when, for the most part, these are simply the virtues and sins inherent in being human and in using language as rhetoric, noble or base, as the case might be.[49] In short, Freud was neither worse nor better than other religious and political leaders who rose to "greatness" over the bodies and souls of executed or execrated enemies.

VIII

That Freud was an angry avenger and a domineering founder of a religion (or cult), rather than a dispassionate scientist or compassionate therapist, is, I believe, epitomized by his lifelong fascination with Moses. Righteous indignation is the mood, more than any other, that characterizes both Moses and Freud. Moses liberated the Jews from Egyptian slavery; Freud sought to liberate the ego from enslavement to the id. Moses took revenge against the Egyptians; Freud, against the Christians. Moses founded Judaism; Freud, psychoanalysis.

Moses and Monotheism, published in 1939, was Freud's last

creative effort.[50] Written when he was over eighty, it supplements his earlier remarks about Moses.[51] Why was Freud, especially at the end of his life, so obsessed with the Moses legend and the origin of Judaism? Jones supplies the evidence for the answer: Freud began his intellectual quest with indignation about anti-Semitism and a resolve to avenge it; he ended it with the same preoccupation and passion. "We cannot refrain from wondering," writes Jones, "how, when nearing his end, Freud came to be so engrossed in the topics described above [*i.e.*, Moses and the origin of Judaism], and to devote to them all his intellectual interest during the last five years of his life."[52] Alluding to Freud's "bitter experiences of anti-Semitism," Jones suggests, I believe correctly, that Freud's interest in these matters derived partly from his unceasing obsession with the "Jewish problem" and partly from the rising tide of Nazism. Jones notes that "Freud's deep conviction of his Jewishness, and his wholehearted acceptance of that fact,"[53] compelled him to concern himself with the origin and nature of Judaism. "We know," adds Jones, "how greatly he admired the great Semitic leaders of the past, from Hannibal onward, and how gladly in his early years he would have been willing to sacrifice his life to emulate their heroic deeds."[54] This, then, was the primary motive for Freud's identification with Moses: "The leader who kindled his imagination above all others was inevitably Moses, the great man who did more than anyone to build the Jewish nation, to create the religion that has ever since borne his name."[55]

Replacing the Mosaic with the Freudian religion satisfied Freud's craving for fame and power. Identifying himself with an avenging Jewish hero gratified his urge to oppose, in his own—rhetorical rather than ethical or political—style, the fresh flood of anti-Semitism issuing from Nazism. "The reason," writes Jones, "that just then narrowed Freud's interest in mankind in general and its religions to the more specific question of the Jews and their religion could only have been the unparalleled persecution of his people getting under way in Nazi Germany."[56]

That, no doubt, was true. However, it is one thing to avenge Medieval Christian or modern National-Socialist anti-Semitism as moral and political evils; it is quite another to call the linguistic justification or literary result of such a revenge a science or treatment. After all, the view that avenging great wrongs, especially against the Jews, is reserved to God has always stood at the center of the Jewish religion. It is articulated repeatedly in the Bible: in Deuteronomy, "To me belongeth vengeance" (32:35); in Psalms, "O Lord God, to whom vengeance belongeth, shew thyself" (94:1); and even Paul, the Jew-become-apostle, writes in Romans, "Vengeance is mine; I will repay, said the Lord" (12:19). Clearly, Freud felt that vengeance was his, too. That, perhaps, is what made him the great religious leader he was.

10

Carl Gustav Jung:
Pastor Without a Pulpit

I

Although Carl Gustav Jung's ideas—especially on religion and psychotherapy—have always had an important following and are now again becoming more influential, his pivotal place in the history of psychotherapy has been slighted. Familiarity with Jung's writings is, however, indispensable for understanding the development of the pseudoreligion we now call "psychotherapy."

II

Jung was born in the village of Kesswil, Switzerland, in 1875, and died in Küssnacht on the shores of Lake Zürich, in 1961. His paternal grandfather was supposedly an illegitimate son of Goethe and was a legendary figure in Basel. Rector of the University of Basel and a successful and sought-after physician, he married three times, had thirteen children, wrote scientific works as well as plays, and was a man of uncommon charm and vitality. Although Jung never knew that grandfather, after whom he had been named, his image of him had a profound influence on his life. Jung's maternal grandfather, almost equally distinguished and important for Jung's life, was Samuel Preiswerk, a respected theologian and Hebraist who not only wrote a Hebrew grammar but was also convinced that Palestine should be given back to the Jews.[1]

In his autobiography, Jung related a childhood episode that, I believe, was very significant both as a motive for his interest in psychiatry and psychotherapy and as a source of his intuitive understanding that so-called mental illness is in reality an imitation of illness. Having been poor in mathematics and inept in gymnastics, the little Jung quickly learned to hate school. Moreover, like most children, he also learned how to play the illness game. When, at the age of twelve, a suitable occasion for playing that game in earnest presented itself, he made the following fateful use of his skills:

> One day in the early summer of 1887 I was standing in the cathedral square, waiting for a classmate who went home by the same route as myself. It was twelve o'clock, and the morning classes were over. Suddenly another boy gave me a shove that knocked me off my feet. I fell, striking my head against the curbstone so hard that I almost lost consciousness. For about half an hour afterward I was a little dazed. At the moment I felt the blow the thought flashed through my mind: "Now you won't have to go to school anymore." I was only half unconscious, but I remained lying there a few moments longer than was strictly necessary, chiefly in order to avenge myself on the assailant. Then people picked me up and took me to a house nearby, where two elderly spinster aunts lived. From then on I began to have fainting spells whenever I had to return to school, and whenever my parents set me to doing my homework. For more than six months I stayed away from school, and for me that was a picnic.[2]

Although the youngster was free to loaf and play, he still was not happy. "I had the obscure feeling," he writes, "that I was fleeing from myself."[3]

His worried parents consulted various doctors. One thought he had epilepsy, which made them worry even more. His sense of achievement at having fooled the doctors, as well as his parents, grew: "I knew what epileptic fits were like and I inwardly laughed at such nonsense."[4] The denouement of that episode became a turning point in Jung's life, twice-over: first, as a child, as he himself notes; and later, as an adult, as the first modern psychotherapist who knew, deep down, that so-called mental patients were not really sick. Here is Jung's description of his realization that he had better stop his pretense:

> Then one day a friend called on my father. They were sitting in the garden and I hid behind a shrub, for I was possessed of an insatiable curiosity. I heard the visitor saying to my father, "And how is your son?" "Ah, that's a sad business," my father replied. "The doctors no longer know what is wrong with him. They think it may be epilepsy. It would be dreadful if he were incurable. I have lost what little I had, and what will become of the boy if he cannot earn his own living?"
>
> I was thunderstruck. This was the collision with reality. "Why, then, I must get to work!" I thought suddenly.[5]

By that time, however, fainting had become a habit with little Jung. So he immediately set himself to breaking the habit:

> From that moment on I became a serious child. I crept away, went to my father's study, took out my Latin grammar, and began to cram with intense concentration. After ten minutes of this I had the finest of fainting fits. I almost fell off the chair, but after a few minutes I felt better and went on working. "Devil take it, I'm not going to faint," I told myself, and persisted in my purpose. This time it took about fifteen minutes before the second attack came. That, too, passed like the first. "And now you must really get to work!" I stuck it out, and after an hour came the third attack. Still I did not give up, and worked for another hour, until I had the feeling that I had overcome the attacks. Suddenly I felt better than I had in all the months before. And in fact the attacks did not recur. From that day on I worked over my grammar and other schoolbooks every day. A few weeks later I returned to school, and never suffered another attack, even

there. The whole bag of tricks was over and done with!
That was when I learned what a neurosis is.[6]

Here it is, clearly and plainly: neurosis is illness-imitative behavior and the habituation of such faking! That simple idea
applies, of course—with the slight modification that the behavior
adopted need not be the imitation of bodily illness—to the so-
called psychoses as well.

III

A few years later, Jung underwent another profound experience, which he does not connect with his later psychiatric ideas
and practices; but I do. It is a test that countless young persons in
Christian countries face, but which few meet with the courage and
honesty that Jung exhibited when he was fifteen. The matter concerned Jung's understanding of the doctrine of the Trinity and the
ritual of Holy Communion. As the time for his confirmation
approached—his father was personally preparing him for it—
Jung felt that the mystery had to be resolved. "I waited longingly
for the moment when we would reach this question," he related.
"But when we got that far, my father said, 'We now come to the
Trinity, but we'll skip that, for I really understand nothing of it
myself.' "[7]

Jung says that though he appreciated his father's honesty, he
was "profoundly disappointed" in this answer. That confrontation
—so undramatic in its staging and with so mild-mannered a pro-
tagonist as his father—shook Jung's faith in dogmatic authority
forever. How could Jung as a grown man believe in the psychoanalytic trinity of the id, ego, and superego, when even as a child he
could not believe in the Christian Trinity?

The religious problem that faced the adolescent Jung could not
be put off. He sought clarification among his fellow pupils in
school, to no avail. Then came his confirmation and the "Communion, on which I had set my last hopes."

This was, I thought, merely a memorial meal, a kind of
anniversary celebration for Lord Jesus who had died
1890–30=1860 years ago. But still, he had let fall certain

hints such as, "Take, eat, this is my body," meaning that we should eat the Communion bread as if it were his body, which after all had originally been flesh. Likewise we were to drink the wine which had originally been blood. It was clear to me that in this fashion we were to incorporate him into ourselves. This seemed to me so preposterous an impossibility that I was sure some great mystery must lie behind it, and that I would participate in this mystery in the course of Communion, on which my father seemed to place so high a value.[8]

Jung duly participated in the ceremony, but felt that it was empty. The more he thought about it, the more repelled he felt by what seemed to him a sham. People pretended to "become one" with Jesus, but in fact they did not. Apparently, neither Jung nor any of the biographers or students of his life and work have noted the striking similarities between Jung's childhood malingering, his subsequent reactions to the mythology of the Holy Communion, and his later rejection of the mythologies of psychiatry and psychoanalysis—parallels of the greatest importance. Although he was still only fifteen, Jung did not flinch from facing the conflict within himself: "Slowly I came to understand that this communion had been a fatal experience for me. It had proved hollow; more than that, it had proved to be a total loss. I knew that I would never again be able to participate in this ceremony. 'Why, that is not religion at all,' I thought. 'It is an absence of God; the church is a place I should not go to. It is not life which is there, but death.' "[9]

Jung's struggles with the problem of transubstantiation were, obviously, not just struggles with an intellectual or religious problem; they were also his struggles with trying to understand his father and his father's life. As his earlier experience with malingering succeeded in diminishing his dependence on parental authority, so his experience with the literalization of the Christian metaphor of the Communion destroyed his dependence on all authorities. "I was seized," he writes, "with the most vehement pity for my father. All at once I understood the tragedy of his profession and his life. He was struggling with a death whose existence he could not admit. An abyss had opened between him and me, and I saw no possibility of ever bridging it, for it was infinite in extent."[10]

Jung, the Christian, had thus fully emancipated himself from the Christian religion and devoted the better part of his life to helping himself and others find their own faiths as befits intelligent adults in the twentieth-century West. However, Freud, the Jew, had never emancipated himself from the Mosaic religion and devoted the better part of his life to an effort to destroy traditional Western faiths and to replace them with one of his own creation.

These, then, are some of the crucial events and experiences that lay behind the man who became Freud's great collaborator, competitor, and critic. Through them, and perhaps through others like them, Jung became just as fearless a thinker as Freud. Moreover, Jung did not need a Breuer, a Fliess, and a "Committee" for the development of his thought and work. To be sure, Jung learned from Freud, which he always generously acknowledged. But he neither leaned on friends and colleagues, nor did he systematically exploit, vilify, and persecute them, as Freud had.

IV

After completing his medical studies, Jung, aged twenty-five, turned immediately to the study of psychiatry: he obtained an assistantship at the Burghölzli Mental Hospital in Zürich, then one of the most prestigious psychiatric institutions in the world. Why Jung chose psychiatry, and chose it so clearly and decisively, is important. In those days, psychiatry was by no means a glamorous field, as Jung's following remarks remind us:

> In the medical world at that time psychiatry was quite generally held in contempt. No one really knew anything about it, and there was no psychology which regarded man as a whole and included his pathological variations in the total picture. The director was locked up in the same institution with his patients, and the institution was equally cut off, isolated on the outskirts of the city like an ancient lazaret with its lepers. No one liked looking in that direction. The doctors knew almost as little as the layman and therefore shared his feelings. Mental disease

was a hopeless and fatal affair which cast its shadow over psychiatry as well. The psychiatrist was a strange figure in those days, as I was soon to learn from personal experience.[11]

What, then, was there about psychiatry in 1900 that appealed to Jung? He had already sensed, on the basis of his own experiences, that mental patients were somehow "not really sick"; in other words, that mental diseases were not like regular diseases—that they were spiritual in nature, or had a large spiritual component. Jung recollects his own feelings about his occupational choice: "For me the only possible goal was psychiatry. Here alone the two currents of my interest could flow together and in a united stream dig their own bed. Here was the empirical field common to biological and spiritual facts, which I had everywhere sought and nowhere found. Here at last was the place where the collision of nature and spirit became a reality."[12]

From the beginning of his work at the Burghölzli, Jung's interest centered on the mental patient's personal or private experience. He soon concluded that that experience was a well-kept secret from the psychiatrist, partly because the patient wanted to keep it that way, but mainly because the mental hospital physician showed not the least interest in it. He thus discovered that the patient's personal life is literally a secret, in the sense that it hides a powerfully disturbing piece of truth, often the truth of an actual criminal, or at least sinful, act; that the secreting away of such guilty and painful truths can make people "mentally ill"; and that confessing the secret and confronting its implications can cure the patient, even if he or she suffers from schizophrenia! It is obvious —and it was obvious to Jung—that here was no ordinary illness and no ordinary treatment.

One of Jung's first psychiatric patients at the Burghölzli whom he mentions was a young woman who had been diagnosed as suffering from dementia praecox. Through word-association tests, Jung learned the patient's secret story which she had never confided to anyone. In an effort to rid herself of the burden that her two small children were to her, she had let them drink nonpotable water; as a result, one of them contracted typhoid fever and died. The woman immediately broke down with her mental illness, was institutionalized, and was considered incurably insane when she came under Jung's care. Jung elicited this story from her, confronted her with the crime, and discussed it with her. In two weeks she was discharged, cured, and was never hospitalized again.[13]

Jung's experiences at the Burghölzli must, again, be set in their precise psychiatric-historical context. By 1900, the year Freud published *The Interpretation of Dreams* and Jung began his work as a hospital psychiatrist, the efficacy of electrotherapy in mental disorders was no longer taken seriously in progressive psychiatric circles. Not that any other treatment had taken its place. What replaced it was the idea, an old one resurrected for the occasion, that mental diseases, at least the "severe" ones, were incurable. When, in 1911, Bleuler renamed dementia praecox "schizophrenia," he identified the disease not by its characteristic histopathology, as was customary with diseases of the nervous system, but by its incurability![14] That this is an utterly destructive way of describing a disease—a disease that, moreover, has no objective bodily manifestations and has never been known to be fatal —should be obvious. It was indeed obvious to many people, Jung among them.

Even as a beginning student of psychiatry, Jung was repelled by the absurdity of classifying obscure behavioral symptoms as schizophrenia and schizophrenia as incurable. "While I was still at the clinic [Burghölzli]," he reminisces in his autobiography, "I had to be most circumspect about treating my schizophrenic patients, or I would have been accused of woolgathering. Schizophrenia was considered incurable. If one did achieve some improvement with a case of schizophrenia, the answer was that it had not been a real schizophrenia."[15]

What, then, was the professional role of a prestigious psychiatrist practicing his profession "correctly" around 1900? It consisted of the following acts: 1) He examined mental patients and identified the disease from which they suffered; that is, he was a diagnostician. 2) He studied mental diseases and identified their characteristic features; that is, he was a nosographer. 3) He taught psychiatry to medical students and physicians; that is, he was a teacher. 4) He incarcerated mental patients in psychiatric institutions and called it mental hospitalization; that is, he was a judge, a jailer, and a justifier. 5) He counseled the "healthy" members of the families of mental patients on the prognosis of the patient's illness and on the proper ways of dealing with the patient during his lucid intervals; that is, in the wars between the generations and the sexes, he was an agent and ally of the patient's adversaries.

Here is Jung's own account of what respectable psychiatry and psychiatrists were like in the early 1900s: "Psychiatry teachers were not interested in what the patient had to say, but rather in how to make a diagnosis or how to describe symptoms and to compile statistics. From the clinical point of view which then prevailed, the human personality of the patient, his individuality, did not matter at all. . . . Patients were labeled, rubber-stamped with a diagnosis, and, for the most part, that settled the matter."[16]

Not quite. Even psychiatrists as sensitive to the human personalities of their patients as Jung and Freud never referred explicitly, in just so many words, to the fact that psychiatrists did something else: namely, they locked up innocent people in institutions that were in effect jails and kept them confined there, often for life. Clearly, identifying that dimension of psychiatric practice would have been quite out of bounds with what was then considered acceptable behavior on the part of physicians—as, indeed, it still is!

The real and revolutionary innovation that Freud and his followers brought to this scene was therefore not scientific or technical, but human or moral: they introduced the physician into the world of the madman as an agent and ally of the so-called patient. This was the first time in the history of psychiatry that physicians had tried systematically to assume such a role.[17]

Jung never ceased to credit Freud for this achievement, the significance of which he appreciated better than did Freud himself. Perhaps because he had actually served an apprenticeship in a mental hospital, which Freud never did, Jung was deeply impressed with the destructive atmosphere of the insane asylum—harmful to both patient and doctor. He fled from it as soon as he could.

V

In 1906, Jung sends Freud a complimentary copy of his *Diagnostic Association Studies*. In their subsequent exchange of letters, each man makes numerous informal but highly revealing remarks about mental illness, psychiatric diagnosis, and psychotherapy. Many of Jung's comments on these subjects support and amplify my previous interpretations of his views. For example, on January 8, 1907, he writes: "Megalomania and affectation are practically synonymous."[18] And in those days, megalomania was practically synonymous with dementia praecox or schizophrenia. Hence, Jung is saying here that this most serious of all mental diseases is simply an affectation or play-acting.

In the same letter, Jung refers to hospitalized mental patients as "habitual hysterics," "uneducated hysterics," and "hospital parasites"—suggesting that he viewed these patients not as sick in the ordinary sense, but as malingering. That idea is articulated more explicitly in his letter of January 2, 1908: "The patient plays to perfection and with positively thrilling dramatic beauty the personality that is her dream ideal."[19]

At the same time, when he is frustrated with, and angry at, a patient—especially when the patient is a colleague—Jung, like Freud, calls the patient by a bad psychiatric name. "I am afraid you will already have read from my words the diagnosis I long refused to believe and which I now see before me with terrifying clarity: Dem. praec.,"[20] writes Jung on June 19, 1908, apparently forgetting that only a year earlier he wrote: "There are, however, numerous fluid transitions to what we call D. pr. D. pr. is a most unfortunate term!"[21]

By 1909, Jung's grasp of the nonmedical character of what he and Freud were doing is firm and secure: "It has become quite clear to me that we shall not solve the ultimate secrets of neurosis and psychosis without mythology and the history of civilization. . . . Hence my attacks on 'clinical terminology.'"[22] At this point, however—perhaps partly because of Jung's insistence that psychotherapy is, in effect, just conversation—the two men are beginning to grow apart.

On February 11, 1910, in one of his most revealing letters to Freud, Jung declares: "Religion can be replaced only by religion."[23] Two days later Freud replies: "But you mustn't regard me as the founder of a religion. My intentions are not so far-reaching."[24]

The division between the two men now quickly deepens. Freud is incapable of understanding that "religion," which is a bad word and a bad thing for him, is a good word and a good thing for Jung. In August, 1910, Jung writes: "All these mutterings about sectarianism, mysticism, arcane jargon, initiation, etc. mean something. Even the deep-rooted outrage, the moral indignation can only be aimed at something gripping, that has all the trappings of a religion. . . . Might this become a phase, however unexpected, in the development of psychoanalysis?"[25] In December of the same year, he is even more explicit: "I lectured at the Psychoanalytic Society on my forthcoming opus. The theologians were deeply impressed, especially Pfister. The spiritual trend in psychoanalysis now taking shape in Zürich seems to me much more promising than the Bleuler-Adler attempts to squeeze everything into biology (biophysics)."[26]

Here, then, was the issue that lay at the bottom of the inevitable break and subsequent bad feelings between Freud and Jung: Was psychotherapy (psychoanalysis) to be defined, practiced, and merchandised as a medical, scientific enterprise, or as a religious, spiritual one? Freud, as we know, opted for the former answer— preferring a Platonic lie to a plain truth—and is considered a great scientist. Jung, predictably, opted for the latter—preferring a simple truth to a convenient obfuscation—and is considered a great mystic. Victor von Weizsaecker makes a similar point when he observes:

> C. G. Jung was the first to understand that psychoanalysis belonged in the sphere of religion, more accurately, to the dissolution of religion in our time. To him, neurosis was a symptom of the man who loses his support in religion. Publicly he spoke about that only later, but once he said to me in conversation: '*All* neurotics seek the religious.' At first, he may have been under the sway of scientific psychology and the curiosity of the

researcher in the history of religion. Later he was prevented from speaking more openly about it by an old resentment against Christianity (he was the son of a pastor) and probably by tactical considerations—he was afraid of being identified with a superficial pastoral attitude.[27]

After 1913, Jung begins to refer to psychoanalysis explicitly as a religion. "Our moves," he writes to Poul Bjerre in a letter on July 17, 1914, "are merely reactions to the papal policies of the Viennese."[28] At the same time, Freud begins his campaign to discredit Jung because he no longer practices the new, scientific (that is, good) psychoanalysis, but merely the old, religious (that is, bad) cure of souls. In his "On the History of the Psycho-Analytic Movement," Freud resorts to an extremely revealing tactic in trying to destroy Jung as a modern psychotherapist by identifying him as just another old-fashioned pastor: he quotes the confidential communications of a patient who had been a former patient of Jung's. The method Freud used for this attack—in particular his explicit justification for using a patient's confidential communications for such a purpose—has been overlooked by historians of psychoanalysis and psychotherapy. After denouncing Jung's rejection of the new "scientific" discoveries of psychoanalysis and his "relapse" into mouthing old religious platitudes, Freud cites the patient's following criticism of Jung: "Instead of freeing me by analysis, every day brought fresh tremendous demands on me, which had to be fulfilled if the neurosis was to be conquered—for instance, inward concentration by means of introversion, religious meditation, resuming life with my wife in loving devotion, etc. . . . I left analysis as a poor sinner with intense feelings of contrition and the best resolutions, but at the same time in utter discouragement. Any clergyman would have advised me what he recommended, but where was I to find the strength?"[29]

There is, of course, no way of knowing whether the patient said these things or whether Freud had put the words into his mouth. All we know is that the patient's alleged argument was exactly the same as Freud's and hence suited his polemical purposes perfectly. After quoting the anonymous patient's condemnation of the Jungian "treatment," Freud drives home his point as the franchiser of psychoanalysis: he asserts that Jung's method "no longer has any claim to be called psychoanalysis."[30]

Still, there remained the highly questionable practice of Freud's using a patient's confidential communications to him to defame his most famous colleague. The moral problem this raised evidently troubled Freud enough to prevent his passing over it in silence. But his efforts to justify it caused Freud inadvertently to deliver a profoundly serious ethical blow against psychoanalysis. "I know," he writes, "the objections there are to making use of a patient's reports, and I will therefore expressly state that my informant is a trustworthy person, very well capable of forming a judgment. . . . I make use of his communication without asking his consent, since I cannot allow that a psychoanalytic technique has any right to claim the protection of medical discretion."[31]

At every significant juncture in the intellectual and social history of psychoanalysis, Freud thus acted as a politician—in the worst sense of the word. That is to say, he identified psychoanalysis with science, with medicine, and with religious healing as the occasion demanded, and repudiated such identification when such rejection suited his purposes.

VI

With the passing years, Jung identified himself and his work ever more clearly with the cure of souls. Revealingly, that identification remains somewhat disguised in his formal writings and emerges most unambiguously in his private correspondence, especially during the last two decades of his life.

Although Jung seemingly rejected the idea that a neurosis (or a psychosis, for that matter) is a bona fide illness, in his professional publications he continued to use the term *illness* in an expanded or metaphorical sense. For example, in an essay in 1932, he criticizes Freud for maintaining a medical perspective on mental diseases: "Freud always remained a physician. For all his interest in other fields, he constantly had the clinical picture of neurosis before his mind's eye—the very attitude that makes people ill and effectively prevents them from being healthy."[32]

In his paper on "What Is Psychotherapy?" published in 1935,

Jung speaks of neurosis as a metaphorical sickness rather than as no sickness at all: "The clinical standpoint by itself is not and cannot be fair to the nature of a neurosis, because a neurosis is more a psychosocial phenomenon than an illness in the strict sense. It forces us to extend the term 'illness' beyond the idea of an individual body whose functions are disturbed, and to look upon the neurotic as a sick system of social relationships."[33] However, in his Tavistock Lectures, delivered in the same year, he indicates—in everyday language rather than in psychiatric jargon—that in his view mental illnesses are not illnesses at all: "To be 'crazy' is a social concept; we use social relationships and definitions in order to distinguish mental disturbances. You can say that a man is peculiar, that he behaves in an unexpected way and has funny ideas, and if he happens to live in a little town in France or Switzerland you would say, 'He is an original fellow, one of the most original inhabitants of that little place'; but if you bring that man into the midst of Harley Street, well, he is plumb crazy."[34]

The extent to which Jung often rejected both the medical model of mental illnesses and mental treatments. He subsequently ment is revealed further by his following statements concerning suicide and psychotherapy. "You should not cheat people even for their own good," he writes in the Tavistock Lectures. "I do not want to cheat people out of their mistaken faith. . . . I never hinder people. When somebody says, 'I am going to commit suicide if . . . ,' I say, 'If that is your intention, I have no objection.' "[35] In the same lecture, he explains his method of working as follows: "I reject the idea of putting the patient upon a sofa and sitting behind him. I put my patients in front of me and I talk to them as one natural human being to another."[36]

Clearly, Jung understood perfectly well the metaphorical nature of mental illnesses and mental treatments. He subsequently amplified his rejection of the medical-technical approach to psychotherapy. For example, in an important but rarely quoted paper written in 1953, he says: "I am afraid psychotherapy is a very responsible business and anything but an impersonal application of a convenient medical method. . . . For this reason I object to any kind of prejudice in the psychotherapeutic approach. In Freud's case, I disagree with his materialism, his credulity (trauma theory), his fanciful assumptions (totem and taboo theory), and his asocial, merely biological point of view (theory of neurosis)."[37] However, in some of his later remarks Jung contradicts his here seemingly complete rejection of the medical character of psychotherapy.

During this period of the early 1950s, Jung comes down firmly in his correspondence in favor of the view that psychotherapy is merely a new name for the cure of souls, and that its practice is therefore religious rather than medical. For example, in a letter to Dorothee Hoch, dated September 23, 1952, he writes: "The *cura animarum* has reached its nadir. Instead, one goes in for missions to the heathen. . . . A good example is Albert Schweitzer, who is urgently needed in Europe but prefers to be a touching saviour of savages and to hang his theology on the wall. We have a justification of missionizing only when we have straightened ourselves out here, otherwise we are merely spreading our own disease."[38]

Jung returns to the example of Schweitzer in some subsequent letters, repeating his sharp distinction between the religious cure of souls and the medical cure of bodies. On December 11, 1953, he writes to Pastor Willi Bremi: "Faced with the truly appalling *afflictio animae* [affliction of the soul] of the European man, Schweitzer abdicated from the task incumbent on the theologian, the *cura animarum,* and studied medicine in order to treat the sick *bodies of natives.* . . . Should we all, following Schweitzer's banner, emigrate to Africa and cure native diseases when our own *sickness of soul* cries to heaven?"[39] In this important letter, Jung also rearticulates the individualistic, personal character of genuine psychotherapy: "The sermon is utterly inept as a *cura animarum* since the sickness is an individual affair and cannot be cured in a lecture hall. . . . In even higher degree the *cura animarum* is an individual affair that cannot be dealt with from the pulpit."[40]

In a letter to Hans A. Illing dated January 26, 1955, Jung explicitly extends this caveat to group therapy: "I have no practical objections to group therapy any more than I have to Christian Science, the Oxford Movement, and other therapeutically effective sects. . . . However, in view of the foregoing critical remarks about group therapy, I do not believe that it can replace individual analysis, i.e., the dialectical process between two individuals."[41]

Jung's next letter to Illing, dated February 10, 1955, reaffirms his unconditional commitment to an individualistic ethic: "I still stand up for the inalienable rights of the individual since he alone is the carrier of life and is gravely threatened by the social levelling process today. Even in the smallest group he is acceptable only if he appears acceptable to the majority of its members."[42] It would have been unthinkable for a man who wrote like this to have remained a part of the psychoanalytic movement, even if that movement had been less autocratically controlled by Freud and even if Freud had not mythologized sex as he had. However, it was also inconsistent for such a man to authorize and participate in the activities of a Jungian school and movement.

VII

Although Jung's attitude toward religion was positive, that did not mean that he believed in any particular religion. Jung's detached and yet respectful attitude toward religion is expressed beautifully in the following passage from his letter to Pastor Walter Bernet, dated June 13, 1955: "I stick to my proposal that we take all talk of God as mythological and discuss these mythologems honestly. . . . Let the Protestant theologian therefore abandon his hieratic word-magic and his alleged knowledge of God through faith and admit to the layman that he is mythologizing."[43]

There is an interesting parallel between Jung's and Freud's respective attitudes toward religions and neuroses. Jung regarded both respectfully—religions as collective mythologies and neuroses as individual ones; Freud regarded both contemptuously—religions as neuroses and neuroses as defenses against reality. Thus, in Jung's view religions are indispensable spiritual supports, whereas in Freud's they are illusory crutches. Jung accepted his patients as persons and did not feel compelled to use them; Freud used them either as cases or as recruits to his cause. The distinctions Jung himself makes between psychoanalysis and his own views, and between Freud and himself, suggest that he was aware of such a dichotomy and that he did not want to make a religion of Jungianism as Freud had made of Freudianism: "Analytical psychology," he writes in a letter dated June 15, 1955, "only helps us to find the way to the religious experience that makes us whole. It is not this experience itself, nor does it bring it about."[44] In a similar vein, on March 13, 1956, he writes to Jolande Jacobi: "Freud has a 'theory.' I have no 'theory' but I describe facts. I do not theorize about how neuroses originate, I describe what you find in neuroses. . . . I must emphasize this because people always fail to see that I am talking about and naming facts, and that my concepts are mere names and not philosophical terms."[45]

In the last years of his life, Jung reiterated, more forcefully than ever, the essentially nonmedical and religious character of psychotherapy as he saw it; at the same time, he revealed that he could not go the whole way with his own realization that so-called mental diseases are dramas rather than diseases and made obeisances to medicine quite inconsistent with his psychotherapeutic orientation. For example, in a letter to J. A. F. Swoboda, dated January 23, 1960, Jung asserts that there is no such thing, that indeed there can be no such thing, as a systematized theory of psychotherapy. Like marriage or one's relationships to one's children or friends, psychotherapy is a personal matter. "In medicine," writes Jung, "every conceivable method can be employed without one's being affected by it in any way. This is not possible in psychology, where everything depends on the dialectical process between two personalities. . . . Under these circumstances any organization that proposes collective methods seems to me unsuitable, because it would be sawing off the branch on which the psychotherapist sits."[46] That is an excellent statement of the essence of true psychotherapy by whatever name it might be called. It describes a form of healing repudiated equally, for however different reasons, by the modern psychoanalysts, behaviorists, and organicists.

Jung expresses the same sort of opinion in one of his last letters, written in English on February 11, 1961: "As a neurosis starts from a fragmentary state of human consciousness, it can only be cured by an approximative totality of the human being. Religious ideas and convictions from the beginning of history had the aspect of the mental *pharmakon*. They represent the world of wholeness in which fragments can be gathered and put together again. Such a cure cannot be effected by pills and injections."[47]

However, the purity, if not the force, of Jung's foregoing declaration about psychotherapy and the nature of the "conditions" it seeks to ameliorate is diminished by some of his utterances which back away from acknowledging that these "conditions" are man-made (however unwittingly) and that the "therapy" is non-medical. For example, in a letter dated April 7, 1958, after noting that in French one does not have a dream but rather makes one, he writes: "The summit of European hybris is the French phrase: 'faire un rêve.' But in reality we seem rather to be the dream of somebody or something independent of our conscious ego, at least in all fateful moments."[48] Unfortunately, Jung is here repudiating the fundamental Freudian insight embodied in the grammar of the French language. Freud himself had remarked that we are responsible for our own dreams;[49] and many modern psychotherapists have toyed with the view—perhaps Jung more seriously than most others—that dreams, neuroses, and psychoses are all mental products of the same sort.

Jung consistently held the view that psychotherapy was a dialogue between patient and doctor. In his autobiography, he sums up his position on the subject as follows: "I am often asked about my psychotherapeutic or analytic method. I cannot reply unequivocally to the question. Therapy is different in every case. . . . The cure ought to grow naturally out of the patient himself. Psychotherapy and analysis are as varied as are human individuals. . . . The crucial point is that I confront the patient as one human being to another. Analysis is a dialogue demanding two partners. Analyst and patient sit facing one another, eye to eye; the doctor has something to say, but so has the patient."[50]

Freud believed that, at bottom, both the neuroses and the psychoses were diseases.[51] Jung believed that the neuroses were not diseases, though the psychoses probably were. "I am in favor," he writes, "of non-medical men studying psychotherapy and practicing it; but in dealing with latent psychoses there is the risk of their making dangerous mistakes. Therefore I favor laymen working as analysts, but under the guidance of a professional physician."[52]

In one of his last letters, Jung offers a rather strange argument for why the psychotherapist ought to have a medical degree. On August 13, 1960, he writes to Pastor Werner Niederer: "But lay psychologists, too, are necessarily obliged to work together with doctors because the neuroses are frequently and unavoidably complicated by dangerous psychotic phenomena to which only a man who is protected by a medical diploma can and should expose himself."[53] How does a "medical diploma" protect a psychotherapist from "psychotic phenomena"? The question poses something of a riddle. The most likely interpretation is that Jung was more successful in emancipating himself from the mythologies and rituals of Christian theology than he was in emancipating himself from the mythologies and rituals of psychiatric theology. Confronted with certain horrors of life, he thus fell back on calling them "psychoses" rather than "possessions," and on seeking protection from them by medical rather than theological means—that is, by displaying a caduceus rather than a cross.

Jung thus exhibits some of the same failings as Freud. The sufferer who comes to the psychotherapist brings with him the moral problems of life; the psychotherapist is a secular pastor engaged in the cure of souls. Nevertheless, when the going gets difficult, Jung too falls back on regarding the mental patient as medically sick and the physician-psychotherapist as a medical healer. And, like Freud, Jung succumbs to the temptation of franchising conversation: he, too, becomes the founder of his own school of psychology and psychotherapy—contradicting, in a way even more sharply than did Freud, his most significant insights into the nature of the human predicament and our options for coming to terms with it.

IV

The Politics
of Psychotherapy

11

Psychotherapy: Medicine, Religion, and Power

I

The controversy over whether psychotherapy belongs to medicine or religion is not new. Freud and Jung devoted a great deal of attention to this problem, claiming psychotherapy sometimes for medicine, sometimes for religion. Their ambivalence about this question reflects, in part, their uncertainty about the nature of the mental disorders they were "treating," and in part their unwillingness, because of its practical implications, to commit themselves exclusively to either a medical or a moral perspective on psychotherapy.

Freud was equally eloquent in arguing that mental diseases were organic disorders whose proper treatment was chemical, and in arguing that they were psychological problems whose proper treatment was pastoral. For example, in 1914, Freud asserts: "All our provisional ideas in psychology will presumably some day be based on an organic substructure. This makes it probable that it is special substances and chemical processes which perform the operations of . . . special psychical forces."[1] In 1930, he declares: "The hope of the future lies in organic chemistry or access to it through endocrinology. This future is still far distant, but one should study analytically every case of psychosis because this knowledge will one day guide the chemical therapy."[2] And in 1938, in *An Outline of Psycho-Analysis,* he reiterates this view and extends it to encompass all mental diseases: "The future may teach us to exercise a direct influence, by means of particular chemical substances, on the amounts of energy and their distribution in the neural apparatus. It may be that there are other still undreamt-of possibilities of therapy. But for the moment we have nothing better at our disposal than the technique of psychoanalysis."[3] These excerpts show us Freud as the cryptobiologist and the secret believer in the chemical treatment of mental diseases.

There was, however, another side to Freud, a side that looked upon psychoanalysis not as a poor substitute for a future chemical miracle cure, but as a valuable discovery for probing the unconscious and as an invaluable therapy for the neuroses. For example, in 1919, Freud writes that the analyst's task is "to bring to the patient's knowledge the unconscious, repressed impulses existing in him."[4] In 1928, he repeats his "wish to protect analysis from the doctors (and the priests)."[5] And in 1927, in his essay on lay (nonmedical) analysis, he declares, "I have assumed that psychoanalysis is not a specialized branch of medicine. I cannot see how it is possible to dispute this."[6] But if psychoanalysis is not a branch of medicine, what is it a branch of? This is Freud's answer: "The words, 'secular pastoral worker,' might well serve as a general formula for describing the function of the analyst. . . . We do not seek to bring [the patient] relief by receiving him into the catholic, protestant, or socialist community. We seek rather to enrich him from his own internal sources. . . . Such activity as this is pastoral work in the best sense of the word."[7] Much of what I have written in this book may be regarded as a consequence of my effort to take Freud's foregoing view seriously.[8]

II

Throughout his long life, Jung also struggled with the dilemma of whether to classify psychotherapy as a medical or as a religious enterprise. Although, as I showed, Jung too vacillated in his attitude toward this question, on the whole he assumed a more consistently antimedical and proreligious position on it than did Freud.[9] In fact, the break between Freud and Jung, usually thought to center on their disagreement about the significance of sexuality in the etiology and therapy of the neuroses, lies much deeper, and is, I believe, closely connected with the problem before us.

To put it simply, Freud was more ambitious and less honest about psychotherapy than Jung. Appraising the temper of this time correctly, Freud realized that the great legitimizer of the age was not religion but science. He insisted, therefore, that psychotherapy was a science, and he called his own version of it psychoanalysis.

Jung rejected such an opportunistic hitching of psychotherapy to the wagon of medical science. He maintained that religions were the forerunners of modern psychotherapies and that psychotherapeutic systems were actually ersatz religions. For example, in 1932 he writes: "In this matter [of spiritual needs] both the doctor and the patient deceive themselves. Although the theories of Freud and Adler come much nearer to getting at the bottom of the neuroses than does any earlier approach to the question from the side of medicine, they still fail, because of their exclusive concern with the drives, to satisfy the deeper spiritual needs of the patient. . . . In a word, they do not give meaning enough to life. And it is only the meaningful that sets us free."[10]

"It is," Jung continues, "the priest or the clergyman, rather than the doctor, who should be most concerned with the problem of spiritual suffering. But in most cases the sufferer consults a doctor in the first place, because he supposes himself to be physically ill, and because certain neurotic symptoms can be at least alleviated by drugs."[11] Jung concludes that "healing may be called a religious problem. . . . Religions are systems of healing for psychic illness. . . . That is why patients force the psychotherapist into the role of a priest, and expect and demand of him that he shall free them from their distress. That is why we psychotherapists must occupy ourselves with problems which, strictly speaking, belong to the theologians."[12]

The problems Jung here highlights are still very much with us. Indeed, the positivistic—medical, psychological, and scientific—approach to the psychotherapies is today even more entrenched, concealed behind even thicker smoke screens of semantic and institutional legitimizations than it had been in 1933 when Jung wrote the following words:

> This Freudian father-complex, fanatically defended with such stubbornness and oversensitivity, is a cloak for religiosity misunderstood; it is a mysticism expressed in terms of biology and the family relation. As for Freud's idea of the "super-ego," it is a furtive attempt to smuggle in his time-honored images of Jehovah in the dress of psychological theory. When one does things like that, it is better to say so openly. For my part, I prefer to call things by the names under which they have always been known. The wheel of history must not be turned back, and man's advance towards a spiritual life . . . must not be denied.[13]

Freud's declaration that the psychoanalyst is a "secular pastoral worker" and that psychoanalysis is "pastoral work in the best sense of the word," and Jung's declaration that the psychotherapist occupies the role of the priest and that the problems of psychotherapy "belong to the theologians" have the most far-reaching practical implications. They are comparable to the declarations, two hundred years ago, of the abolitionists and Quakers that Negroes are human beings. As the view that blacks are persons was inconsistent with the institution of chattel slavery, so the view that psychotherapy is religion is inconsistent with the institution of medical psychiatry. Therein, precisely, lies both its threat and its promise.

III

In the New Testament, the words *name* and *power* are synonymous. The power to name things, to classify acts and actors, is the greatest power in the world. Classifying "psychotherapies" and "psychotherapists" thus reflects certain facts about the holders of power. If we now classify certain forms of personal conduct as illness, it is because most people believe that the best way to deal with them is by responding to them as if they were medical diseases. Similarly, if we now classify certain other forms of personal conduct as psychotherapy, it is because most people believe that the best way to legitimize these activities is by authenticating them as medical treatments.[14]

Classifying human acts and actors is political, because the classification will inevitably help some persons and harm others. Categorizing religion, rhetoric, and repression as psychotherapy primarily helps physicians and psychotherapists. If, however, our aim in classifying psychotherapeutic interventions is to help others —in particular those who want to better understand the world they live in—then we shall categorize such interventions as what they are—religion, rhetoric, and repression.

Language thus not only reveals and conceals acts and actors; it also creates what and who they are. For example, in the first century A.D., Roman Christians were heretics; in the fourth century, they were possessors of the true faith. A few decades ago, oral-genital sex was a degrading perversion; now it is a delightful pastime. A few years ago, abortion was an abominable criminal act; now it is an accepted form of medical treatment. Obviously, it makes a great deal of difference to a great many people whether we call certain acts pastoral or psychotherapeutic, religious or medical.

The distinction between rhetoric and science was supremely important to Aristotle. The distinction between talking and treatment, spiritual caring and medical curing is equally important to anyone who wants to think clearly about such matters. As I showed, although some rhetoricians, such as Mesmer and Erb, claimed that their interventions were medical treatments, others, such as Freud and Jung, claimed that their interventions were both medical curings and spiritual carings. Such a dual claim has, indeed, continued to be advanced on behalf of psychiatry and psychotherapy by most of its propagandists. The fact that this claim has been accepted as valid by the intellectual, legal, and political authorities of most modern societies has had beneficial consequences for the claimants and baneful consequences for nearly everyone else. The result is that modern psychiatry and psychotherapy claim to be scientific religion or religious science, combining in a powerful alliance the forces of both religion and science. When that power is then allied with the modern state, the result is a fresh political force—a force at once arrogant and arbitrary, despotic and destructive.

IV

My contention that all forms of psychotherapy comprise one or several elements of religion, rhetoric, and repression finds striking confirmation in the writings of Pierre Janet, one of the pioneers of modern medical psychotherapy. In his book, *Psychological Healing,* Janet considers the moral objections raised against suggestive therapy—especially that the hypnotist or suggestionist deceives his patient—and tries to refute them with the following argument: "I am sorry that I cannot share these exalted and beautiful scruples. . . . My belief is that the patient wants a doctor who will cure; that the doctor's professional duty is to give any remedy that will be useful, and to prescribe it in the way in which it will do most good. Now I think that bread pills are medically indicated in certain cases and that they will act far more powerfully if I deck them out with impressive names. When I prescribe such a formidable placebo, I believe that I am fulfilling my professional duty."[15]

The old rhetoric of patriotism is here transformed into the new rhetoric of therapeutism. The words and the imagery conjure up an irresistible justification, or so it seems to Janet. Who could object to a remedy that cures a sick patient? According to Janet, no one could, or should: "We are faced here with one of those conflicts between duties which are continually arising in practical life; and, for my part, I believe that the duty of curing my patient preponderates enormously over the trivial duty of giving him a scientific lecture which he would not understand and would have no use for."[16]

Janet premises his claims on the tacit assumption that patients want to be lied to, that they want to infantilize themselves and paternalize their therapists. "There are some [patients]," he declares, "to whom, as a matter of strict moral obligation, we must lie."[17] Why lying should be a matter of moral obligation on the part of a physician, Janet does not further explain. Perhaps, once more, he assumes as obvious that the doctor's relationship to his patient ought to be like that of a Platonic guardian to the citizen: the former "owes" it to the latter to pacify him with "noble lies." Thus does deception become the cornerstone of modern medical psychotherapeutics. Indeed, Janet explicitly asserts that hypnosis rests not only on deception but also on despotism, that is, on the domination of the subject by the hypnotist: "The relationship of a hypnotisable patient to a hypnotist does not differ in any essential way from the relationship of a lunatic to the superintendent of an asylum. By accepting this outlook, those who practice suggestion and hypnotism would escape a good many moral difficulties— difficulties which never trouble alienists."[18] The ethical and political implications of this admission—namely, that hypnosis in particular and mad-doctoring in general depend on the pseudomedical tyrannization of the patient by the doctor—have been widely ignored. Thus, hypnosis enjoys periodic revivals as a "medical treatment" and the false analogy between chemical anesthesia and the so-called hypnotic trance persists.

Janet himself was, of course, an accomplished base rhetorician. For example, he tries to persuade the reader of the validity of his claims by pretending to be wholly empirical and therapeutic. "The only thing that really matters," he declares, "is that we should know whether hypnotism is practically effective. Have notable cures been achieved through hypnotic suggestion, employed in a definite fashion and to the exclusion of other methods? Generally speaking, the answer is in the affirmative."[19] Like Freud, Janet dons the robes of the positivistic scientist and pronounces himself in possession of a scientific psychotherapy. Hence, to disagree with him is to deny science itself. "Hypnotic suggestion," asserts Janet, "is no longer a vague theriac. . . . It is a definite treatment whose results can be ascertained. . . . These characteristics [of hypnosis] . . . enable us to emerge from the religious and moral epoch of psychotherapeutics and to enter the genuinely scientific epoch."[20]

Hypnosis does indeed remain a useful model for exposing the true nature of all psychotherapies. It is the paradigm of ritualized repression and of medicalized mendacity, displaying, in a dramatically enacted form of personal pairing, both the faith and the folly that animate all attempts to transform the tragedies and triumphs of real life into the therapies of a fake science.

V

One of the most successful recent psychotherapeutic movements is Couéism or so-called autosuggestion. Its doctrine and practice illustrate dramatically the combination, in the concepts and claims of a modern psychotherapist, of the clerical cure of souls with the clinical treatment of minds.

Émile Coué (1857–1926) was a French pharmacist who became interested in the then-popular practice of hypnosis. At about the same time that Freud hit upon the idea that the royal road to the unconscious led through the analysis of dreams, Coué hit upon the idea that the royal road to mental health led through the sufferer's own inner self. The patient did not need to be hypnotized. He did not even need a therapist. The essential element in hypnotic "treatment" was the subject's own resolution to recover from his "illness." Armed with that idea, Coué instructed persons suffering from nervous disorders to tell themselves—morning, noon, and night—that "every day and in every way I am getting better and better." During the first two decades of the twentieth century his popularity and success were phenomenal.[21]

Instead of stressing interpretation and insight, as Freud did, Coué emphasized resolution and ritual. "Don't think of what you are saying," he told his patients. "Say it as you say the litany in church."[22] Freud demanded that the patient "admit" that he is "ill" and promise to "free-associate," that is, tell his analyst everything that goes through his mind. Coué's rules of psychotherapy were almost exactly the opposite. He insisted that the patient not give a name to his alleged disease, as if he had realized that such disorders were metaphorical in nature and acquired a literal existence only through being named; and he insisted that the patient articulate his resolve to recover in the present rather than in the future tense, as if he had realized that decisions promised for future delivery have no moral reality. Remarking on the magico-religious character of modern psychotherapies, Leslie Weatherhead offers this comment about Coué's method: "It is strange, as one contemplates Coué's instructions to a patient to repeat the words *'Ca passe'* ('It will pass') and to count the number of times he says those words by fingering knots in a cord, to compare so modern a direction with the practices of antiquity, in which the magician untied a knot in a cord as he recited each new spell."[23]

Coué had thus rediscovered an age-old wisdom—namely, that when a respected authority instills faith in a person and admonishes him to "get better," and that when such a person places faith in the authority and resolves to "recover" from an "illness" that consists largely or wholly of his having assumed the sick role, then he is likely to derive a "therapeutic" benefit from the interaction and from his own attitudes and actions. The question is: How should such a simple and straightforward moral exhortation be categorized? Let us see how Couéists and modern psychotherapists classify it.

An English exposition of Couéism was published in 1922 by C. Harry Brooks. Entitled *The Practice of Autosuggestion by the Method of Émile Coué,* it includes a foreword by Coué himself. In keeping with the demands of the scientific age in which he was writing, Brooks declares that "autosuggestion is not a religion like Christian Science. . . . It is a scientific method based on the discoveries of psychology."[24] Having unburdened himself of that ritual incantation required of the modern faith healer, Brooks is free to preach his, and Coué's, faith: "Say it [the magic formula] with faith! You can only rob Induced Autosuggestion of its power in one way—by believing that it is powerless. . . . The greater your faith the more radical and the more rapid will be your results."[25]

In the concluding chapter of his book, Brooks reiterates that autosuggestion is both a science and a religion: "We should approach autosuggestion in the same reasonable manner as we approach any other scientific discovery."[26] But only six lines later, he declares: "Like religion, autosuggestion is a thing to practice. A man may be conversant with all the creeds in Christendom and be none the better for it; while some simple soul, loving God and his fellows, may combine the high principles of Christianity in his life without any acquaintance with theology. So it is with autosuggestion."[27] To Coué and his followers, then, autosuggestion was at once a religious and a medical enterprise. They emphasized one or the other aspect of it, depending on the argument they wanted to put forward.

Actually, it would be difficult to imagine how anything could be more clearly a secular prayer for health than reciting Coué's formula. "Is not the affirmation contained in Coué's formula a kind of prayer?" asks Brooks, only to offer the standard denial of our age in reply to it: No, it is not prayer but "a mere scientific technique!"[28]

Although Coué was a pharmacist and hence a layman, psychiatrists and psychiatric historians count him as one of their own. For example, Alexander and Selesnick, with their unflagging zeal for flattering the medical profession, call Coué a "hypnotist, psychotherapist, and autosuggestionist"[29]—despite the fact that Coué explicitly repudiated hypnotism. All this betokens still another aspect of the implacable resolve of psychotherapy to rob religion of as much as it can, and to destroy what it cannot: contrition, confession, prayer, faith, inner resolution, and countless other elements are expropriated and renamed as psychotherapy; whereas certain observances, rituals, taboos, and other elements of religion are demeaned and destroyed as the symptoms of neurotic or psychotic illnesses.

VI

I submit that we ought to distinguish more sharply than is customary in contemporary medical, psychiatric, legal, and political thought between language and lesions, between lies and leukemia. My suggestion that we separate medical from psychiatric interventions may be countered with the assertion that persuasion constitutes an inseparable part of medical practice. For example, physicians persuade diabetics to use insulin and patients with cancer to submit to operations. Are such medical recommendations, so this argument might run, not an integral part of what we call "medical treatment"? And if so, does not this fact contradict the supposedly sharp demarcation between the physician's prescription of drugs and surgical therapy and the psychiatrist's prescription of drugs and psychotherapy?

The similarities between the prescriptive acts of regular physicians and those of psychiatrists rests on the same illusion as do the similarities between the sick-role performances of bodily and mentally ill patients. Both medical and mental patients usually *act as if* they were sick. And both regular physicians and psychiatrists usually *act as if* they were prescribing treatments. To the extent that each of these actors plays his role well—whether as patient or doctor—his performance will be convincing; and to that extent the demarcation between histopathology and psychopathology, between medical and psychiatric treatment, may seem contrived or false. I have described elsewhere the pretenses of neurotics and psychotics claiming to be patients,[30] but I have not heretofore described the corresponding pretenses of psychiatrists and psychotherapists claiming to be therapists.

What makes a physician a therapist? Certainly not the mere fact that he is a physician. Not all physicians treat patients and not all are therapists. Pathologists and diagnostic radiologists, to name only two obvious examples, do not treat patients and are not therapists. What makes a physician a therapist is that he performs a physicochemical act on the patient's body that is, or is considered, therapeutic. A pathologist or radiologist may recommend the removal of a tumor; but such an act is not a form of therapy. Only the removal of the tumor is. In the course of medical treatment the physician may use persuasion as a part of, or preliminary to, his actual therapeutic performance; but persuasion is not, in itself, a form of medical treatment.

Psychiatric treatment differs from this, and it does so in different ways in the so-called somatic therapies and the psychotherapies. Somatic therapies—for example, the use of drugs or shock or lobotomy—involve the employment of physicochemical interventions on the patient's body. But since the intervention is not aimed at any demonstrable pathological lesion, but on the contrary is aimed at the patient's undesirable behavior, it is wrong to classify it as therapy. Poisoning and electrocuting criminals are, after all, also physicochemical interventions on human bodies. But since the subjects are not patients, we do not call these procedures treatment.

In psychotherapy the situation is altogether different from that obtaining in regular medical therapy. Psychotherapy, as I have shown, is religion or rhetoric (or repression, a contingency about which I shall say no more here). The result of psychotherapy can thus only be that the subject is, or is not, converted or persuaded to feel, think, or act differently than has been his habit. The "patient" changes some of his ways; or he remains the same. The psychotherapist does not do anything but talk. If there is any change in the "patient," it is, in the last analysis, brought about by the "patient" himself. Hence, it is false to say that the psychotherapist *treats* or is a therapist. It would be more accurate to say that the "patient" in psychotherapy treats or is a therapist, because he treats himself. But that, too, would be using the term *treatment* metaphorically, inasmuch as such a person treats himself only in the sense in which any person who submits himself to and actively cooperates with athletic, educational, or religious influence or instruction treats himself.

VII

Still, physicians and patients insist that psychotherapy *is* medical treatment. This is no more surprising than that Medieval Catholic priests insisted that ceremonial wine *is* human blood. Such a confusion and conflation of ceremonial and scientific concepts and performances is rarely accidental. In the case of the Eucharist, the mythologized category error was an integral part of Medieval Christian theology; in the case of psychotherapy, it is an integral part of modern medical theology. In medicine, and especially in psychiatry, the clear distinction between science and religion, so typical of contemporary thought, is obscured.[31] In the natural sciences, we distinguish between astrology and astronomy, between alchemy and chemistry. But in medicine we do not distinguish— often we are officially forbidden to distinguish—between healing by spiritual and moral influences on the one hand, and by chemical and physical interventions on the other. It is, of course, mainly through psychiatry, and its core concepts of mental illness and psychotherapy, that the distinction between the cure of bodies and the cure of souls is confused, condemned, and cast out of official science.

Whether we classify religion, rhetoric, and repression as psychotherapy, or vice versa, has, of course, the most obvious and far-reaching practical implications. Religion (morals and ritual), rhetoric (speech and gestures), and repression (constraint and punishment) are all matters of the utmost concern to every legal and political system, especially to the American legal and political system where the precise sphere of action of each—particularly their freedom from government interference and their exclusion from government support—is clearly defined.

There is, however, no comparable definition of the proper sphere of the state with respect to medical matters. Insofar as the role of the state in relation to health is examined and articulated, it is usually in the spirit of naïve medicalism, reflecting the false premise that in the area of treatment, unlike that of salvation, there are no fundamental conflicts between the individual and the state. As a result, the most varied interests have sought, in the name of health, to enlist the support of the modern state. They have all succeeded. For example, we saw how Heinroth based his whole psychiatric program on the premise that the financial support and legal imposition of mental treatment were the self-evident duties of the state. Since then, the idea that the preservation and promotion of health are obligations the government owes its citizens has become, the whole world over, an article of faith compared to which the Medieval belief in Christianity is veritable skepticism.

As a result, most people now believe that it is a good thing that the state defines what is sickness and what is treatment and that the state pays for whatever treatment people need. What most people do not understand, indeed seem disinclined to understand, is that the state may, and therefore will, define as sickness whatever the people might want to do for themselves; that it may, and therefore will, define as treatment whatever the government might want to do to the people; and that it may, and therefore will, tax the people for "medical" services that range from denying Laetrile to those persons who want it to imposing psychiatric imprisonment on those who do not want it. Clearly, the future scope of such "services" promises to include an array of therapeutic prohibitions and prescriptions of truly Orwellian proportions.

12

Psychotherapy and Language: Contemporary Uses and Abuses

I

After the First World War, Germany was the scene of a momentous monetary inflation. The government printed more and more money. Soon a postage stamp cost billions of marks. Was there then more money in Germany than in other countries in which a postage stamp cost only a small fraction of the unit of the currency? Or was there simply more state-authorized counterfeit in circulation?

For a good many decades, and more rapidly since the end of the Second World War, the whole "civilized" world—but especially the United States—has been the scene of a similar phenomenon, involving not money, but ideas about and names for mental diseases and mental treatments. The American government has thus created and authenticated more and more psychiatric diagnoses and psychiatric therapies. Soon virtually any behavior displeasing to a person himself or to others could be labeled a mental illness, and any behavior pleasing to a person himself or to others could be labeled a mental treatment. Is there now more mental illness and mental treatment in the United States than in another country less psychiatrically blessed? Or is there simply more state-authorized diagnostic and therapeutic counterfeit in circulation?

I have discussed and documented elsewhere the semantic inflation—indeed, hyperinflation—that has given us our rich store of psychopathologies—that has, in other words, resulted in the transformation of the ordinary behaviors of ordinary persons into the extraordinary and awe-inspiring symptoms of mental diseases. Here I want to document, by means of a series of characteristic quotations from the contemporary literature, the similar, indeed symmetrical, hyperinflation that has given us our rich store of psychotherapies—that has, in other words, resulted in the transformation of the ordinary behavior of professionally authenticated persons into the extraordinary techniques of mental treatments. I offer the following illustrative quotations, without internal comment.

II

"There is a growing realization among thoughtful persons that our culture is sick, mentally disordered, and in need of treatment. . . . The conception of a sick society in need of treatment has many advantages for diagnosis of our individual and social difficulties and for constructive therapy."
Lawrence K. Frank, "Society as the Patient," American Journal of Sociology, 42 (1936), pp. 335–36.

"Surrogate Wife. The story of a Masters and Johnson sexual therapist and the nine cases she treated. . . . Valerie was employed by the Masters and Johnson Research Foundation in St. Louis as an 'in-bed' therapist. The nature of this therapy may be shocking to some but has proved its value."
"Valerie X. Scott," as told to Herbert d'H. Lee, Surrogate Wife (New York: Dell, 1971), front and back cover.

"Sandi Enders, an attractive brunette of 26 who intends to become an occupational therapist, is earning her way through San Jose State University by working as a sexual therapist. She charges $50 for a two-and-a-half-hour session—including love-

making—in her sensuously decorated apartment with its incense burner and heated water bed."
"All About the New Sex Therapy," *Newsweek,* November 27, 1972, p. 71.

"Today, pelvic congestion . . . is treated by various psychotherapeutic methods. Achievement of orgasm plays an important part in therapy."
"Pelvic Congestion. Commentary by Hans Lehfeldt," *Medical Aspects of Human Sexuality,* 7 (May, 1973), pp. 25–26.

"Dr. Abraham Maslow, this year's president of the American Psychological Association, described psychologists' training groups as 'a kind of psychological nudism under careful direction.' Maslow speculated that if physical nudity were added, 'people would go away more spontaneous, less guarded, less defensive, not only about the shape of their behinds, but freer and more innocent about their minds as well. That clinched it for [Psychotherapist Paul] Bindrim. If some patients respond better in groups than to individual therapy, he reasoned, then nude groups might be even more effective. . . . All the professionals who have participated agree that nude marathons are worth further trials, provided they are conducted by a trained leader. Nude psychotherapy has achieved enough respectability to be the subject of a two-hour program at a recent meeting of the California State Psychological Association."
"Psychotherapy: Stripping Body and Mind," *Time,* February 23, 1968, p. 68.

"Prostitution is not an option for women but an addiction that requires long-range support and encouragement for cure, Samuel S. Janus, Ph.D., said at the annual meeting of the American Psychiatric Association. Eighteen of 22 New York prostitutes who had renounced the trade had returned to prostitution after 5 years; this is a recidivism rate equal to that among narcotics addicts, said Dr. Janus, director of group therapy, New York Medical College."

"Prostitution Called an Addiction Requiring Long-Term Treatment," *Clinical Psychiatry News,* 5 (June, 1977), p. 12.

"A doctor here has reported a drug cure for pathological jealousy. Dr. Neda Herceg, in a report he circulated among the medical profession, said two women had been cured after a two-month treatment with the drug thiotizene, previously used for schizophrenia."
"Australian Reports Cure for Jealousy," *International Herald Tribune,* April 11, 1976, p. 5.

" 'When marital therapy began in the 1940s, one unhappy spouse would go to a psychiatrist and complain. That didn't work out too well, so the therapy changed: Both spouses went to different psychiatrists, and the psychiatrists met to discuss the problem. By 1960, spouses were seeing the same psychiatrist, but separately. Today they usually see the psychiatrist together, and sometimes even the children are invited. In 1940, the divorce rate was 2.0 per 1,000 population; in 1976, it was 5.4.' "
Delia Ephron, quoted in *Medical Economics,* May 2, 1977, p. 198.

"Marriage counseling fees paid to clergymen are not deductible. A couple consulted with a clergyman associated with a nonprofit marriage counseling center. As a result of the counseling, they feel they are healthier. . . . The IRS fails to see such fees as deductible medical expenses. . . . In connection with this ruling, one accounting firm advised a marriage-counselor client to call himself a 'therapist in sexual inadequacy and incompatibility.' The firm asserted the cost of treating those problems to be still deductible."
"Tax Shorts," *Physician's Financial Letter,* October 20, 1975, p. 7.

"Divorce Therapy. In divorce therapy, partners who are allergic to each other are helped to disengage from their relationship with a minimum of destructiveness to themselves, each other, and to the children."

Workshop 304, American Orthopsychiatric Association, 50th Anniversary Meeting, May 29–June 1, 1973; from the *Preliminary Program*, p. 40.

"Father Tom Smith [a former Broadway actor] uses dance therapy in helping patients at Woodside State Mental Hospital. The Roman Catholic priest emphasizes he does not teach dance. 'We teach meaningful dance movements,' he said. . . . 'Dance therapy is a therapeutic art whereby the dance therapist establishes an atmosphere of confidence with the aid of acoustic space provided by music,' Father Smith said."
"Dance Therapy Is Used To Help the Mentally Ill." New York *Times,* August 7, 1973, p. 46.

"In their efforts to understand the mental illnesses they treat, therapists sometimes encourage their patients to express themselves in painting, music, dance and drama. Now they are turning to yet another art form: poetry. . . . Formal training in poetry therapy is now available. Patients in poetry therapy are encouraged to read verse, write it, or both. The technique seems to be effective in both individual and group treatment."
"Poetry Therapy," *Time,* March 13, 1972, p. 45.

"Generally the psychiatrist is at a loss when confronted by a patient who faithfully appears for therapy sessions each week but who seems to be making little progress. Analyzing the patient's resistance, coaxing, cajoling, and threatening do little good to resolve the problem. The implicit authority of simple directions on a prescription form—for instance, go to one movie this week, call a friend for lunch—seems to motivate the patient and helps to achieve desired goals."
"The Prescription Pad: A Motivational Force," *Modern Medicine,* January 1, 1977, p. 117.

"There is no better therapy than a job and a paycheck."
William Menninger, quoted in Steven Rosner, "Treatment in China," *Mental Hygiene,* 60 (Summer, 1976), p. 9.

"Creative Art Therapy, *by Arthur Robbins, Ed.D., A.T.R. and Linda Beth Sibley, M.P.S., A.T.R. Art therapy as an emerging profession is still establishing an identity and a role among the helping professions. . . . To the individual attempting to integrate the principles of psychodynamics with creativity in therapeutic endeavors, this volume will not only contribute to personal and professional growth but also provide advice for practical everyday experiences with art therapy."*
Advertisement, Brunner/Mazel Publishers, New York, January 1977.

" *'Friendship can be a valuable therapy,' says this picture. It was taken by Mrs. William Hunter. The picture was taken for a community organization seeking volunteers. You probably have a camera. . . ."*
Advertisement for the Eastman Kodak Company, New York *Times Magazine,* November 25, 1973, p. 9.

"Although shopping excursions were recommended as therapy for a woman who was under psychiatric care, the Tax Court held that, even though the shopping trips were undoubtedly therapeutic, their costs could not be deducted as medical expenses. . . . The court felt that a more explicit statement of a medical purpose was needed."
Rabb v. *Commissioner,* Tax Court Memo (May 22, 1972), p. 119, cited in "Costs of 'Therapeutic' Shopping Trips Not Medical Expenses," *Citation,* 26 (April 1, 1973), 187–88.

"Now you can release pent-up pain, anger, and fear through Dr. Casriel's own technique of 'scream therapy'—often more effective and less expensive than traditional methods."
Advertisement for *A Scream Away from Happiness,* by Daniel Casriel, M.D., New York *Times Book Review,* October 8, 1972, p. 14.

"The psychologist treated the patient with 'Rage Reduction Therapy,' a therapy method which involves physical stimulation of the rib cage area. As a result of this therapy, the patient was physi-

cally and mentally abused for 11 hours, resulting in severe bruising of the upper half of the body. Also, there was a complete kidney failure for seven days. . . . In a malpractice action against the psychologist . . . [the patient] was awarded $170,000 for physical and mental injuries."

Abraham v. Zaslow, California Superior Court, Santa Clara County, Docket No. 245862 (1972), cited in "Psychologist Liable for Injuries Due to 'Rage Reduction' Therapy," *Citation,* 26 (March 15, 1973), 169–70.

"The controversial 'Z therapy' developed by Robert Zaslow may benefit nonpsychotic children who have severe antisocial personality disorders, Dr. Foster W. Cline said at the annual meeting of the American Association for the Advancement of Science. . . .
'Z therapy' is based on the assumption that children who are unable to love because they were unloved must have love forced on them before they can develop other loving attachments, he said. The therapy exploits the close association of rage, relief, touch, eye contact, and midbrain and/or vestibular stimulation to generate the disordered child's ability to form loving relationships. . . .
Although Z therapy enrages the child and sometimes arouses anger and indignation in observers, it may result in deeply loving relationships, he asserted."

" 'Z Therapy' May Aid Nonpsychotic, Antisocial Children," *Clinical Psychiatry News,* 5 (June, 1977), p. 50.

"Camping Therapy: Its Uses in Psychiatry and Rehabilitation. . . . *This collection of 18 articles describes camping programs for normal as well as emotionally and physically disordered children and adults. . . . It is a brief introduction to its practice and possibilities."*

David J. Muller, Review, *American Journal of Psychiatry,* 132 (February, 1975), p. 213.

"Thumb Therapy. Thumb Therapy emanates from soothing Mexican onyx: Just rub gently with your thumb for diversion from minor pressures and tension. Thumb Therapy is universal. . . . Thumb Therapy is inexpensive. It costs only $2.75 each and

comes smartly pouched for safe-keeping in a tan cloth bag. . . .
Rich Lane Associates, 521 Fifth Avenue, New York."
Advertisement (full page), New York *Times,* April 12, 1976,
p. 34.

"Medical researchers at Ohio State University are making use of
the master-dog relationship in the clinic—specifically as an impor-
tant aid in psychotherapy. . . . OSU psychobiologist Dr. Samuel
Corson . . . has done a formal study of 'pet-facilitated psycho-
therapy' on some sixteen mentally ill hospital patients. . . . Pet
therapy for emotional illness has also been utilized by Dr. Boris
Levinson of Sunnyside, NY, but Corson claims his study is the
first systematic attempt to evaluate the technique."
"My Dog, the Therapist," *Newsweek,* April 22, 1974, p. 80.

"It was a cold, bleak night in January. . . . That particular eve-
ning my companions and I found ourselves exploring two ques-
tions: Is sailing really different from other sports? May it actually
be a form of therapy? . . . Sailing, we had already decided, is
different and therapeutic. But how so? All sports are essentially
regressive endeavors and sailing is particularly so. . . . The
gratification derived from joining with nature . . . perhaps uncon-
sciously represents reunion with the mother and thus enables one
to recapture childhood bliss with an adult sense of power and
mastery. Moreover, the opportunity to comfortably regress in a
primal setting, while setting the pace of regression, can provide
the necessary milieu for self-therapy to take place."
Norman B. Levy, "The Therapeutics of Sailing," *Psychiatric*
Worldview, 1 (April/June, 1977), p. 2.

"A new technique is gaining ground in addiction therapy: skydiv-
ing. . . . Radical therapy? . . . 'Not all that radical,' says pedia-
trician Henry Bruyn, the program's medical advisor. . . . 'Tech-
nically, we are an encounter group, with a Gestalt basis. . . . It's
become very valuable therapy.'"
"Ex-Addict Sky Jumpers: 'Sky-high' on Mutual Trust," *Medical*
World News, September 1, 1972, p. 7.

"An International Congress . . . THE PSYCHOLOGY OF CONSCIOUS-NESS AND SUGGESTOLOGY, *May 2, 3, 4, 1975, International Hotel, Los Angeles, California. A unique and important Congress on consciousness, learning, and emerging breakthroughs in the development of human potential—introducing Suggestology, a new science of suggestion and its role in learning, attitudinal change, and therapy."*
Advertising flier, Pepperdine University, Los Angeles, 1975.

"The saying 'Try it, you'll like it' has become as American as apple pie. . . . *However, down in Miami's Center of Psychological Services the more you try to eat your favorite food the more you'll hate it. The Center is using what it describes as 'aversion therapy' for such problems as alcoholism, drug addiction, smoking, and compulsive eating. The aversion therapy is simple enough: the more one eats, the more one is punished. Psychologists Michael Stokols and Edward Wallach seem nice enough fellows to their patients. They serve lots of ice cream and ham sandwiches or French fries, whatever the patient's heart—or stomach—desires. But the patient is in for quite a shock. Attached to the spoon or fork are electrodes. Every time a patient takes a mouthful, he receives a shock—just enough to be painful, not really enough to hurt."*
"Painful," *Auckland Star* (New Zealand), October 7, 1972, p. 15.

"LaVerne Kowalski never went to college. But she's got a diploma anyway. And it's a special one at that. For Mrs. Kowalski is one of the nation's first few graduates of a new course of study to turn bartenders into amateur psychiatrists. . . . *It is an innovative counseling road being taken increasingly across the country, according to the National Association for Mental Health."*
Andrew H. Malcolm, "Bartenders Being Trained To Provide Counseling as Well as Drinks," New York *Times,* October 13, 1975, p. 75.

" 'While we were gambling [says a member of Gamblers Anonymous] we begged, borrowed, and in some cases stole from other people to support our illness. . . .' The word illness plays an im-

portant part because 'compulsive gambling is an illness, progressive in nature, that can never be cured but can be arrested.' . . . The basis of the meetings are the therapies, the speeches that begin 'I am a compulsive gambler.' . . . It's called therapy because it's a chance to unburden oneself, to find inner strength."
Jeffrey Robinson, " 'I Am a Compulsive Gambler,' " International Herald Tribune, June 4–5, 1977, p. 14.

"In San Francisco one has been able to buy conversation—more or less sensitively tuned instant friendship—as reported in Psychiatric News previously. Now New York . . . not to be outdone, has a new service for the emotionally forlorn—'Dial-A-Shrink.' "
"Couple Runs Phone Therapy Operation in New York City," Psychiatric News, June 18, 1975, p. 23.

"Biofeedback relaxation training (BFT) is an 'electronic' version of the familiar behavioral therapy. . . . Monitoring devices give the patient visual and auditory displays of his alpha (EEG) wave, blood pressure, muscle tension, or galvanic skin response; the patient's task is to modify these biofeedback signals through methods that focus his concentration, heighten suggestibility, and induce a 'relaxed' state. . . . Like behavioral therapy, then, BFT has its roots in the animal learning laboratories of the American, Thorndike (circa 1898) and the Russian, Pavlov (circa 1920). . . . BFT simply took psychiatry the next step in the electronic age."
Ari Kiev, "BFT: Psychiatry Goes 'Electronic,' " Drug Therapy, June, 1976, pp. 169–70.

"Every year, thousands of Americans turn to healers like the Rev. Mr. [John] Scudder who claims that through prayer, meditation or the use of 'psychic energy' they can cure the sick and the crippled. Some healers, like the now-retired Oral Roberts or the irrepressible Kathryn Kuhlman, rely on belief in God. Others are not religious at all but believe that by altering their states of consciousness, they can produce curative effects in patients. 'The demand for psychic healing is spreading like wildfire, rapidly

outdistancing the supply of healers, says Sally Hammond, author of a recent book called 'We Are All Healers.'"
"Healing: Mind Over Matter?" *Newsweek*, April 29, 1974, p. 67.

"Psychologists have replaced the religious priesthood in many of its functions—determining proper behavior, 'soul healing,' and ministering to the dying. . . . They are now extending it to another priestly domain—giving last rites to condemned prisoners. Florida State Prison officials are planning a course and series of seminars to 'psychologically prepare death row inmates for the electric chair,' they announced. The counseling is similar to therapy given to terminally ill cancer patients."
"Freud Giveth and Freud Taketh Away," *State and Mind* (November–December, 1976), p. 4.

"In this field, in which so much contradictory advice has been given, and in which so many vague statements have been made, it is necessary to formulate the material with some precision. Orderliness, however, does not mean rigidity. Many of the methods of psychotherapy which are listed below are not sharply defined, but shade over into each other.

Methods of Psychotherapy
A. Methods for the General Practitioner, for use in suitable cases.
1. *Physical Examination as Psychotherapy*
2. *Physical Treatment as Psychotherapy*
3. *Medicinal Treatment as Psychotherapy*
4. *Reassurance*
5. *Hydrotherapy as Psychotherapy*
6. *Occupational Therapy*
7. *Diversion and Entertainment*
8. *Establishment of a Daily Routine*
9. *Development of Hobbies*
10. *Authoritative Firmness*
11. *Suggestion Therapy*
12. *Hospitalization, including the 'Rest Cure'*
13. *Giving of Information*
14. *Removal of External Strain*

15. *Changing the Attitudes in the Environment*
16. *Guidance and Advice*
17. *Fostering of Socialized Living*
18. *Provision of Acceptable Outlets for Aggressiveness*
19. *Provision of Acceptable Compensations for Fears and Inferiority Feelings*
20. *Non-Condemning Constructive Relationship*
21. *Ignoring of Certain Symptoms and Attitudes*
22. *Satisfaction of Frustrated Basic Needs*
23. *Satisfaction of Neurotic Needs*
24. *Opportunity for Healthy Identifications*
25. *Bibliotherapy*

B. *Advanced Methods for the General Practitioner (who has some added training and aptitude) for use in suitable cases.*
1. *Confession and Ventilation*
2. *Life-History Discussion*
3. *Desensitization*
4. *Persuasion and Reeducation*
5. *Applications of Psychoanalysis*

C. *Methods for the Specialist*
1. *Psychotherapy Associated with Shock Therapy*
2. *Hypnosis*
3. *Psychoanalysis*
4. *Modified Psychoanalytic Methods—Short-Term Psychotherapy.*
5. *Psychoanalytic Prescriptions*
6. *Child Analysis*
7. *Group Psychotherapy*
8. *Individual Play Therapy*
9. *Group Play Therapy*
10. *Distributive Analysis"*

Maurice Levine, *Psychotherapy in Medical Practice* (New York: Macmillan, 1952), pp. 17–20.

"There is a widespread prejudice among mental health professionals that treatment must be voluntary to be effective and/or ethical. . . . Patients are coerced into treatment by pain, fear, and despair as well as by spouses, employers, and judges. Volun-

tary treatment is a myth. . . . Thomas Szasz has helped to dispel some naivete about institutional treatment, but his fundamenal premise is erroneous and regressive, denying the valid services psychiatry can offer to a society much in need. To serve, we risk the abuse of our powers; to avoid that risk is not to serve at all."
Richard R. Parlour, "The Myth of Voluntary Therapy" (Letter to the Editor), *American Journal of Psychiatry,* 131 (May, 1974), p. 606.

"In my department at the Vienna Polyclinic, we use drugs, and use electro-convulsive treatment. I have signed authorization for lobotomies without having cause to regret it. In a few cases, I have even carried out transorbital lobotomy. However, I promise you that the human dignity of our patients is not violated in this way. . . . What matters is not a technique or therapeutic approach as such, be it drug treatment or shock treatment, but the spirit in which it is being carried out."
Viktor E. Frankl, " 'Nothing but—': On Reductionism and Nihilism," *Encounter* (November, 1969), p. 56.

"Restraints may be imposed [on the patient] from within by pharmacologic means or by locking the door of a ward. Either imposition may be a legitimate component of a treatment program."
Council of the American Psychiatric Association, "Position Statement on the Question of Adequacy of Treatment," *American Journal of Psychiatry,* 123 (May, 1967), p. 1,459.

III

Because psychiatrists study and influence certain kinds of behaviors and persons, the critical student of psychiatric history must scrutinize what kinds of behaviors and persons psychiatrists and their predecessors have studied, and what sorts of influence they have sought to bring to bear on them. Treating the medical metaphors of modern psychiatry as literal reflects and reinforces our modern aversion to moral conflict, human tragedy, and plain language. If we can succeed in stripping away the mask from the ideology of modern psychotherapy, we discover the perennial interests and institutions of mankind—sex and significance, power and prestige, race, religion, and the family—whose nature has always been, and perhaps always will be, what the genuine students of man, writers and poets, have endeavored to comprehend and to convey.

Because many human problems are the result of conflicts between people, a therapist can exercise influence only if one of the parties to the conflict enlists his services, or if, through the powers vested in him by the state, the therapist imposes himself on one or another of the conflicting parties. Since the Freudian revolution, we have divided psychiatry into two broad classes: one, comprising the neuroses or minor mental disease, characterized by arrangements in which the patient seeks the psychiatrist's services; and another, comprising the psychoses or major mental diseases, characterized by arrangements in which the psychiatrist imposes his services on the patient. In the former the relationship between patient and therapist is voluntary, in the latter it is involuntary. Yet, according to official psychiatry, in both cases the therapist "gives" and the patient "receives" a form of medical treatment often called "psychotherapy." I maintain that this entire imagery and understanding of the essential nature and purpose of the psychiatrist-patient relationship is mistaken, misleading, and mischievous.

What, then, are psychotherapists and what do they sell to or impose on their clients? Insofar as they use force, psychotherapists are judges and jailers, inquisitors and torturers; insofar as they eschew it, they are secular priests and pseudomedical rhetoricians. Their services consist of coercions and constraints imposed on individuals on behalf of other persons or social groups, or they consist of contracts and conversations entered into by individuals on their own behalf.

IV

Today we also distinguish two broad classes of psychiatric treatments—namely, psychological and organic. But since all psychiatric treatments achieve their effect through psychosocial—that is, cognitive, ceremonial, or social—means, it would be more accurate to identify three broad classes of psychiatric treatments—namely, institutional, physicochemical, and rhetorical. The paradigmatic institutional method is involuntary mental hospitalization. The paradigmatic physicochemical method is the use of drugs or electroshock. And the paradigmatic rhetorical method is psychoanalysis. These procedures came into being not so much because they work—though, depending on one's expectations, of course, they all do or don't—but rather because they satisfy a reciprocal need in the mental patient or those he disturbs and in the person who treats mental illness. In short, "psychopathology" and "psychotherapy" stand in the same sort of relation to each other as do the negative and positive images of a photograph.

The two most important methods of psychotherapy are confinement and conversation. Why is confining a madman treatment? Because his affront against society is an illness? The psychotic infringes on the freedom of others, by injuring their person, property, or privacy. Insofar as such behavior is seen not as criminal or sinful but as sick, it requires and justifies such therapeutic interventions. The pretense that the patient's coercive behavior is an illness is thus matched by the pretense that the psychiatrist's counter-coercive behavior is a treatment. Insofar as the patient's complaints about his body or his boss, his family or his fortune, are regarded as the manifestations of a disease of his brain, they require and justify therapeutic interventions aimed at that organ. The pretense that the patient's brain is sick is thus matched by the pretense that the doctor's use of a faradic or alternating current, of camphor or compazine, is a treatment.

In other words, what characterizes all the various "psychopathologies" is that the patient and/or the psychiatrist (and society) pretend and profess that the patient's words and actions are the symptoms of a disease; what characterizes all the various "psychotherapies" is that the psychiatrist and/or the patient (and society) pretend and profess that the psychiatrist's words and actions are the methods of a treatment. Thus, almost every human encounter has been described as both "mental illness" and "mental treatment."

V

The promiscuous use of the term *psychotherapy* is an important sign of the debauchment of the language of healing in the service of dehumanizing and controlling persons by technicizing and therapeutizing personal relations. Although such a fundamental cultural problem cannot be changed merely by changing our language, we must, if we want to extricate ourselves from our difficulties, begin with our language. Accordingly, if we want to rescue the cure of souls from the medical morass in which it is now mired, we must call psychotherapy by its proper name. To do so, we must create a neologism, a practice not without grave hazards of its own. That is why, both in my previous writings and in the present work, I have continued to use and to paraphrase accepted terms. Now, however, I should like to propose a new name for psychotherapy.

The name should fulfill two basic requirements: it should denote correctly the activities to which it points, and it should be free of the misleading contemporary medical implications of the term *psychotherapy.* As I noted at the beginning of this study, Aeschylus actually had such a name for what we now call psychotherapy. He called it the employment of *iatroi logoi,* or "healing words." In those ancient roots, then, lies our proper term for the modern, secular cure of souls: *iatrologic.*

Thus conceived, iatrologic would be a branch of rhetoric and logic. Its practitioners, specialists in rhetoric and logic, would be known as iatrologicians. Their activities would constitute, and be classified as, art rather than science.

The implications of such a change in terminology are immense. And so are its aims—namely, resurrecting the human soul from the therapeutic grave in which our technological age has buried it, and preserving the dignity and discipline of art from modern man's insatiable passion for professionalism.

Notes

INTRODUCTION

1. M. Ganz, "Moonies' parents given custody; 'Deprogramming' sessions begin today," Baton Rouge *State Times*, March 25, 1977, p. 14B.
2. Ibid.
3. L. Ledbetter, "Custody rule upheld for Moon disciples," New York *Times*, March 29, 1977, p. 54.
4. Ganz, "Moonies," Baton Rouge *State Times*, March 25, 1977, p. 14B.
5. B. Hayward, *Haywire* (New York: Alfred A. Knopf, 1977), pp. 298–99.
6. J. Leonard, Review of *Haywire*, *International Herald Tribune*, March 12, 1977, p. 14.
7. P. S. Prescott, "Surviving a Greek Tragedy," *Newsweek*, March 14, 1977, pp. 48–49.
8. J. M. Maze, "Council Reviews Past Six Months, Therapeutic Leaves," *The Bulletin, Area II District Branches APA*, 19 (February, 1977), p. 3.
9. L. Linn, "Therapeutic Leave," Ibid.
10. Maze, "Therapeutic Leaves," Ibid.
11. Ibid.
12. J. Herbers, "Jesuit at the White House defends Nixon," New York *Times*, May 9, 1974, pp. 1 and 34.
13. Ibid., p. 34.
14. See T. S. Szasz, *The Manufacture of Madness* (New York: Harper & Row, 1970), Chapter 11.

15. H. S. Kaplan, *The New Sex Therapy: Active Treatment of Sexual Dysfunctions* (New York: Brunner/Mazel, 1974), p. 208.
16. Ibid., p. 181.
17. J. S. Annon, *Behavioral Treatment of Sexual Problems: Brief Therapy* (New York: Harper & Row, 1976), p. 69.
18. "Nude Therapy Expenses May Be Tax Deductible," *Modern Medicine,* March 6, 1972, p. 154.
19. "Women Deny Husbands Sex," *Parade,* September 17, 1972, p. 7.

CHAPTER I

THE MYTH OF PSYCHOTHERAPY

1. In this connection, see, especially, T. S. Szasz, *The Ethics of Psychoanalysis: The Theory and Method of Autonomous Psychotherapy* (New York: Basic Books, 1965), and "The Myth of Psychotherapy," *American Journal of Psychotherapy,* 28 (October, 1974), pp. 517–26.
2. L. C. Kolb, *Noyes' Modern Clinical Psychiatry* (7th ed., Philadelphia: Saunders, 1968), p. 546.
3. Quoted in G. J. Sarwer-Foner, "Psychotherapy in Relation to the Changing Canadian Scene," *Canadian Psychiatric Association Journal,* 10:98–108 (April, 1965), p. 98.
4. See T. S. Szasz, *The Myth of Mental Illness* (Rev. ed.; New York: Harper & Row, 1974); *The Second Sin* (Garden City, N.Y.: Doubleday, 1973); and *Heresies* (Garden City, N.Y.: Doubleday, 1976).
5. L. Wittgenstein, *Zettel* (Oxford: Blackwell's, 1967), p. 82e.
6. See T. S. Szasz, "Scientific Method and Social Role in Medicine and Psychiatry," *A.M.A. Archives of Internal Medicine,* 101 (February, 1958), pp. 228–38; T. S. Szasz, "Bad Habits Are Not Diseases," *Lancet* (London), 2 (July 8, 1972), pp. 83–84; L. Goldman, "Exactly What Is a Doctor For?" *Doctor* (London), December 2, 1976, p. 2.
7. See pp. 194–205, herein.
8. S. Freud, "On the History of the Psycho-Analytic Movement" (1914), *The Standard Edition of the Complete Psychological Works of Sigmund Freud,* trans. by James Strachey (24 vols.; London: The Hogarth Press, 1953–74), Vol. XIV, pp. 14–15; hereinafter cited as SE.
9. See T. S. Szasz, *Schizophrenia: The Sacred Symbol of Psychiatry* (New York: Basic Books, 1976), Chapter 1.

CHAPTER II

PERSUADING PERSONS

1. See T. S. Szasz, "The Myth of Psychotherapy," *American Journal of Psychotherapy*, 28 (October, 1974), pp. 517–26.
2. See, generally, R. L. Johannesen, R. Strickland, and R. T. Eubanks (eds.), *Language Is Sermonic: Richard M. Weaver on the Nature of Rhetoric* (Baton Rouge: Louisiana State University Press, 1970); and T. S. Szasz, *Karl Kraus and the Soul-Doctors: A Pioneer Critic and His Criticism of Psychiatry and Psychoanalysis* (Baton Rouge: Louisiana State University Press, 1976).
3. Plato, *Phaedrus*, trans. by W. C. Helmbold and W. G. Rabinowitz (Indianapolis: Bobbs-Merrill, 1956), p. 61.
4. Quoted in P. Lain Entralgo, *The Therapy of the Word in Classical Antiquity*, trans. by L. J. Rather and J. M. Sharp (New Haven: Yale University Press, 1970), p. xxi.
5. Ibid.
6. Ibid., p. 66.
7. Ibid., p. 95; in this connection, see also T. S. Szasz, *Ceremonial Chemistry: The Ritual Persecution of Drugs, Addicts, and Pushers* (Garden City, N.Y.: Doubleday, 1974).
8. Ibid., p. 136.
9. Plato, *Charmides*, trans. by Benjamin Jowett, in E. Hamilton and H. Cairns (eds.), *The Complete Dialogues of Plato* (Princeton: Princeton University Press, 1961), pp. 99–122, see esp. p. 103, line 157a.
10. Lain Entralgo, *The Therapy of the Word*, pp. 137, 126.
11. Aristotle, *Rhetorica*, in *The Basic Works of Aristotle*, ed. with intro. by Richard McKeon (New York: Random House, 1941), pp. 1325–1454, esp. p. 1325.
12. Ibid., p. 1335.
13. Ibid., p. 1325.
14. Ibid., p. 1337.
15. Ibid., p. 1353.
16. Ibid.
17. Ibid., p. 1360.
18. G. Willis, *The Philosophy of Speech* (London: George Allen & Unwin, 1919), p. 198.
19. G. Weiler, *Mauthner's Critique of Language* (Cambridge, England: Cambridge University Press, 1970), p. 158.
20. Ibid., p. 141.
21. Ibid., pp. 141–42.
22. Ibid., p. 142.

23. A. Janik and S. Toulmin, *Wittgenstein's Vienna* (New York: Simon and Schuster, 1973), p. 123.

24. F. Mauthner, *Beiträge zu einer Kritik der Sprache: Vol. I, Sprache und Psychologie* (*Contributions to a Critical Study of Language: Vol. I, Language and Psychology*) (Stuttgart: J. G. Cotta, 1901), pp. 23, 214–15. The translation is mine.

25. Johannesen, Strickland, Eubanks (eds.), *Language Is Sermonic*, pp. 224, 181.

26. Ibid., p. 206.

27. Ibid.

28. Ibid., p. 184.

29. See Szasz, *Kraus*, esp. Chapter 3.

30. R. M. Weaver, *The Ethics of Rhetoric* (Chicago: Regnery, 1953), p. 11.

31. Ibid., pp. 11–12.

32. Ibid., p. 25.

33. W. Sargant, *Battle for the Mind: A Physiology of Conversion and Brainwashing* (New York: Harper & Row, 1971), p. viii.

34. Ibid., p. ix.

35. Ibid., p. 37.

36. Ibid., pp. 48–49.

37. Ibid., p. 129.

38. Ibid., p. 137.

39. Ibid., p. 138.

40. Ibid., p. 139.

41. Ibid.

42. Ibid., pp. 139–40.

43. Ibid., p. 350.

CHAPTER III

CURING SOULS

1. See G. Zilboorg, *A History of Medical Psychology* (New York: Norton, 1941); and F. G. Alexander and S. T. Selesnick, *The History of Psychiatry: An Evaluation of Psychiatric Thought and Practice from Prehistoric Times to the Present* (New York: Harper & Row, 1966).

2. H. F. Ellenberger, *The Discovery of the Unconscious: The History and Evolution of Dynamic Psychiatry* (New York: Basic Books, 1970), pp. 43–46.

3. See p. 15, herein.

4. J. T. McNeill, *A History of the Cure of Souls* (New York: Harper & Row, 1951), p. 320.

5. Ibid., p. vii.

6. T. Papadakis, *Epidaurus: The Sanctuary of Asclepios* (München-Zürich: Verlag Schnell & Steiner, 1971), p. 16.
7. Ibid.
8. Ibid., p. 17.
9. W. Jaeger, *Paideia: The Ideals of Greek Culture,* trans. by Gilbert Highet (2 vols.; New York: Oxford University Press, 1965), Vol. I, pp. 353, 481.
10. McNeill, *Cure of Souls,* p. viii.
11. Ibid.
12. Plato, *Socrates' Defense (Apology)*, trans. by Hugh Tredennick, in Hamilton and Cairns (eds.), *Complete Dialogues of Plato,* pp. 1–26, esp. p. 15.
13. Ibid., p. 16.
14. Quoted in McNeill, *Cure of Souls,* p. 27.
15. Ibid., p. 28.
16. Quoted in ibid., p. 34.
17. Ibid., p. 2.
18. Jeremiah, 18:18.
19. Ecclesiasticus or the Wisdom of Jesus, Son of Sirach, in *The New English Bible with the Apocrypha* (Oxford and Cambridge: Oxford and Cambridge University Presses, 1970), Part II, pp. 117–91; 37:7–8.
20. Ibid., 37:14.
21. Matthew, 23:13–17.
22. Quoted in McNeill, *Cure of Souls,* p. 70.
23. Ibid.
24. Matthew, 4:20.
25. Mark, 12:38–40.
26. McNeill, *Cure of Souls,* p. 85.
27. Ibid., p. 111.
28. See, generally, Szasz, *Heresies.*
29. McNeill, *Cure of Souls,* p. 117.
30. Ibid.
31. Ibid., p. 119.
32. Ibid., p. 134.
33. F. MacNutt, *Healing* (Notre Dame, Ind.: Ave Maria Press, 1974), p. 14.
34. McNeill, *Cure of Souls,* p. 164.
35. Ibid., p. 163.
36. In this connection, see also Szasz, *The Manufacture of Madness* and *Ceremonial Chemistry.*
37. McNeill, *Cure of Souls,* p. 164.
38. Ibid.
39. Ibid., p. 166.
40. Ibid., p. 167.

41. Ibid.
42. Ibid., p. 168.
43. Ibid., p. 169.
44. See Szasz, *The Ethics of Psychoanalysis.*
45. McNeill, *Cure of Souls,* p. 176.
46. W. Haller, *The Rise of Puritanism* (Philadelphia: University of Pennsylvania Press, 1972), p. 25.
47. Ibid., p. 33.
48. Quoted in ibid., p. 41.
49. Ibid., p. 153.
50. E. S. Morgan, *Visible Saints: The History of a Puritan Idea* (Ithaca: Cornell University Press, 1965), p. 113.
51. Ibid., p. 121.
52. See T. S. Szasz, *The Theology of Medicine: The Political-Philosophical Foundations of Medical Ethics* (Baton Rouge: Louisiana State University Press, 1977).
53. McNeill, *Cure of Souls,* p. 319.
54. See Szasz, *The Myth of Mental Illness* and *Heresies.*

CHAPTER IV

FRANZ ANTON MESMER

1. R. Darnton, *Mesmerism and the End of the Enlightenment in France* (Cambridge, Mass.: Harvard University Press, 1968), p. 15.
2. Ibid., p. 166.
3. See Szasz, *Schizophrenia,* esp. Chapter 2.
4. S. Zweig, *Mental Healers: Franz Anton Mesmer, Mary Baker Eddy, Sigmund Freud,* trans. by Eden and Cedar Paul (New York: Frederick Ungar, 1962), p. 11.
5. Ibid., pp. 11–12.
6. M. Goldsmith, *Franz Anton Mesmer: A History of Mesmerism* (New York: Doubleday, 1934), p. 59.
7. Zweig, *Mental Healers,* p. 15.
8. Ibid., p. 17.
9. Ibid., p. 21.
10. Ibid., p. 22.
11. Goldsmith, *Mesmer,* p. 68.
12. Ibid., p. 72.
13. Ibid.
14. Ibid.
15. V. Buranelli, *The Wizard from Vienna* (New York: Coward, McCann and Geoghegan, 1975), p. 107.

16. Zweig, *Mental Healers,* p. 27.
17. Ibid., p. 28.
18. Ibid., pp. 28–29.
19. Ibid., p. 29.
20. Ibid.
21. Ibid.
22. Ibid.
23. Ibid., p. 36.
24. Goldsmith, *Mesmer,* p. 94.
25. Ibid., p. 95.
26. Ibid., p. 96.
27. Ibid., p. 97.
28. Ibid., p. 98.
29. Ibid., pp. 99–100.
30. Ibid., p. 100
31. Zweig, *Mental Healers,* p. 41.
32. Ibid., p. 42.
33. Buranelli, *Wizard,* p. 84.
34. Ibid.
35. Ibid., p. 85.
36. See, generally, L. Freeman, *The Story of Anna O.* (New York: Walker, 1972).
37. Goldsmith, *Mesmer,* pp. 117–21.
38. Ellenberger, *Discovery of the Unconscious,* p. 65.
39. Buranelli, *Wizard,* p. 172.
40. Ibid.
41. Goldsmith, *Mesmer,* p. 148.
42. Ibid.
43. Ibid.
44. Ibid.
45. Ibid., p. 150.
46. Ibid.
47. Buranelli, *Wizard,* p. 162.
48. Goldsmith, *Mesmer,* p. 151.
49. Ibid., p. 153.
50. Buranelli, *Wizard,* p. 165.
51. Ibid., p. 174.
52. F. A. Mesmer, *Memoir of F. A. Mesmer, Doctor of Medicine, on His Discoveries,* trans. by Jerome Eden (1799; Mt. Vernon, N.Y.: Eden Press, 1957), p. ix.
53. Ibid., pp. 3–4.
54. Ibid., p. 15.
55. Ibid., pp. 21–22.
56. Ibid., p. 51.
57. Ibid., p. 52.

CHAPTER V

JOHANN CHRISTIAN HEINROTH

1. J. C. Heinroth, *Textbook of Disturbances of Mental Life, or Disturbances of the Soul and Their Treatment* (1818), trans. by J. Schmorak, with intro. by George Mora (2 vols.; Baltimore: Johns Hopkins University Press, 1975).
2. Ibid., Vol. I, p. 25.
3. Ibid., p. 21.
4. Ibid., p. 136.
5. Ibid.
6. Ibid., p. 138.
7. Ibid., p. 16.
8. Ibid.
9. Ibid., p. 124.
10. In this connection, see Szasz, *Schizophrenia*, esp. Chapter 1, and this book, Chapters 8, 9, and 10.
11. Heinroth, *Mental Life*, Vol. I, p. 220.
12. Ibid.
13. Ibid., p. 25.
14. Ibid.
15. Ibid.
16. Ibid., p. 28.
17. Ibid., p. 29.
18. See T. S. Szasz, *Psychiatric Slavery: When Confinement and Coercion Masquerade as Cure* (New York: Free Press, 1977).
19. Heinroth, *Mental Life*, Vol. I, p. 236.
20. Ibid., p. 250.
21. Ibid., p. 284.
22. Ibid., pp. 286–89.
23. Ibid., p. 291.
24. Ibid.
25. Ibid., pp. 292–96.
26. Ibid., p. 292.
27. Ibid., pp. 292–93.
28. Ibid., p. 294.
29. Ibid., p. 295.
30. Ibid., p. 332.
31. Ibid.
32. Ibid., p. 337.
33. Ibid.
34. Ibid., p. 413.
35. Ibid., pp. 413–14.

36. Ibid., p. 415.
37. Ibid., p. 419.
38. Ibid., p. 420.
39. See Szasz, *Schizophrenia*, esp. Chapter 4, and *Psychiatric Slavery*, esp. Chapters 1 and 2.
40. Zilboorg, *A History of Medical Psychology*, p. 470.
41. Alexander and Selesnick, *History of Psychiatry*, p. 141.
42. Ibid., p. 143.
43. Ellenberger, *Discovery of the Unconscious*, p. 212.
44. Ibid.

CHAPTER VI

WILHELM ERB, JULIUS WAGNER-JAUREGG, AND SIGMUND FREUD

1. Zilboorg, *A History of Medical Psychology*, pp. 591–606.
2. S. Arieti (ed.), *American Handbook of Psychiatry* (3 vols.; New York: Basic Books, 1959–1966), Vol. II, pp. 2009–98, and Vol. III, pp. 761–78.
3. W. Erb, *Handbook of Electro-Therapeutics*, trans. by L. Putzel (New York: William Wood & Company, 1883).
4. Ibid., p. 228.
5. Ibid.
6. Ibid., p. 290.
7. Ibid.
8. Ibid.
9. Ibid., p. 291.
10. Ibid.
11. Ibid., p. 349.
12. Ibid., p. 352.
13. Ibid.
14. See, generally, Szasz, *The Manufacture of Madness*.
15. E. Jones, *The Life and Work of Sigmund Freud* (3 vols.; New York: Basic Books, 1953–1957), Vol. III, p. 21.
16. S. Freud, "Memorandum on the Electrical Treatment of Neurotics" (1920), SE, Vol. XVII, pp. 211–15, esp. p. 212.
17. Ibid., p. 213.
18. See Szasz, *The Myth of Mental Illness*, esp. pp. 17–47.
19. S. Freud, "Memorandum," SE, Vol. XVII, p. 213.
20. Ibid.
21. Ibid., pp. 213–14.
22. Quoted in Jones, *Freud*, Vol. III, p. 23.
23. Ibid.

24. M. S. Gunther, "Freud as Expert Witness; Wagner-Jauregg and the Problem of the War Neuroses," in J. E. Gedo and G. H. Pollock (eds.), *The Annual of Psychoanalysis* (New York: International Universities Press, 1975), Vol. II, pp. 6, 7.
25. See, generally, Szasz, *The Myth of Mental Illness.*
26. J. Breuer and S. Freud, *Studies on Hysteria* (1893–1895), SE, Vol. II, pp. 1–335, esp. p. 135.
27. Ibid., p. 136.
28. Ibid., p. 138.
29. Ibid.
30. Ibid.
31. See T. S. Szasz, "Psychoanalysis and Suggestion," *Comprehensive Psychiatry,* 4 (1963), 271–80.
32. S. Freud, "The Future Prospects of Psycho-Analytic Therapy" (1910), SE, Vol. XI, pp. 139–51, esp. p. 147.
33. S. Freud, "On the History of the Psycho-Analytic Movement" (1914), SE, XIV, p. 9.
34. S. Freud, "Preface to Reik's *Ritual: Psycho-Analytic Studies*" (1919), SE, Vol. XVII, pp. 257–63, esp. p. 259.
35. S. Freud, "A Short Account of Psycho-Analysis" (1923), SE, Vol. XIX, pp. 189–209, esp. p. 192.
36. S. Freud, *An Autobiographical Study* (1925), SE, Vol. XX, pp. 1–74, esp. p. 16.

CHAPTER VII

THE PSYCHOANALYTIC MOVEMENT

1. Jones, *Freud,* Vol. I, p. 198.
2. Ibid., p. 199.
3. See Freeman, *The Story of Anna O.*
4. Ibid., pp. 150, 167.
5. Ellenberger, *Discovery of the Unconscious,* p. 484.
6. Lain Entralgo, *The Therapy of the Word,* pp. 186–87.
7. See Szasz, *The Myth of Mental Illness,* Chapter 14.
8. See, generally, M. Douglas, *Purity and Danger: An Analysis of the Concepts of Pollution and Taboo* (Harmondsworth, Eng.: Pelican, 1970).
9. F. Kafka, *Wedding Preparations in the Country, and Other Posthumous Prose Writings,* with notes by Max Brod; trans. by Ernst Kaiser and Eithne Wilkins (London: Secker and Warburg, 1954), p. 330.
10. Ibid., p. 443.
11. See Szasz, *Kraus.*
12. Jones, *Freud,* Vol. I, p. 234.

13. Ibid., pp. 234–35.
14. See Chapter 6, herein.
15. Jones, *Freud,* Vol. I, p. 243.
16. Breuer and Freud, *Studies on Hysteria,* SE, Vol. II, p. 266.
17. S. Freud, "Heredity and the Aetiology of the Neuroses" (1896), SE, Vol. III, p. 151.
18. M. Bonaparte, A. Freud, and E. Kris (eds.), *The Origins of Psycho-Analysis, Letters to Wilhelm Fliess, Drafts and Notes, 1887–1902, by Sigmund Freud,* trans. by Eric Mosbacher and James Strachey (New York: Basic Books, 1954), p. 355.
19. Ibid., p. 360.
20. Ibid., p. 55.
21. Ibid., p. 57.
22. Ibid., p. 5.
23. Ibid., p. 66.
24. Ibid.
25. Ibid., p. 68.
26. See Szasz, *The Manufacture of Madness,* Chapter 11.
27. S. Freud, "Findings, Ideas, Problems" (1938), SE, Vol. XXIII, p. 299.
28. Ibid., p. 300.
29. Bonaparte, A. Freud, and Kris (eds.), *Origins,* p. 68.
30. Ibid., p. 71.
31. Ibid., pp. 71–72.
32. Ibid., p. 73.
33. Ibid., p. 74.
34. Jones, *Freud,* Vol. II, pp. 69–70.
35. S. Freud, "On the History of the Psycho-Analytic Movement" (1914), SE, Vol. XIV, p. 42.
36. Ibid., p. 43.
37. Ibid., p. 50.
38. Ibid.
39. Jones, *Freud,* Vol. II, p. 129.
40. S. Freud, "On the History of the Psycho-Analytic Movement," p. 42.
41. Ibid., p. 50.
42. Quoted in Jones, *Freud,* Vol. II, p. 171; in this connection see also this volume, pp. 157–62B.
43. S. Loránd, "The Founding of the Psychoanalytic Institute of the State University of New York Downstate Medical Center: An Autobiographical History," *Psychoanalytic Review,* 62 (Winter, 1975/76), p. 677.
44. Ibid., p. 678.
45. Ibid.

46. Ibid., p. 679.
47. Ibid., pp. 679–80.
48. Ibid., p. 680.

CHAPTER VIII

PSYCHOANALYSIS AS BASE RHETORIC

1. See, generally, T. S. Szasz, *Pain and Pleasure: A Study of Bodily Feelings* (2nd ed., New York: Basic Books, 1975), pp. xi–xlvii, and *The Myth of Mental Illness*, Chapters 7 and 8.
2. S. Freud, *The Psychopathology of Everyday Life* (1901), SE, Vol. VI, p. 253.
3. Ibid.
4. Ibid., p. 254.
5. Ibid.
6. S. Freud, "Leonardo da Vinci and a Memory of His Childhood" (1910), SE, Vol. XI, p. 63.
7. Ibid., p. 68.
8. Ibid.
9. Ibid.
10. Ibid., p. 69.
11. Ibid.
12. Ibid., pp. 71–72.
13. Ibid., p. 87.
14. Ibid., p. 82.
15. S. Freud, "A Special Type of Choice of Object Made by Men" (1910), SE, Vol. XI, p. 171.
16. S. Freud, *Three Essays on the Theory of Sexuality* (1905), SE, Vol. VII, p. 226.
17. S. Freud, *An Autobiographical Study* (1925), SE, Vol. XX, p. 36.
18. S. Freud, "On the History of the Psycho-Analytic Movement" (1914), SE, Vol. XIV, p. 62.
19. Ibid.
20. Ibid., p. 63.
21. My account of the legend is based on R. Graves, *The Greek Myths* (2 vols.; New York: Braziller, 1959), Vol. II, pp. 9–15.
22. Ibid., p. 14.
23. Ibid., p. 13.
24. D. Wormell, "Oedipus," *Encyclopaedia Britannica*, 14th ed., Vol. XVI, p. 868.
25. P. Roazen, *Freud and His Followers* (New York: Knopf, 1975), p. 243.

26. S. Freud, *Introductory Lectures on Psycho-Analysis* (1915–16), SE, Vol. XV, p. 207.

27. S. Freud, *An Outline of Psycho-Analysis* (1938), SE, Vol. XXIII, p. 192.

28. Ibid., p. 189.

29. Ibid., p. 192.

30. S. Freud, *New Introductory Lectures on Psycho-Analysis* (1933), SE, Vol XXII, p. 126 (W. W. Norton & Company, Inc. U.S. edition).

31. Ibid., p. 127.

32. Ibid., p. 132.

33. Ibid., p. 135.

34. S. Freud, *The Future of an Illusion* (1927), SE, Vol. XXI, p. 43.

35. E. L. Freud (ed.), *Letters of Sigmund Freud,* trans. by Tania and James Stern (New York: Basic Books, 1960), p. 431.

CHAPTER IX

SIGMUND FREUD

1. See Ellenberger, *Discovery of the Unconscious,* pp. 418–77.

2. D. Bakan, *Sigmund Freud and the Jewish Mystical Tradition* (Boston: Beacon, 1958), p. 49.

3. Ibid., p. 50.

4. Ibid., p. 52.

5. Jones, *Freud,* Vol. III, p. 352.

6. S. Freud, *The Future of an Illusion* (1927), SE, Vol. XXI, p. 31.

7. Voegelin, E., *Order and History, Vol. III: Plato and Aristotle* (Baton Rouge: Louisiana State University Press, 1957), p. 264.

8. Plato, *Laws,* Book X, 908 c–e, in Hamilton and Cairns (eds.), *Complete Dialogues of Plato,* pp. 1463–1464.

9. See Szasz, *Kraus,* Chapter 4.

10. A. J. P. Kenny, *Mental Health in Plato's Republic.* Dawes Hicks Lecture on Philosophy, British Academy, 1969. (London: Oxford University Press, 1969), p. 240.

11. S. Freud, *An Autobiographical Study* (1925), SE, Vol. II, p. 7.

12. Ibid., p. 9.

13. K. Popper, *Unended Quest: An Intellectual Autobiography* (La-Salle, Ill.: Open Court Publishing Co., 1976), p. 105.

14. E. L. Freud (ed.), *Letters of Sigmund Freud,* p. 22.

15. Bonaparte, A. Freud, and Kris (eds.), *Origins,* p. 238.

16. Ibid., p. 312.

17. H. C. Abraham, and E. L. Freud (eds.), *A Psycho-Analytic Dialogue: The Letters of Sigmund Freud and Karl Abraham,*

1907–1926, trans. by Bernard Marsh and Hilda C. Abraham (New York: Basic Books, 1965), p. 63.

18. Ibid., p. 64.
19. Ibid., p. 46.
20. Ibid.
21. Ibid., p. 54.
22. Quoted in Jones, *Freud*, Vol. II, p. 119.
23. Ibid.
24. E. Meng and E. L. Freud (eds.), *Psychoanalysis and Faith: The Letters of Sigmund Freud and Oskar Pfister* (New York: Basic Books, 1963), p. 63; hereinafter cited as *Freud/Pfister Letters*.
25. E. L. Freud (ed.), *Letters of Sigmund Freud*, pp. 427–28.
26. Ibid., p. 365.
27. See Szasz, *Kraus*, p. 11.
28. S. Freud, *The Interpretation of Dreams* (1900), SE, Vol. IV, pp. 196–97.
29. C. E. Schorske, "Politics and Patricide in Freud's *Interpretation of Dreams*," *American Historical Review*, 78 (April, 1973), p. 337.
30. Ibid.
31. S. Rothman, and P. Isenberg, "Freud and Jewish Marginality," *Encounter* (December, 1974), p. 48.
32. Ibid.
33. Ibid.
34. Ibid.
35. Ibid., p. 49.
36. See, generally, J. M. Cuddihy, *The Ordeal of Civility: Freud, Marx, Levi-Strauss, and the Jewish Struggle with Modernity* (New York: Basic Books, 1974).
37. Quoted in Ellenberger, *Discovery of the Unconscious*, p. 462.
38. F. Field, *The Last Days of Mankind: Karl Kraus and his Vienna* (New York: St. Martin's Press, 1967), p. 59.
39. Ibid.
40. Ibid.
41. Szasz, *Kraus*, pp. 22–42.
42. K. Eissler, *Talent and Genius: The Fictitious Case of Tausk Contra Freud* (New York: Quadrangle, 1971), p. 299.
43. Jones, *Freud*, Vol. III, p. 160.
44. Eissler, *Talent and Genius*, p. 299.
45. *The Theodosian Code and Novels and the Sirmondian Constitution*, trans., with commentary, glossary, and bibliography, by Clyde Pharr (Princeton: Princeton University Press, 1952), p. 440.
46. See especially Szasz, *The Manufacture of Madness*.

47. W. McGuire (ed.), *The Freud/Jung Letters: The Correspondence between Sigmund Freud and C. G. Jung,* trans. by Ralph Manheim and R. F. C. Hull (Princeton: Princeton University Press, 1974), p. 325.

48. Jones, *Freud,* Vol. II, p. 116.

49. In this connection, see Szasz, *Kraus,* esp. Chapter 3.

50. S. Freud, *Moses and Monotheism: Three Essays* (1939), SE, Vol. XXIII, pp. 1–137.

51. See, for example, S. Freud, "The Moses of Michelangelo" (1914), SE, Vol. XIII, pp. 209–38.

52. Jones, *Freud,* Vol. III, p. 367.

53. Ibid.

54. Ibid.

55. Ibid.

56. Ibid., p. 368.

CHAPTER X

CARL GUSTAV JUNG

1. See, generally, Ellenberger, *Discovery of the Unconscious,* pp. 657–63.

2. C. G. Jung, *Memories, Dreams, Reflections,* ed. by Aniela Jaffe, trans. by Richard and Clara Winston (New York: Pantheon, 1963), p. 30.

3. Ibid., p. 31.

4. Ibid.

5. Ibid.

6. Ibid., pp. 31–32.

7. Ibid., p. 53.

8. Ibid.

9. Ibid., p. 55.

10. Ibid.

11. Ibid., p. 108.

12. Ibid., pp. 108–9.

13. Ibid.

14. E. Bleuler, *Dementia Praecox, or the Group of Schizophrenias* (1911), trans. by Joseph Zinkin (New York: International Universities Press, 1950); see also Szasz, *Schizophrenia,* Chapter 1.

15. Jung, *Memories,* p. 128.

16. Ibid., p. 114.

17. See Szasz, *The Ethics of Psychoanalysis,* esp. Chapters 5 and 6.

18. McGuire (ed.), *Freud/Jung Letters,* p. 21.

19. Ibid., p. 108.

20. Ibid., p. 156.
21. Ibid., p. 279.
22. Ibid., p. 279.
23. Ibid., p. 295.
24. Ibid.
25. Ibid., p. 345.
26. Ibid., p. 383.
27. V. von Weizsaecker, "Reminiscences of Freud and Jung," in B. Nelson (ed.), *Freud and the 20th Century* (New York: Meridian, 1957), p. 72.
28. G. Adler (ed.), *C. G. Jung Letters,* trans. by R. F. C. Hull (2 vols.; London: Routledge, 1976), Vol. II, p. xxix.
29. Freud, "On the History of the Psycho-Analytic Movement" (1914), SE, Vol. XIV, pp. 63–64.
30. Ibid., p. 64.
31. Ibid.
32. C. G. Jung, "Sigmund Freud in His Historical Setting" (1932), *The Collected Works of C. G. Jung,* trans. by R. F. C. Hull, ed. by H. Read, M. Fordham, G. Adler, and W. McGuire (18 or more vols. planned; Princeton: Princeton University Press, 1953–), Vol. XV, p. 45; hereinafter cited as CW.
33. C. G. Jung, "What Is Psychotherapy?" (1935), CW, Vol. XVI, p. 24.
34. C. G. Jung, *Analytical Psychology: Its Theory and Practice.* Tavistock Lectures, 1935; original in English. (New York: Vintage, 1968), pp. 37–38.
35. Ibid., p. 107.
36. Ibid., p. 155.
37. C. G. Jung, "Answers to Questions on Freud" (1953), in C. G. Jung, *Critique of Psychoanalysis,* trans. by R. F. C. Hull (Princeton: Princeton University Press, 1975), p. 237.
38. Adler (ed.), *Jung Letters,* Vol. II, p. 85.
39. Ibid., pp. 140–41.
40. Ibid., p. 142.
41. Ibid., p. 219.
42. Ibid., p. 221.
43. Ibid., p. 262.
44. Ibid., p. 265.
45. Ibid., p. 293.
46. Ibid., p. 534.
47. Ibid., p. 625.
48. Ibid., p. 427.
49. S. Freud, "Some Additional Notes on Dream-Interpretation as a Whole" (1925), SE, Vol. XIX, pp. 123–38, esp. pp. 131–34.
50. Jung, *Memories,* p. 131.

51. See, for example, S. Freud, *An Autobiographical Study* (1925), SE, Vol. XX, p. 25; in this connection, see also Szasz, *Schizophrenia,* esp. Chapter 1.
52. Jung, *Memories,* p. 136.
53. Adler (ed.), *Jung Letters,* Vol. II, p. 582.

CHAPTER XI

PSYCHOTHERAPY: MEDICINE, RELIGION, AND POWER

1. S. Freud, "On Narcissism: An Introduction" (1914), SE, Vol. XIV, p. 78.
2. Freud, to Marie Bonaparte, January 15, 1930, quoted in Jones, *Freud,* Vol. III, p. 449.
3. S. Freud, *An Outline of Psycho-Analysis* (1938), SE, Vol. XXIII, p. 182.
4. S. Freud, "Lines of Advance in Psycho-Analytic Therapy" (1919), SE, Vol. XVII, p. 159 (W. W. Norton & Company, Inc. U.S. edition).
5. Quoted in Meng and E. L. Freud (eds.), *Freud/Pfister Letters,* p. 126.
6. S. Freud, "Postscript to the Question of Lay Analysis" (1927), SE, Vol. XX, p. 252.
7. Ibid., pp. 255–56.
8. In this connection, see also T. S. Szasz, "The Theology of Therapy: The Breach of the First Amendment Through the Medicalization of Morals," *New York University Review of Law and Social Change,* 5 (Spring, 1976), pp. 127–35, and *The Theology of Medicine* (Baton Rouge: Louisiana State University Press, 1977).
9. Chapter 10, herein.
10. C. G. Jung, "Psychotherapists or the Clergy?" (1932), in his *Modern Man in Search of a Soul* (New York: Harcourt, Brace, 1933), pp. 221–44, pp. 224–55.
11. Ibid., p. 227.
12. Ibid., pp. 237, 241.
13. C. G. Jung, "Freud and Jung—Contrasts," ibid., pp. 115–24, pp. 122–23.
14. See T. S. Szasz, *Ideology and Insanity: Essays on the Psychiatric Dehumanization of Man* (Garden City, N.Y.: Doubleday, 1970), Chapter 12.
15. P. Janet, *Psychological Healing: A Historical and Clinical Study,* trans. by Eden and Cedar Paul (2 vols.; New York: Macmillan, 1925), Vol. II, p. 338.

16. Ibid.
17. Ibid.
18. Ibid., p. 340.
19. Ibid.
20. Ibid., p. 367.
21. See, generally, L. D. Weatherhead, *Psychology, Religion, and Healing* (Rev. ed.; New York: Abingdon Press, 1952), pp. 122–28.
22. Ibid., p. 122.
23. Ibid., p. 22.
24. C. H. Brooks, *The Practice of Autosuggestion by the Method of Émile Coué,* with a foreword by Émile Coué (Rev. ed.; New York: Dodd, Mead and Co., 1922), p. 47.
25. Ibid., p. 85.
26. Ibid., p. 114.
27. Ibid., pp. 114–15.
28. Ibid., p. 119.
29. Alexander and Selesnick, *History of Psychiatry,* p. 84.
30. See, generally, Szasz, *The Myth of Mental Illness, The Second Sin,* and *Heresies.*
31. In this connection, see Szasz, *Ceremonial Chemistry* and *The Theology of Medicine,* esp. Chapters 9 and 12.

Index

About the Author

Thomas Szasz is one of the most controversial and influential psychiatrists in the United States today, and also one of the most productive. He is Professor of Psychiatry at the Upstate Medical Center of the State University of New York, maintains a private practice in psychiatry and psychoanalysis, lectures widely both in the United States and abroad, and frequently serves as an expert witness in court on behalf of individuals injured by psychiatric interventions. Dr. Szasz is a co-founder of the American Association for the Abolition of Involuntary Mental Hospitalization and a member of the American Humanist Association, which in 1973 named him Humanist of the Year. In 1974, he received the Jefferson Award of the American Institute for Public Service. He is the author of fifteen books and over three hundred articles.